D1125099

Whiskey & Spirits For Dummies

Calculating the Amount of Alcohol in a Bottle of Spirits

By law, the labels on containers of distilled spirits and wine must show alcohol by volume (ABV) or proof. Beer labels aren't required to provide this information.

Percent ABV = percent alcohol by volume, which is the percentage of the liquid that is pure alcohol

Proof = two times ABV

So 40 percent ABV = 80 proof

Measuring for Moderation

The Dietary Guidelines for Americans, written by the U.S. Department of Health and Human Services and the U.S. Department of Agriculture, defines moderate drinking as two drinks a day for a man, one drink a day for a woman. But how much alcohol should that one drink contain?

One drink =

- ✔ 1.5 ounces distilled spirits (80 proof)
- ✔ 5 ounces wine
- ✔ 12 ounces (regular) beer

For Dummies: Bestselling Book Series for Beginners

Whiskey & Spirits For Dummies®

Cheat Sheet

Foods from Which Spirits Are Distilled

Grains

- Barley, corn, oats, rye wheat: whiskeys
- Wheat: vodka

Fruit/Vegetables

- Agave: tequila
- Apples, grapes, and other fruits: brandies
- Potatoes: vodka

Sweeteners

- Sugar cane, molasses, honey: rum, cachaça, cordials/liqueurs

Talking Distillation

The following terms come in handy when you're discovering all there is to know about distillation:

- **Batch:** Alcohol distilled in one limited run through the still.
- **Fermentation:** The process by which microorganisms digest and convert carbohydrates (sugars and starches) to a liquid (alcohol) and a gas (carbon dioxide).
- **Milling:** Procedure to strip away the outer covering of grains used in making distilled spirits.
- **Mash:** Soupy mass of fermenting food from which spirits are distilled; the process of creating a mash is called *mashing*.
- **Neutral spirits:** The ethyl alcohol collected and condensed during distillation.
- **Still:** The container in which the alcohol/water liquid from fermented food is distilled.

For Dummies: Bestselling Book Series for Beginners

Whiskey & Spirits

FOR

DUMMIES®

Whiskey & Spirits

FOR

DUMMIES®

by Perry Luntz

BICENTENNIAL
1807
WILEY
2007
BICENTENNIAL

Wiley Publishing, Inc.

Whiskey & Spirits For Dummies®

Published by
Wiley Publishing, Inc.
111 River St.
Hoboken, NJ 07030-5774

Copyright © 2008 by Wiley Publishing, Inc., Indianapolis, Indiana

Published by Wiley Publishing, Inc., Indianapolis, Indiana

Published simultaneously in Canada

WILEY

About the Author

Perry Luntz has been involved in one way or another with the beverage alcohol business most of his adult life. For more than 20 years he has been publisher and editor of *Beverage Alcohol Market Report,* an international e-letter for marketing executives in beer, wine, and spirits. He served as Director of Marketing Communications for Seagram Distillers for a decade, worked on the creative side of several advertising agencies, including a spell as a creative director of a Young & Rubicam division, and for several years headed his own marketing communications agency.

A consultant, lecturer, teacher, and news media source, Perry is frequently interviewed in newspapers, radio, and television, including the BBC. He is chairman emeritus of the Wine Media Guild, proving he knows his way around vineyards and breweries, as well as distilleries.

Like many native New Yorkers, Perry is a political junky. He served several years as president of a highly regarded NYC political club.

For the past decade, Perry has been Senior Editor of the Beverage Media Group, a network of trade magazines read by 140,000 licensed retailers. He also writes a weekly column for the group's B-to-B Internet site.

He lives with his wife Carol Ann Rinzler in the Center of the Known Universe — Midtown Manhattan — occasionally visiting his home town of Brooklyn, where his son Russell lives with wife Lisa Di Gennaro. In the winter, he and Carol often become "snow birds" to descend on the rest of their family, Ira, Jacky, and grandsons Ari and Eli, who live in Sarasota, Florida.

Dedication

For Lloyd, whose light is gone but whose spirit is always with us.

Acknowledgments

It's impossible to say how much I owe to Carol Ann Rinzler, my wife, confidant, love of my life, and a damned good editor as well as a prolific and terrific author. I'll settle for saying just this: I couldn't have done it without you!

For my children, Ira and Jackie, Russell and Lisa, and my grand-children Ari and Eli — my cheering section — most appreciation and love.

On a professional level, my blessings are extended to the many friends and mentors in the spirits business with whom I've worked over the years. They are the most generous and forthcoming people in the world, and I love them all.

In particular, I want to thank Bill Slone, whose support made this book possible. Special acknowledgment goes to my oldest and wisest friends in the business, Gerry Slone, Ron Kapon, and Herbert Silverman, as well as the two best mixologists in the world, Dale De Grof and Ray Foley.

Particular thanks to Lisa Hawkins of DISCUS and Chris Morris of Brown-Forman, who helped make sure the chapter on distillation was accurate. In all cases, any errors are mine, not those who helped me.

And of course where would this book have been without the gentle editorial ministrations of Wiley's Michael Lewis, Tim Gallan, Sarah Faulkner, and my guardian angel agent Phyllis Westberg.

It was a long time coming, but I hope all who contributed to it enjoy reading this book as much as I enjoyed writing it.

Publisher's Acknowledgments

We're proud of this book; please send us your comments through our Dummies online registration form located at www.dummies.com/register/.

Some of the people who helped bring this book to market include the following:

Acquisitions, Editorial, and Media Development

Senior Project Editor: Tim Gallan

Acquisitions Editor: Michael Lewis

Copy Editor: Sarah Faulkner

Technical Reviewers: William Greenman, Mike Tully

Editorial Program Coordinator: Erin Calligan Mooney

Editorial Managers: Christine Meloy Beck, Michelle Hacker

Editorial Assistants: Joe Niesen, David Lutton, Leeann Harney

Cover Photo: © Dorling Kindersley/ Getty Images

Cartoons: Rich Tennant (www.the5thwave.com)

Composition Services

Project Coordinator: Erin Smith

Layout and Graphics: Stephanie D. Jumper, Shelley Norris, Christine Williams

Anniversary Logo Design: Richard Pacifico

Proofreaders: Todd Lothery, Nancy L. Reinhardt

Indexer: Becky Hornyak

Publishing and Editorial for Consumer Dummies

Diane Graves Steele, Vice President and Publisher, Consumer Dummies

Joyce Pepple, Acquisitions Director, Consumer Dummies

Kristin A. Cocks, Product Development Director, Consumer Dummies

Michael Spring, Vice President and Publisher, Travel

Kelly Regan, Editorial Director, Travel

Publishing for Technology Dummies

Andy Cummings, Vice President and Publisher, Dummies Technology/General User

Composition Services

Gerry Fahey, Vice President of Production Services

Debbie Stailey, Director of Composition Services

Contents at a Glance

Introduction..1

Part 1: Entering the Spirits World.......................7
Chapter 1: Discovering Distilled Spirits 9
Chapter 2: How Distilled Spirits Are Created.............................23
Chapter 3: Enjoying Spirits..43

Part 11: Whiskeys from Around the World...........59
Chapter 4: Sipping the Irish Whiskeys......................................61
Chapter 5: Saluting the Scots..79
Chapter 6: American Cousins: Bourbon and Tennessee Whiskey 97
Chapter 7: More Whiskeys from America
    and Other Parts of the World 115
Chapter 8: Channeling the Canadians.......................................131

Part 111: Surfing the White Waters:
A Guide to "Clear" Spirits..................................147
Chapter 9: Getting the Goods on Gin.......................................149
Chapter 10: Vodka: Toasting the Russians 169
Chapter 11: Tequila: Unearthing the Aztecs 191
Chapter 12: Yo Ho Ho and a Bottle of Rum 209

Part 1V: Enjoying the "After Dinner" Specials...231
Chapter 13: Cultivating Brandy 233
Chapter 14: Collecting Cordials, Lining Up Liqueurs.......................255

Part V: The Part of Tens....................................275
Chapter 15: Ten (or so) Classic Spirits Cocktails.............................277
Chapter 16: Ten Spirited Dishes 291
Chapter 17: Ten Nutrition Profiles of Alcohol Beverages.................303
Chapter 18: Ten (or so) Health Benefits of Moderate Drinking........307

Index...317

Table of Contents

Introduction *1*

Conventions Used in This Book..2

What You're Not to Read...2

Foolish Assumptions 3

How This Book Is Organized..3

    Part I: Entering the Spirits World....................................4

    Part II: Whiskeys from Around the World.....................4

    Part III: Surfing the White Waters:

       A Guide to "Clear" Spirits...................................4

    Part IV: Enjoying the "After Dinner" Specials...............4

    Part V: The Part of Tens...5

Icons Used in This Book...5

Where to Go from Here 5

Part 1: Entering the Spirits World *7*

Chapter 1: Discovering Distilled Spirits. 9

A Brief History of Distilled Spirits...9

    Eureka! Wine! Beer!..10

    Advancing the art 10

    Distillation arrives 12

    The secret gets out...12

    The process goes global 14

Setting Standards for Producing Modern Distilled Spirits...15

    The not-so-noble experiment 15

    New rules for better times..16

The Types of Spirits...17

    The clear spirits..17

    The dark spirits...18

A Word about the Words...19

Chapter 2: How Distilled Spirits Are Created 23

The Distillation Process in a Nutshell 23

The Basic Material for Distilling...26

Milling and Mashing..26

    Starting the fermentation process.............................27

    Bringing on the micros...28

Distilling: The Main Event...28

    The pot still 29

    The column still 33

Aging Gracefully 35
    The classic oak barrel 36
    Is getting older always better? 37
Blending Science with Art 37
    Straight spirits 38
    Blended spirits 38
Bottle, Bottle, Who's Got the Bottle? 40
    Choosing a model bottle 40
    The bottling line 40

Chapter 3: Enjoying Spirits 43

Assembling the Accoutrements 43
    Choosing your spirit 44
    Setting the tasting table 45
    Creating the tasting sheet 46
Getting to the Good Part 48
    Enjoying the view: Color and legs 48
    The nose knows 49
    The tasting technique 50
    Describing what you're tasting 51
Serving Spirits Day to Day 53
    Choosing a liquor store 53
    Surfing the Net 54
    Reading a spirits label 54
    Protecting your investment 55
    Taking temperature into account 56
    Avoiding glass warfare 56

Part II: Whiskeys from Around the World 59

Chapter 4: Sipping the Irish Whiskeys 61

Entering the Emerald Isle 61
    Tracking the origins of Irish whiskey 62
    Sailing the Irish seas 63
    Beginning well: The early days
       of the Irish whiskey trade 63
    Go west, young distiller 64
    Losing — and again finding — the luck of the Irish ...65
The Uniqueness of Irish Whiskey 66
    Beginning with barley 66
    Following the flow 67
    Firing the spirit 67
The Leading Irish Whiskeys 68
    Midleton 69
    Bushmills 71
    Cooley 71

Tasting Irish Whiskey 73
    Creating the tasting sheet.................................73
    Setting up the tasting 73
    Observing and tasting the whiskeys 73
Planning a Blended Meal...76
Touring the Source 76

Chapter 5: Saluting the Scots 79

Which Came First: Whiskey or Whisky?.................79
    From monastery to market...............................80
    The "smugglers" take to the high seas 81
Making Scotch Whisky 82
    The Scottish difference 82
    Distilling the whisky 84
The Styles of Scotch Whisky 85
    The whisky-making regions of Scotland: Where the
       single malts come from and the blends are born ...86
    Blended Scotch whiskies 89
Tasting Scotch Whisky 91
    Creating the tasting sheet.................................92
    Choosing your samples.....................................92
    Appreciating the appearance...........................93
    Inhaling the aromas 93
    Tasting the flavors 94
Planning a Scotch-Friendly Meal.............................95
Traveling through Distillery Land............................96

Chapter 6: American Cousins: Bourbon
and Tennessee Whiskey 97

Life, Liberty, and the Pursuit of . . . Whiskey? 98
    Rumbling to rebellion..99
    Over the mountains...100
    Bourbon beginnings 100
    The great schism: Bourbon gets its name,
       and Tennessee splits 101
Making Bourbon and Tennessee Whiskey 104
    Selecting the grain and making the mash.................104
    Fermenting and producing distillate..........................105
    Distilling the whiskey 106
    Changing the color and building the flavor:
       Aging..106
    Filtering 107
The Types of Bourbon...107
Tasting Bourbons and Tennessee Whiskeys 108
    Gentlemen, choose your whiskeys.............108
    What your senses sense when you taste
       Bourbon or Tennessee whiskey.................110
Pairing Foods with Bourbon and Tennessee Whiskey 111
Touring the Bourbon and Tennessee Whiskey Distilleries ...112

Chapter 7: More Whiskeys from America and Other Parts of the World 115

The Character of American Blended Whiskey 116
  The birth of the blends 116
  A man with a plan 117
Building a Blended Whiskey 119
  Producing a unique American flavor...................119
  Choosing whiskeys for the blend 120
Tasting American Blended Whiskeys 121
  Choosing the whiskeys 121
  What you see, taste, and smell when sampling
    American blended whiskey 123
Planning an American Blended Meal........................124
Traveling the American Whiskey Trail.....................125
Off the Beaten Whiskey Trails 126
  Japan 126
  India...127
  New Zealand 128
  Wales 129

Chapter 8: Channeling the Canadians. 131

Starting at the Top (of the World) 131
  Molson's multitudinous accomplishments 131
  Entering the modern era with a bang 132
  Moving into the modern markets 135
What Makes a Whisky Canadian? 136
How Canadian Whisky Is Made 137
Tasting the Best of Canada 139
  Selecting the whiskies for your tasting.............140
  Savoring the flavor of Canadian whisky 143
Pairing Foods with Canadian Whisky......................144

Part III: Surfing the White Waters: A Guide to "Clear" Spirits............................147

Chapter 9: Getting the Goods on Gin 149

The Origins of Gin.......................................149
  Hello, Holland; welcome, jenevre 150
  Holland's balm for British soldiers................150
The Brits Take Charge 151
  Protecting the home teams 151
  Spreading the gin gospel............................152
  Riding out the rougher years 153
Making Modern Gin 154
  Protecting the secret..............................154
  Creating the flavor 155

Touring the World of Gin...156
  British gins...156
  American gins..159
  Holland gins..161
  Gins from other countries 161
Tasting the World's Gin 163
  What to look for when tasting gin 164
  What to sniff and sip 165
Serving Gin...167

Chapter 10: Vodka: Toasting the Russians 169

What Is Vodka, Anyway? 169
The Birth of a "Breathless" Spirit 170
  The monks move north................................170
  The Russians stake a claim 171
  Huzzah for Ivan IV, the not-so-terrible czar 171
  Regulations, regulations, and more............172
Vodka Takes a Long Voyage..............................172
  "Why would people pay money for this stuff?" 173
  With a kick like a Moscow mule..................174
  Yesterday, the Cold War; today, the world 175
Distilling Vodka..176
  First comes the mash 177
  Next comes fermentation 177
  Don't forget the water 177
  Into the still 178
  And then into the bottle 178
The Second Vodka Revolution: The Flavor Factor 179
Tasting Vodkas 181
  Creating the tasting sheet...........................181
  Classifying vodkas 182
  Tasting vodka neat 186
  Sampling vodkas: What to see, sniff, and taste........186
  Serving vodka after the tasting....................187
The Foods That Match the Drinks 188

Chapter 11: Tequila: Unearthing the Aztecs. 191

The First North American Spirit 192
  Ancient history 192
  Tequila's middle ages 194
  Tequila's trek north 196
Defining Tequila: New Standards for
  a New Global Spirit 196
How Tequila Is Made 198
  Choosing the base material.........................198
  Pressing the agave.....................................199
  Preparing the mash 200
  Fermenting the wort....................................201

Distilling not once but twice 201
Aging the spirit...201
Blending and bottling...202
The Different Brands of Tequila 203
Tasting Tequila and Mezcal 205
Making a tasting sheet 205
Choosing the Tequilas to taste 206
Tasting the Tequilas 206
Pairing Food with Tequila..207

Chapter 12: Yo Ho Ho and a Bottle of Rum 209

The History of Rum 209
From arak to rum 210
Hooray for Christopher Columbus............................210
Rum rises 211
Sugar into rum: A trade bonus.................................211
How Rum Is Produced 212
The base...213
Fermentation 214
Distillation 214
Aging...215
Blending 215
Flavoring a favorite..216
Where That Rum Is From and Why It Matters.....................217
Hola! Rums from the Caribbean...............................217
Other places, other rums 224
Tasting the World's Rums 227
Prepping your tasting sheet 227
Selecting the rums you want to sample....................227
Gettin' to tastin' 228
Trying the rum with mixers..229

Part IV: Enjoying the "After Dinner" Specials ...231

Chapter 13: Cultivating Brandy. 233

The "Champagne" of Distilled Spirits 234
Where Do Brandies Come From? 234
France...235
Spain...239
Italy...239
United States 240
Other places, other brandies 241
Brandy by Type..244
Wine brandies 244
Fruit brandies...244
Pomace brandies 244

Distilling Brandies...245
    Choosing a base..245
    Bringing out the spirit...245
    Aging..246
    Blending..247
Tasting Brandy 248
    Tasting by type...248
    Tasting by country 249
    Tasting by price 250
    What you taste (and smell) when
        you sniff and sip..250
Serving Brandy: Neat or Mixed? Warm or Cool?.................251
Pairing Brandy and Food 252
    Flambé — with care..252

**Chapter 14: Collecting Cordials,
Lining Up Liqueurs 255**

The Birth of the Liqueur 256
    The first "medicines"..257
    Cordial? Liqueur? A tale of two words 258
Cordially Yours: The Making 258
    Choosing the base spirit...259
    Marking the differences 259
    Adding the flavor 260
    The final touches 261
    The two types of cordials 262
Cordials by the Ingredients 263
    Fruit flavors 264
    Seeds and nuts 266
    Branded, spirit-based...268
    Cream liqueurs 269
    Bitters...270
    Two classic liqueurs 271
A Cordial Tasting..271
Pairing Foods with Cordials and Liqueurs..........................273

Part V: The Part of Tens.................................275

Chapter 15: Ten (or so) Classic Spirits Cocktails 277

Oops! Tomato Juice on My Blouse: The Bloody Mary 277
Alexander! Another Brandy! 279
War Is Hell, so Pass the Rum — in a Daiquiri,
    if You Please..280
A Shipboard Romance: The Gimlet.....................................281
Uptown, Downtown: The Manhattan...................................282
If You Knew Margie Like I Know Margie: The Margarita.....283
The World's Most Famous Cocktail: The Martini................284

A Cuban Cup of Cheer: The Mojito 285
The Highland Fling: Rob Roy 286
Simple Perfection: The Whiskey Sour 287
Horses, Grass, and Mint: The Mint Julep 288

Chapter 16: Ten Spirited Dishes 291

Chilled Melon Pepper Soup with Glazed Shrimp 292
Game Pâté Terrine 293
Marinated Salmon 295
Penne à la Vodka 296
Chicken Fajitas 297
Filet Mignon with Whiskey Sauce 298
Green Beans with Toasted Pine Nuts 299
Tennessee Whiskey Candied Apples 300
AppleJack Pound Cake 301
Nut Ball Cookies 302

**Chapter 17: Ten Nutrition Profiles
of Alcohol Beverages 303**

Rum..304
Gin..304
Vodka...304
Whiskey..304
Coffee Liqueur 305
Coffee with Cream Liqueur 305
Whiskey Sour (Cocktail, Made from a Powdered Mix).......305
Tequila Sunrise (Cocktail, Canned) 306
Piña Colada (Cocktail, Canned) 306
Daiquiri (Cocktail, Canned) 306

**Chapter 18: Ten (or so) Health Benefits
of Moderate Drinking 307**

Heartening News 308
Lowering Bad Cholesterol, Raising Good Cholesterol 309
Busting Blood Clots 310
Lowering the Pressure 310
Staving Off Stroke..312
Deterring Diabetes 312
Protecting Intelligence 313
Preserving the Brain...314
Boosting Bones 314
Enhancing Appetite 315
Controlling Weight 315
Countering the Common Cold...316

Index *317*

Introduction

*F*or thousands of years man and womankind celebrated major events — religious and secular — by having a taste or even two of a fermented beverage that contained alcohol. Things got even tastier around 800 CE — the height of development of the Moorish culture. That's when a brilliant alchemist in the perpetual search for a way to turn lead into gold attempted to urge the release of the "essence" of various fruits and grains. The result was not only better than anything ever enjoyed before, but it also could be repeated over and over again.

That brilliant alchemist had found distillation. The art of making the most noble of beverages was created by nature and perfected by men and women. This book is dedicated to giving you a full explanation of distillation from the simplest and most popular spirit (vodka) to the most complicated (whiskey and brandy).

No, *Whiskey & Spirits For Dummies* definitely won't tell you how to set up your very own still in the basement (or bathtub) so that you can whip up a batch of your very own whiskey, gin, vodka, Tequila, rum, cordial, or Cognac.

Instead, this book aims to increase your appreciation of the qualities in fine distilled spirits, enabling you to make wise choices from the myriad products on the shelves in your local liquor store or in the literally hundreds of cocktails available for serving or drinking on social occasions. Drinking alcohol beverages is indeed a social thing to do. It's also part of religious services, and its use as a psychic benefit is unquestioned. There are other sides to these noble beverages as well.

This book also presents some ways in which a measured drink or two a day can create a more healthful way to live. I also talk about how to avoid any of the unpleasant results that can come from drinking too much.

For those readers who know absolutely nothing about distilled spirits other than that these beverages enhance a social setting and dining experience, this book is a good place to start to pick up the basics.

More experienced connoisseurs will find this a refresher course that can confirm their own good taste, introduce them to a few new types and brands of distilled spirits, and provide the kind of odds and ends — for example, why whiskey is spelled *whiskey* in Ireland and *whisky* in Scotland — that enliven cocktail conversation. And, yes, I give you several classic cocktail recipes in here, too.

Conventions Used in This Book

To make the text consistent and easier to read, *Whiskey & Spirits For Dummies* follows the usual Dummies style. For example:

- ✔ All Web addresses are printed in `monofont`.

- ✔ When this book was printed, some Web addresses may have needed to break across two lines of text. If that happened, rest assured that I didn't put in any extra characters (such as hyphens) to indicate the break. So, when using one of these Web addresses, just type in exactly what you see in this book, pretending that the line break doesn't exist.

- ✔ New terms appear in *italic* type and are followed by an easy-to-understand definition.

- ✔ **Bold** type is used to highlight the action parts of numbered steps.

What You're Not to Read

Imagine: An author telling you that you don't have to read every word that appears in his book. The truth is that some small parts of this book are fun or provide information that you may not find anywhere else, but they aren't absolutely essential to your under-standing of the basic facts about distilled spirits. For example:

- ✔ **The text in sidebars:** These shaded boxes are exactly that — sidebars to the main event — a little anecdote here, a special factoid there. Fascinating, but not essential.

✔ **The text next to a Technical Stuff icon:** Readers who want to
know every single fact about how things work will find these
paragraphs a delight. Readers who can do without the technical details can surf on by.

✔ **The text on the copyright page:** Really. This page is for pub-
lishers and libraries. If my editor put the dedication there to
save space, I think you should read about the people who
helped make this book possible, but the publisher's address?
The number of editions? The Library of Congress identification number? Nah.

Foolish Assumptions

If an author clicks the computer, hits typewriter keys, or pushes a
quill pen across the page, what's in front of him or her is an image
of the person for whom the book is being written. These are some
of the assumptions I made about you:

✔ You know the names of the different types of distilled spirits,
but you may not be totally familiar with the characteristics
that differentiate a whiskey from a Tequila (you may even
know why Tequila is spelled with a capital letter and whiskey
is not).

✔ You've read conflicting reports about the risks and benefits of
spirits (and other kinds of alcohol beverages), and you want
to pin down the real facts.

✔ You want the basic information about these products and how
they're made, but you have no intention of opening your own
distillery. That's good, because a few paragraphs back you were
told that this book isn't designed to tell you how to do that.

✔ Most important, you enjoy the flavor, aroma, and panache of
distilled spirits — but only and always in moderation.

How This Book Is Organized

The following is a brief summary of each part of *Whiskey & Spirits
For Dummies.* You can use this as a fast guide to check out the stuff
you want to go to first, because the best thing about a *For Dummies*
book is that no one expects you to start at Chapter 1 and work your
way straight through to the end. Each chapter here is a whole little
book of its own, which means that you can start anywhere and still
come out with a wealth of new information about distilled spirits.

Part 1: Entering the Spirits World

Chapter 1 is (what else?) a general introduction to the universe of distilled spirits. Chapter 2 is more technical: A detailed description of the distillation process in all its traditional glory. Chapter 3 tells you how to serve, evaluate, and enjoy the products produced in Chapter 2.

Part 11: Whiskeys from Around the World

Chapter 4 is all about how the Irish introduced the first whiskeys. Chapter 5 explains how the Scots adopted the Irish spirits — and changed the spelling to "whisky," thus confusing generation after generation of whiskey (or is it whisky?) drinkers.

Chapter 6 salutes two quintessential Americans — Bourbon and Tennessee whiskey. Chapter 7 describes the other great American innovation, American blended whiskey, and tells you all about upstarts from India, Japan, and New Zealand. Chapter 8 goes north to talk about a Canadian contribution to New World whisky choices.

Part 111: Surfing the White Waters: A Guide to "Clear" Spirits

Chapter 9 focuses on gin, from its birth in the Netherlands, toward its perfection in London, through its Prohibition adolescence, to its present presence. Chapter 10 is about vodka, the clear Russian spirit now often enjoyed in totally unexpected flavors. Chapter 11 is all about Tequila, the Aztec contribution to your drinking pleasure. Chapter 12 focuses on rum, the spirit made from sugar cane first carried to the Western hemisphere by Christopher Columbus. Yes, *that* Christopher Columbus.

Part 1V: Enjoying the "After Dinner" Specials

The subject of Chapter 13 is Winston Churchill's favorite spirit, brandy. Chapter 14 rewards the sweet tooth with info about the sweet stuff: cordials and liqueurs.

Part V: The Part of Tens

This is the part of the book regular *For Dummies* readers never skip. Chapter 15 pours recipes for ten classic cocktails (with an extra from the bartender). Chapter 16 dishes out menu choices — entrees, main dishes, veggies, and desserts — whose ingredients include at least one type of spirit. Chapter 17 tells what nutrients (!) are in one serving of each type of distilled spirits. Chapter 18 concludes with the actual health benefits of moderate spirits consumption.

Icons Used in This Book

This icon points out general good ideas, such as serving suggestions, buying advice, and so forth.

I use this icon to highlight important concepts that you shouldn't forget.

This icon flags nonessential information that may be too technical or detailed for some readers. You can skip it if you want.

Where to Go from Here

Now the question is where to begin reading. The real answer is anywhere your curiosity takes you in the Table of Contents. However, one good starting point is Chapter 2, the one that explains how distilled spirits are made. A second good starting point is Chapter 3, the one that shows you how to enjoy distilled products. Both chapters have information that applies to all types of spirits.

Wherever you start, hopefully it will be a trip you'll remember for a long time. Good traveling.

Part I
Entering the Spirits World

The 5th Wave   By Rich Tennant

"Jekyll, old man—I think you've made my wife's drink a bit too strong."

In this part . . .

Just like that first sip of your favorite spirit, this part is pure pleasure. Here I trace the history of distilled spirits, right from the beginning in the 11th century. I also explain the distillation process, and I offer tips on how to serve and enjoy distilled spirits. I recommend reading the chapters in this part if you're new to the spirits world; this information is bound to whet your appetite for the various alcohol beverages you can read about in the rest of the book. Pour yourself a glass of whiskey, settle into your most comfortable chair, and start reading.

Chapter 1

Discovering Distilled Spirits

. . . .

In This Chapter

▶ How distilled spirits were invented

▶ How distilled spirits became popular

▶ The foods from which spirits are made

▶ The varieties of distilled spirits

. . . .

*T*his chapter is called "Discovering Distilled Spirits," but "Distilled Spirits 101" would also do nicely because this is a down-to-earth basic guide to the multicultural history of the wonderful beverages human beings produce via distillation.

Naturally, the chapter includes some spirits history, starting with a graceful bow to other types of alcohol beverages and how they differ from the distilled varieties. The different types of spirits are listed here, as are the foods from which they're made. And just for kicks, I give you a quiz about famous spirits (okay, famous ghosts) in classic movies.

A Brief History of Distilled Spirits

The road to distilled spirits begins with those *other* beverages, wine and beer.

The story starts one day back in the dim, distant past at a point that most anthropologists peg between 5000 and 6000 BCE. A goatherd in the Tigris-Euphrates valley (now Iraq), where human beings created their first agricultural communities, noticed that his flock was friskier than usual.

Looking closely, he saw the goats feasting on rotting grapes fallen from a nearby vine. Being a curious goatherd, he tasted a few grapes himself. Then he tried a few more, and maybe another handful after that, and soon goats and goatherd ambled happily back to their village to share their discovery with others.

Of course, you know what that anonymous goatherd didn't: Those "rotten" grapes had fermented.

In other words, naturally occurring microorganisms in the air had landed on the grapes and started feeding on the fruit, digesting the grape sugars, and turning them into gas (carbon dioxide) and liquid ethanol/ethyl alcohol, which is the same alcohol used in all modern alcohol beverages.

Eureka! Wine! Beer!

Very quickly, the goatherd's friends, neighbors, and acquaintances far and near grasped the idea that squeezing rotten, sorry, *fermented,* fruit released a pleasantly intoxicating beverage called wine (from the Greek *vinos,* the Latin *vinum,* the Old English *win,* and the Germanic *winam*).

And then they discovered that fermenting grains released an equally pleasant intoxicating beverage called beer (from the Latin *bibere* [to drink], the German *bier,* and the Old English *beor,* pronounced *beer*).

After that, a jolly good time was had pretty much everywhere fruits and grains were grown. And it was a profitable time, as well: The oldest known Sumerian tablet is a receipt for a shipment of beer from Mesopotamia to some lucky merchant in Northern Greece. This tablet is a hunk of clay that made it possible for modern scholars to translate the language of Sumer, the nation of Middle Eastern city-states that was one of the world's earliest civilizations.

Advancing the art

At first, folks were content with wine and beer. But being human and naturally inquisitive, they began to experiment with ways to standardize the fermentation process because they wanted to manage the production and improve the quality of alcohol beverages.

Not all alcohol is "alcohol"

Ethanol (ethyl alcohol) is the only alcohol used in food and beverages, but it isn't the only alcohol used in consumer products.

Other alcohols that may be sitting on the shelf in your bathroom or workshop are:

- **Methyl alcohol (methanol):** Methanol is a poisonous alcohol made from wood. It's used as a chemical solvent (a liquid that dissolves other chemicals). During Prohibition, when the sale of beverage alcohol was illegal, some unscrupulous illegal producers would substitute methanol for ethanol, thus leading to many truly unpleasant results, such as blindness and even death, among people who drank it.

- **Isopropyl alcohol (isoproanol, "rubbing alcohol"):** Isopropyl alcohol is a poisonous alcohol made from propylene, a petroleum derivative. It's *denatured,* which means that it includes a substance that makes it taste and smell bad so you won't drink it by mistake.

- **Denatured alcohol:** When ethanol is used in cosmetics, such as hair tonic, it, too, is treated to make it smell and taste bad. Treated ethanol is called *denatured alcohol.* Some *denaturants* (the chemicals used to denature the alcohol) are poisonous, so some denatured alcohol is also poisonous when taken internally. In other words, it's definitely not a good idea to drink your hair tonic.

The first step was to take control of fermentation by adding specific microorganisms (yeasts) to the fruit and grains rather than simply allowing miscellaneous little buggers to waft in and ferment the fruit by accident.

The second step was to distill alcohol from the liquid released by the fermented food.

Unlike the discovery of fermentation, which seems to have been a happy coincidence, learning how to distill alcohol was the result of a deliberate series of experiments conducted by an Arab scholar named Abu Musa Jabir ibn Hayyam (?–803 CE). Most modern scientists generally accept Jabir, known in the West as Geber, as the Father of Modern Chemistry.

Sometime during the eighth century CE — these dates are never quite as clear as one might like them to be — Geber was puttering around with his *al-ambiq,* a round pot with a tall spout rising from the top, sort of like an oversized tea kettle. When liquid was heated in the pot, the vapors rose through the spout to be cooled, condensed, and collected as a liquid in a vessel conveniently positioned under the spout.

The al-ambiq was standard equipment for alchemists, the medieval practitioners who spent their lives trying to turn base metal into gold and, as a sideline, looking for the magical "elixir of life" that would make men immortal.

But Geber, who may have been a wine aficionado, took a different tack. He wondered what would happen if he poured wine into the al-ambiq and boiled it.

In other words — "Eureka!" will do nicely — the man was about to invent distillation.

Distillation arrives

It's a physical fact that alcohol boils at a lower temperature than water, so when Geber poured his wine into his al-ambiq and set the pot over a fire, the alcohol in the fermented grape juice or the fermented grain and water mixture used to make beer vaporized before the rest of the liquid in the pot.

The alcohol vapors rose through the spout on the al-ambiq, were collected and condensed, and, just like that, Geber produced the world's first distilled spirit. And it needed a new name.

The solution was simple: While some alchemists were playing around with longevity tonics, early cosmeticians used their al-ambiqs to boil up powdered antimony in water, producing a dark liquid called *kohl* or *al-kohl*.

Al-kohl became *alcohol*. The al-ambiq became the alembic still, also known as the pot still, which is described in detail in Chapter 2. And that's how your favorite distilled spirit drink was born.

The secret gets out

Geber died in 803 CE, but his distillation process lived on among his Arab compatriots who used the distillate they produced not as a beverage but as a medicine.

The Arabs kept distillation to themselves for several centuries, taking their secrets with them to the Iberian Peninsula when they conquered Spain. When Spain expelled its non-Christian citizens in 1492 and Portugal followed suit in 1597, the secrets of how to make grain and fruits into a potent medicine remained behind to be taken in hand by those doctors of the Middle Ages — monastery monks. Like the Arabs, the monks prescribed the distillates, including some that they originated — such as Benedictine and Chartreuse liqueurs — for medicinal purposes.

The missionary/medicine men met with enough successes to convince the European pagans that these liquids carried the blessings of God to assure a long, healthy life. Around the year 1300, Arnald of Villanova, a professor of medicine at Montpellier (France), one of the earliest European medical schools, compiled the first (hand) written instructions for distilling alcohol from wine.

Arnald christened distilled alcohol *aqua vitae* (Latin for "water of life"), which translated to *eau de vie* in French, *uisege beatha* among the Celts, *akavit* in Scandinavia, and *vodka/wodka* ("dear little water") in Russia and Poland. By any name, the distillate was reputed, in Villanova's words, to "prolong life, clear away ill-humors, revive the heart, and maintain youth." Others claimed it also alleviated diseases of the brain, nerves, and joints; calmed toothaches; cured blindness, speech defects, and paralysis; and warded off the Black Death.

Moderation is the message

In 1478, 48 years after Gutenberg invented the printing press, an Austrian physician named Michael Puff von Schrick published the very first book on distillation. Puff's piece immediately hit the 15th-century bestseller list, going through 14 editions in 20 years.

Most readers probably bought the book to use as a medical reference, but a significant number likely picked it up in order to learn how to make distilled spirits with local fruits and other produce for pleasure.

The new distilled spirits were very popular, so much so that in 1496, a doctor in Nuremberg, Germany, whose name is unfortunately lost to history, offered a word to the wise imbiber: "In view of the fact that everyone at present has gotten into the habit of drinking aqua vitae, it is necessary to remember the quantity one can permit oneself to drink, and learn to drink it according to one's capacity, if one wishes to behave as a gentleman."

Sounds as good today as it did then.

Not surprisingly, nobody at all complained about having to take Arnald's medicine instead of the crushed leaves, boiled grains, and pressed herbs it came from.

The process goes global

Serendipitously, the spread of distillation occurred just as Europeans began to seriously explore and colonize the world, establishing regular trade routes between Europe and the East and Europe and the New World.

The Spanish and the Portuguese were leaders in the exploration game, bringing back new products and taking their alcohol beverages with them. Spirits, in particular, were a win-win trade-off because they were

- ✔ Virtually unknown in the lands the explorers explored
- ✔ Easy to produce
- ✔ A really smart way to turn an excess crop, such as grain, into a cash product rather than leaving it to rot in the field
- ✔ A stable beverage that resisted spoilage and turned tastier as it aged in wooden barrels

Best of all, distilled spirits were a totally natural product that — after distillation became common knowledge — could be produced from virtually any local plant anywhere in the world. As a result, by the 19th century, distilled spirits of one sort or another were available pretty much anywhere a traveler traveled.

Table 1-1 is a list of the plant foods that can be fermented to provide the base for making distilled spirits.

Table 1-1	Foods Used in Distillation
This Food . . .	*. . . Makes This Distilled Spirit*
Grains	
Oats	Scotch whisky
Rice	Sake (distilled rice wine), Japanese whiskey
Rye	Whiskey
Wheat	Whiskey, vodka

This Food . . .	. . . Makes This Distilled Spirit
Fruits and Vegetables	
Agave fruit (piña)	Tequila
Apples	Apple jack, brandy
Grapes	Brandy, eau de vie, grappa
Other fruits	Brandy, cordials, liqueurs
Potatoes	Vodka
Sweeteners	
Sugar cane, molasses	Rum, aguardiente, cachaça
Honey	Cordials, liqueurs
Botanicals (Herbs and Seeds)	Gin, cordials, liqueurs

Setting Standards for Producing Modern Distilled Spirits

Distilled spirits came to the United States just as they had everywhere else — with the explorers and the immigrants. The Irish brought their own whiskey and so did the Scots. The Brits and Dutch brought gin, the French brandy, and Slavic people vodka.

The only difference was that while religious objections led to forbidding the use of any alcohol beverages (including spirits) in some countries, the United States stands alone in having once prohibited drinking for political reasons. (State legislatures under pressure from their constituents passed bans of varying severity on beverage alcohol production and distribution. So many states had bans, in fact, that ultimately the federal government had to follow suit or face interstate warfare.)

The not-so-noble experiment

In 1917, following years of agitation by anti-alcohol activists and the passage of prohibition laws in a number of states, the United States Congress passed the 18th Amendment to the Constitution prohibiting distribution or sale of alcohol beverages nationally. One exception: Medical purposes with a prescription only.

Two years later, after ratification by the requisite three-fourths of the states, Prohibition became the law of the land. Congress then passed the Volstead Act (the National Prohibition Enforcement Act) defining an alcohol beverage as any liquid containing more than 0.5 percent alcohol.

The result was an increase in crime as Americans in general said, "No way," to what President Herbert Hoover called "the Noble Experiment." Americans did their drinking at home or in speakeasies (nightclubs hidden behind locked doors, opened only to a secret password such as "Joe sent me"). Alcohol was shipped in surreptitiously by bootleggers sneaking across the country's seacoasts or its northern or southern borders. Worse yet, there was also an increase in illness due to the fact that much of the alcohol making its way into America's drinking glasses and teacups was unregulated, unsafe, and sometimes deadly.

By 1933, the country had had enough: On December 5, the 21st Amendment to the Constitution was ratified, repealing the 18th, and Americans could once again legally enjoy alcohol beverages, including those of the distilled variety.

New rules for better times

The bad news about Prohibition is that it increased crime and reduced the safety of alcohol beverages. The good news is that after the country recovered from its dry spell, the federal government sat down to write the Alcohol Administration Act on what exactly constituted a specific spirit.

Since then, other countries and economic entities such as the European Union have followed suit. As a result, when you buy Scotch whisky or Bourbon or any other distilled spirit from a recognized distiller anywhere in the world, you know that you're getting a standardized, reliable product.

The American rules, known formally as *Standards of Identity,* are contained in *Title 27 of the Code of Federal Regulations, Chapter 1, Part 5, Section 5.22.*

If you want to know every single little detail about what makes a distilled spirit a whiskey, say, or a vodka, every single fact is available online at www.atf.treas.gov/regulations/27cfr5.html. If your eyes glaze at the very thought of making your way through government-ese, you can find a slightly more user-friendly version posted online by an organization called The Online Distillery Network for Distilleries & Fuel Ethanol Plants Worldwide at www.distill.com/specs/USA10.html.

Or you can read the clear descriptions in the next section, which lays out the basics minus the boring factoids only distillers really need to know to make sure their product meets U.S. standards. And of course, each chapter in this book is devoted to a specific spirit and presents the important facts about the drink.

In essence, the take-away points are:

- ✔ No, a distiller can't just pour some ethanol into a bottle and call it whiskey or one of the other popular distilled spirits.
- ✔ Yes, when you buy your favorite brand, you're getting a standardized product that meets all the relevant government standards.

The Types of Spirits

All distillates come off the still as clear liquids. How the distiller processes the liquid determines the taste, smell, and appearance of the final product.

As a rule, however, all spirits fall into one of two broad categories: *clear spirits* and *dark spirits.* Put in the simplest terms, clear spirits are the ones you can see though; dark spirits range in color from warm amber to deep brown.

The clear spirits

All clear spirits are clear, but depending on the foods from which they were distilled, some have a specific flavor.

- ✔ **Gin** comes in two basic styles. There's the original Dutch jenevre (which the French called *genievre*), a distillate of malt spirits that include juniper berries. London dry gin is a clear spirit that's redistilled with juniper berries and further flavored with aromatic botanicals (plant products).

✔ **Rum** is distilled from molasses or sugar cane. All rums start out as totally clear spirits; some are aged in barrels, a process described in Chapter 2. Aging turns the rum golden, amber, or very dark.

✔ **Sake** is a clear spirit distilled from rice wine.

✔ **Tequila** is distilled from the fruit of the blue agave plant. Like rum, all tequilas start out clear, but some turn golden or amber with aging.

✔ **Vodka** is a true neutral spirit, crystal clear, with no discernible flavor or aroma. Modern vodka producers, however, may flavor their vodkas, changing the taste and sometimes the color to match the color of the fruit juice or synthetic flavoring.

The dark spirits

With the exception of brandy, which is distilled from wine (remember Geber from earlier in this chapter?), dark spirits are beverages distilled from grains.

Like clear spirits, the dark spirits start out clear, but aging in barrels and the addition of coloring agents such as caramel (burnt sugar) to maintain color consistency from year to year turns them characteristically golden amber.

✔ **Brandy** is a spirit distilled from wine or a mash (fermented mass) of any fruit, most commonly grapes.

✔ **Whiskey** is a spirit distilled from grain, such as barley, corn, rye, or wheat. A straight whiskey is made from the distillate produced by one operation of a still and added neutral spirits. A blended whiskey contains several straight whiskeys and added neutral spirits.

✔ **Bourbon** and **Tennessee Whiskey** are distilled spirits made only in the United States; by law, they must be made of 51 percent corn.

✔ **Canadian Whisky** is a distilled spirit made in Canada, generally from a mix of grains, primarily corn, plus rye, wheat, and barley.

✔ **Irish Whiskey** is a distilled spirit made in Ireland from a mix of grains dominated by barley.

✔ **Scotch Whisky** is a distilled spirit made in Scotland from a mix of grains, primarily barley, plus "small grains" — so-called because they're used in limited amounts. The small grains usually include oats.

For spirits, every year is a good year

Unlike wine and with the exception of some brandies, spirits aren't classified by vintage.

For wine, quality and flavor depend to a great extent on the characteristics of the grapes from which the wine is made. Specifically important is their sugar content, which may vary from year to year along with the weather.

Distillation, on the other hand, produces a liquid (distillate) free of all sugars; it's the still master's skill, not the weather, that determines the quality of the liquor.

Ditto for aging. Wines age in the bottle as active microorganisms continue to digest and process residual sugars, maturing and mellowing the flavor of the wine. Spirits, on the other hand, age only in barrels. After they're bottled, they are what they are: Time doesn't change them.

Yes, some distillers, notably the Scots, promote high-priced specialty whiskies that have been aged for more than 21 years and proudly display the year in which they were bottled. But what matters isn't the year they were bottled, but the time they spent in the barrel.

Of course, a very old, very rare, and maybe very dusty bottle of whiskey may be valuable to a collector, but before you plunk down multi-dollars for one of these bottles, remember: Poor storage in varying temperatures, exposure to sunlight, or a loose cap can turn even the very best spirit unpalatable.

A Word about the Words

Like other fine craftsmen, distillers cringe when folks describe their products in derogatory terms.

Prime example: *booze.* The word comes either from the old English word *blouse* (to drink heavily) or, more likely as the *Online Etymology Dictionary* suggests, from the name of early Philadelphia distiller E.G. Booze. Either way, it's a no-no in the company of serious spirits connoisseurs.

Another no-no is *hooch,* short for *Hoochinoo,* the name of a native Alaskan Tlingit Indian tribe whose distilled spirits were a fave with miners during the Alaskan Gold Rush. The *Merriam Webster Online Dictionary* says this one first popped up around 1880. But it really took off during Prohibition, possibly because someone discovered that the tribe's name comes from an Indian word for *grizzly bear fort* and figured that the hooch packed the punch of a big, bad bear. Or not.

Entertaining spirits

Check out the following list to see how many entertaining spirits you can match with the actors who embodied them.

On the left, the name of a famous motion picture starring a member of the spirit world. On the right, a list of actors and actresses who starred in the films. Match 'em up. Answers follow.

Movie	*Star(s)*
1. Ghost (1990)	a. Bill Murray
2. The Ghost and Mrs. Muir (1947)	b. Bob Hope, Paulette Goddard
3. The Ghost Breakers (1940)	c. Gene Tierney, Rex Harrison
4. Ghost Story (1981)	d. Fred Astaire
5. Ghost Busters (1984)	e. Patrick Swayze, Demi Moore
6. The Ghost Goes West (1935)	f. Charles Laughton
7. The Canterville Ghost (1944)	g. Robert Donat
8. Ghost Catchers (1944)	h. Nancy Sinatra, Harvey Lembeck
9. Ghosts of Mississippi (1996)	i. (John Sigvard "Ole") Olson and (Harold Ogden) Johnson
10. The Ghost in the Invisible Bikini (1966)	j. Whoopi Goldberg, Alec Baldwin

Answers: 1. e; 2. c; 3. b; 4. d; 5. a; 6. g; 7. f; 8. i; 9. j; 10. h

By preventing Americans from enjoying safely made alcohol beverages, Prohibition triggered the production of some fairly nasty homemade substitutes with equally nasty names. One example is *rot gut,* a pretty clear description of what happens to your innards if you drink alcohol beverages made by careless amateurs.

As for *bathtub gin,* yes, people really did whip up this stuff in their bathtubs using medical alcohols and flavorings. Unfortunately, as the sidebar "Not all alcohol is 'alcohol'" explains, the alcohols used in medicinal products, such as rubbing alcohol, aren't safe to drink. Which brings us back to — you got it — rot gut, a term that's been pretty much discarded now that alcohol beverages are legal and safe when consumed in moderation.

But that doesn't stop people from calling spirits *hard liquor* to differentiate them from beer and wine. Actually, because no liquid is either hard or soft, the more sensible terms are *higher proof* or *higher ABV* (more about that in Chapter 2), descriptions based on the alcohol content of the beverage.

Finally, the term *alcoholic beverages* (rather than *alcohol beverages* or *beverage alcohol*) is just plain silly. Who ever heard of a whiskey, gin, vodka, or whatever, that drank too much whiskey, gin, vodka, or whatever? No one, that's who.

Chapter 2

How Distilled Spirits Are Created

In This Chapter

▶ Tracking spirits from distiller to consumer

▶ Exploring the chemistry of distillation

▶ Defining the still master's job

▶ Showing the various stills used in distillation

*N*o, this chapter doesn't explain how to cook up spirits at home. Even if the United States government didn't frown on *moonshining* (producing distilled spirits without having the required licenses), you'd still find it difficult, not to mention costly, to install a still in your basement or garden shed.

Instead, this chapter addresses the Real Deal: the multitudinous steps a licensed distiller must take from start ("I think I'll sell a new vodka."), to middle ("Wow! The marketing guy's decision to put it in a blue bottle is terrific!"), to end ("Here, dear customer, try my product.").

It's a hard job, but somebody has to do it. Luckily, so many people do it well enough to enable the rest of us to enjoy the fruits (and/or grains) of their labor.

The Distillation Process in a Nutshell

All beverage alcohol — beer, wine, spirits — begins with the action of microorganisms (yeasts) added to a food-and-water mix, such as grains and water.

The microorganisms ferment carbohydrates in the food. Translation: They convert the starches in food and produce a liquid (alcohol), a gas (carbon dioxide), and flavoring agents (congeners).

For brewers and winemakers, the fermentation process ends when the microorganisms have digested enough carbohydrates to produce a liquid that's 25 percent alcohol, which is much higher than the concentration of alcohol in most beers and just about right for a lot of wines.

However, 25 percent alcohol is too low for most distilled spirits. To obtain sufficient quantities of *neutral spirits* (the virtually pure alcohol used as a base for spirits products), the distiller must distill the *wash* (the liquid drained from the food/yeast/water mix) to separate out the alcohol.

 Distillation is a physical separation process that's so simple, in fact, that as you read this, it's a good bet that somewhere in the world a freshman student in a chemistry class is heating a liquid until it boils and watching the steam rise into a collector where it cools and condenses back into a liquid. But making the alcohol is only one step in the process that yields distilled spirits.

There are only five steps needed to arrive at a distilled spirit. Here they are:

- ✔ **Step 1:** Choosing the food from which to distill the alcohol
- ✔ **Step 2:** Preparing the food for distillation
- ✔ **Step 3:** Heating the prepared mixture to produce (distill) a specific spirit type
- ✔ **Step 4:** Maturing the distilled spirit
- ✔ **Step 5:** Packaging (and shipping) the finished product

Steps 1, 2, 3, and 5 apply to all distilled spirits; some types, such as vodka, aren't aged — no Step 4 for them. (I talk about maturing, called *aging,* in the "Aging Gracefully" section later in this chapter.)

At every step along the way — from carbs to spirits to you — the process is monitored by a still master and his assistants (yes, it's still a very masculine profession) to make certain that the ethanol the distiller turns out meets health and safety standards for use in beverages. The still master totals every ounce of alcohol produced during each distillation period so that the revenue agents have a clear record for tax purposes.

Yay team.

Talking the distillation talk

Like all professionals — doctors, lawyers, chemists, wrestlers — distillers have a language all their own. The following table lists some of the basic vocabulary.

ABV (alcohol by volume)	A measurement term used to describe the concentration of alcohol in a bottle of beer, wine, or spirits
Batch	Alcohol distilled in one limited run through the still; also used to describe selecting barrels for use in making a special product
Congeners	Flavoring agents and alcohols generated by reactions and procedures in making spirits
Ethanol, ethyl alcohol	The chemical name for the alcohol used in food and beverages
Fermentation	The process by which microorganisms digest and convert carbohydrates (sugars and starches) to a liquid (alcohol) and a gas (carbon dioxide)
Milling	Procedure to strip away the outer covering of grains used in making distilled spirits
Mash	Soupy mass of fermenting food from which spirits are distilled; the process of creating a mash is called *mashing*
Mash bill	The recipe for amounts and types of foods used in the mash
Neutral spirits	The ethanol collected and condensed during distillation at or above 190 proof
Proof	An increasingly outmoded measurement term used to describe the concentration of alcohol in a bottle of beer, wine, or spirits
Still	The container in which the alcohol/water liquid from fermented food is distilled
Still master	The person who determines the "recipe" for a distilled spirit and who watches over its creation
Wort	Soup of milled and soaked ingredients mixed with water

The Basic Material for Distilling

Virtually any carbohydrate-rich food can be used as a base from which to distill alcohol.

With the exception of milk — which contains lactose (milk sugar) and is often used after it ferments to produce an alcohol beverage called *kumis* — foods from animals don't contain carbs, which is why nobody's ever made a chicken, fish, or hamburger whiskey, gin, or vodka.

Plant foods, on the other hand, are carb rich; grains, fruits, nuts, seeds, and at one time or another flowers have all been used as the base for a distilled spirit.

Picking the right food(s) is the job of the still master, who, along with other members of the distillery staff, is charged with creating a shopping list called a *mash bill,* a recipe listing the food(s) to be used in distilling a specific whiskey, gin, vodka, or other spirit.

In most countries, including the United States, the government plays a role in drawing up the mash bill, laying down some basic rules to govern how much of which foods go into what kinds of spirits. For example, a Bourbon must be distilled from a minimum of 51 percent corn with the remainder being other grains. What's in the balance is left up to the individual distiller, which is why all Bourbons have a similar flavor with slightly different flavor notes, depending on the "house style" of the source.

Distillers use neutral spirits in blending dark spirits, such as whiskey, and to produce clear spirits, such vodka and gin. These neutral spirits may be distilled from any of the following:

- ✔ Any grain, such as barley, corn, rice, rye, or wheat
- ✔ Any high carbohydrate food, such as potatoes, agave, sugar cane, and others
- ✔ Fruits, such as grapes for brandy. Unfermented fruits, nuts, herbs, and seeds are also used as flavoring agents.

Milling and Mashing

Milling and mashing may sound like the name of a really good law firm, but they're actually two processes used in creating distilled spirits. In this example, I use grains because distilling from them is basic to all other plant and vegetable products used to make potable spirits.

Warning: Yeasty beasties at work

Sailors crossing the Equator for the first time are often subject to an initiation that ranges from the fun (being splashed with water) to the more rigorous (actually being dunked in the ocean).

People visiting a distillery for the first time may also run into a rite of passage. When they enter the mash room, the distillery guide may open the top of the fermentation vat and invite the victim, sorry, visitor, to step closer and take a really deep breath.

Ooops.

Gases produced during fermentation collect right under the covering, so that really deep breath may lead to sudden — but temporary — dizziness.

If the distillery folks offer a taste of the fermenting product, the smart answer is a polite, "No, thank you." Why? Because consuming the active yeasts in the vat has been known to trigger certain gastric discomforts best left to the imagination. In all fairness, you should know that the folks who work in distilleries do taste the fermenting mash without suffering any consequences. Perhaps repeated exposure acclimates their tummies.

Of course, when the product is finished and bottled, the yeasty beasties are gone, leaving a delicious and totally drinkable liquid. Pick up a bottle as you leave: Sampling the finished spirit inside is far and away the best way to remember your distillery visit.

In the first process, the grains that are used as a base for distilling go through a *mill* where mechanical rollers, hammers, and/or grinders break and strip away the husk (outer covering) of the grain to expose as much of the surface of the grain as possible.

In the second of these two processes, the grains are plunked into water and mushed into a *mash*. The water pulls carbs out of the grains into a solution so that those determined microorganisms can get to work.

Before distillation can take place, the mash is heated and fermented by adding yeast.

Starting the fermentation process

After the grain is mixed into a mash, the mash is heated in a large vat so that naturally occurring enzymes in the grains (malt enzymes) soften the grains into a soupy mass called a *wort*.

The wort is then pumped into a large vat called a *mash tun*. The mash tun may be either a wooden container with an open top or a steel or copper container with a closed top. Either way, the bottom of the tun is a strainer through which the liquid flows from the mash into a separate container (the *fermentation tank*). Protein-rich residue is left atop the strainer in the mash tun, and it's compacted and used as animal feed.

Bringing on the micros

Now the still master adds microorganisms — the yeasts — to the liquid in the fermentation tank. Two kinds of yeast work together at this point:

- **Cultivated yeast:** Distillers guard their cultivated yeasts as closely as Fort Knox to prevent the competition from stealing the strain and preserving it in temperature-controlled splendor for future growth for generations (of yeasts).

- **Wild yeast:** These yeasts enhance flavor differences even in products from distilleries located within short distances apart. Wild yeasts are a lot less trouble to handle than their often richer relatives, cultivated yeasts. Leave the fermentation tank open and zap, you've got local yeasts dropping in to help out. Although still masters don't often talk about it, there's a difference in yeasts. It's tough fitting these uncontrolled rascals into the ultimate taste profile desired, but adding complexity is often worth the effort.

Almost immediately, the yeasts go to work digesting carbohydrates in the liquid, emitting alcohol and carbon dioxide. As the carbon dioxide rises to the surface, the solution bubbles. Poetic distillers may describe this phenomenon as "the dance of life." You can call it — what else? — fermentation.

As the yeasts continue to digest the carbs, the amount of alcohol in the liquid steadily rises. When the alcohol concentration reaches 3 percent, the still master transfers the liquid — now known as *distiller's beer* — from the fermentation tank into the still for the main event: distillation.

Distilling: The Main Event

In the distillery, the distiller pours or pumps the water/alcohol mash from the fermentation tank into the *still* (a vessel used for distillation) and heats the still until the liquid inside boils.

Distillation: Up close and personal

Here's a Mr. Wizard–like experiment for you:

Put 1 cup of plain water in a small (1-quart) pot with its own lid.

Put the lid on the pot, put the pot on the stove, and heat the pot until you can hear the water boiling inside. (Yes, if you listen really carefully, you can hear the boil.)

Let the water boil for a minute or so.

Turn off the heat, and lift the lid off the pot.

See the drops of water on the underside of the pot lid? That water is steam that rose from the boiling water to collect and condense as (huzzah!) distilled water.

Ain't science grand?

Because alcohol boils at a lower temperature than water, vapors from the alcohol rise first, to be collected and condensed as liquid ethyl alcohol, the alcohol used in beverages. The alcohol produced in the still is also known as *neutral spirits* because it's free (or relatively free) of flavoring and aroma compounds.

The modern still master works with two distinct types of stills: l the *pot still* and the *column still.*

The pot still

The first pot still was the *alembic still* used by the Arabs who invented distillation sometime during the 11th century CE (for more on the historic discovery and the men who accomplished it, turn to Chapter 1).

The classic alembic still is a simple copper pot with a rounded bottom and an elongated spout (or *swan's neck*) on top that traditionally ends in a twisted coil called the *worm.*

So perfect is the design that modern distillers still use the alembic still centuries after it was designed. The process goes something like this:

1. A distillers pours his mash into the pot still.

2. He heats the vessel over an open fire.

3. The fire sends the alcohol vapors up into the swan's neck.

4. The vapors go into a water-cooled condenser or jacket.

5. In the condenser, the vapors are condensed into liquid alcohol.

6. The liquid alcohol runs out of the worm into a waiting container.

What pot stills are used for

The pot still turns out relatively small amounts of alcohol. As a result, modern distillers most commonly reserve it for *batch distilling,* the distillation of limited amounts of alcohol to make *hand-crafted spirits.* These spirits are small quantities of what the still master considers unusual (read: unusually good) brandies, Bourbons, Irish and Scotch whiskeys, vodkas, rums, and gins. You can see the modern pot still in Figure 2-1.

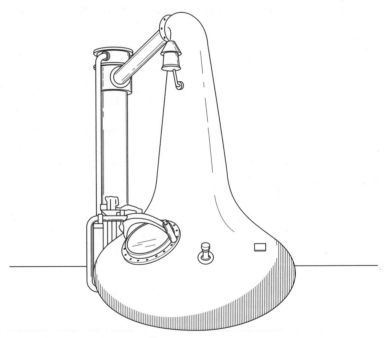

Figure 2-1: The modern pot still.

With the increased interest in whiskey and other types of distilled spirits, a growing number of small distilleries have sprung up around the United States doing all their production on pot stills. Pot stills also are used by mass market operations to produce spirits that offer a more complex or deeper flavor to particular brands.

One example of this is Brown-Forman's Woodford Reserve Kentucky Bourbon, which is made exclusively on pot stills. As a result, sampling craft whiskeys and other spirits — whether from giant distilleries or limited production brewpubs or wineries — can be an exciting experiment. Of course it can also be a waste of time and money.

The American Distilling Institute is a good source of information for fans of hand-crafted spirits. The Institute publishes its own newsletter (*American Distiller*), runs conferences on craft distilling, and maintains a list of reputable, fully licensed craft distillers. You have to be a member to enjoy the full range of benefits. Interested? Check it out at www.distilling.com, or send an e-mail to bill@distilling.com. You can also go the snail mail route by writing to American Distilling Institute, Box 577, Hayward, California, 94543-0577.

How pot stills work

To use a pot still, today's distiller pumps the liquid from the fermentation tank into the still; applies heat via piped-in steam, coils, or an open fire under the still; and then collects the liquid that forms as the alcohol vapors rise through the condenser (the worm).

Actually, the distiller goes through this process twice: Distilling alcohol with a modern pot still means distilling in two pot stills (and sometimes three). They're called *wash stills* and *spirits stills* depending on when they're used in the distillation process.

The trip through the first pot still

The liquid that comes off the first still, or wash still, is called *low wine.* Low wines are suitable for making spirit products because they contain substantial amounts of compounds called *congeners,* which are formed during fermentation.

The primary congeners are

- ✔ **Aromatic esters:** Aroma compounds formed by chemical reactions between alcohol and acids

- ✔ **Aldehydes:** Flavor and aroma compounds formed by chemical reactions between alcohol and oxygen

- ✔ **Fusel oils** (from the German word *fusel,* which translates to the English *rot gut*): Highly flavored alcohols that can be found in alcohol distilled at less than 190 proof and used only in very small quantities, if at all

To obtain the alcohol he needs to make a good-tasting, pleasant-smelling, safe bottle of distilled spirits, the still master must eliminate all or most of these congeners. The amount of congeners the still master allows in the alcohol depends on the product in which the alcohol will be used; whiskeys have some congeners, vodkas have virtually none (and some claim no flavor at all).

The trip through the second pot still

The distiller pours or pumps the low wine from the wash still into a smaller spirits still. Once again, the still is heated, and the alcohol vapors rise to be collected and condensed into liquid alcohol called the *distillate*.

The distillate comes off the still in three distinct phases:

- ✔ **Phase 1:** The *foreshots* (or *heads*) of the batch are low-boiling compounds generally not fit to drink.

- ✔ **Phase 2:** The *potable spirits* (or *mid-cut*) of the batch is the alcohol you can drink.

- ✔ **Phase 3:** The *feints* or *tails* of the batch are unpleasant, oily, smelly, bad-tasting compounds that would make the product, well, oily, smelly, and bad-tasting.

How the still master earns his big bucks

The still master's job is to collect the distillate at exactly the right moment. In other words, like Goldilocks and her Three Bears, whose chairs, beds, and bowls were "too big, too small, and just right," the still master must contend with distillates that are too early, too late, and just right.

These "just right" potable spirits are set aside to be bottled unblended just as they are or blended with other spirits of the same type. The too-early foreshots and too-late feints are poured back into the spirits still and put through again with the next run of low wines.

The three-phase process is repeated until the distiller has the amount of potable spirits — with the precise amount of flavoring and aroma congeners — that he needs to make his product. The residue left in the still at the end, called *spent lees,* is discarded. Then the pot still is cleaned, and soon enough the whole process begins again.

Beauty is as beauty does

Copper pot stills with their graceful "swan necks" are often beloved by their still masters, who are likely to give the pot a pet name such as "Old Bess" or "General Lee." Kinda makes ya feel warm all over, doesn't it?

The column still

Column stills were invented in the 19th century to enable distillers to meet the growing demand for distilled spirits.

The column still's greater capacity remains its greatest virtue. Its second selling point is that, unlike the pot still, it doesn't have to be cleaned at the end of a distillation — a point that anyone who's ever wanted to throw out the dinner dishes rather than wash them one more darned time will appreciate.

As a result, the column still predominates in large commercial distilleries in producing just about any type of mass-market spirit from whiskey to rum and certainly vodka. Figure 2-2 shows a diagram of a typical column still.

Working the column still

The column still itself is an enormous piece of equipment that has two huge stainless steel or copper cylinders that may stand as high as a three-story building.

Inside each cylinder are perforated, heated copper or steel plates placed evenly apart. The plates at the top of the first column in the still are cooler than the plates farther down the column. As a result, when the alcohol/water wash from the fermentation tank is pumped into the column, the alcohol — which has a lower boiling point than water — boils first, producing vapors that collect near the top of the column. The vapors at the top of the column move into a cooled condenser tube where they turn back into liquid alcohol, spilling down the tube to an opening at the bottom of the second column in the still.

If two columns are used, the second column also has heated, perforated copper or stainless steel plates that are hotter at the bottom and cooler at the top. As the alcohol enters the second column, it's again heated. The alcohol vapors rise to an opening near the middle of the second column and flow through the opening to a cooling condenser tube. From there, they spill as distillate into a holding vat. (As with the pot still, the still master must choose the "just right" distillate with which to make his spirits product; see the earlier section, "How the still master earns his big bucks," for more info.)

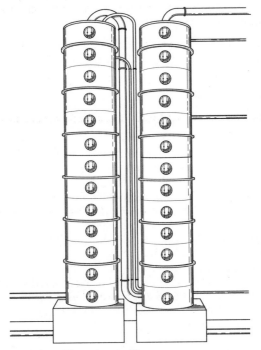

Figure 2-2: The column still.

And then the distiller pours more wash into the first column, and the whole process continues without interruption. Remember: There's no need to clean the column still between distillation sessions, which, of course, is why the column still is also known as the *continuous still.*

Two columns or three?

Like the pot still, the column still produces foreshots, potable spirits, and feints. The potable spirits are drawn off for use in spirits products. The flavor and aroma of the potable spirits can vary with the amount of congeners remaining in the liquid.

Coffey's still

In Ireland the column still is often called the Coffey still in honor of Aneas Coffey. In 1832, as the Inspector General of the Irish Excise, he came up with the idea for a new still large enough to increase production of whiskeys. Coffey went into partnership with a Scottish engineer named Robert Stein, a member of the Haig family of the Haig & Haig distillery. Together they patented their design for the column still, which is why this still is also known as the patent still.

As a side note, when reading the previous paragraph, did you catch the fact that the men who invented a new way to make alcohol were named Coffey and Stein, the latter being the name for a beer mug?

What a small (and fascinating) world . . .

To remove as many congeners as possible, some distillers — usually those making vodkas — put their wash through a still with three columns. This procedure makes it possible for them to label the finished product as *triple distilled,* which is a fancy way of saying, "Hey, our still has a third column and yours doesn't."

Does removing more congeners through the extra column make a better product? If *better* means more flavorful or safer to drink, the answer is no. On the other hand, if *better* means less flavor and virtually no aroma, the answer is yes. In other words, for a distiller making vodka, triple distilling may make sense. For those making whiskey, the two-column column still is just dandy.

Aging Gracefully

All neutral spirits flow colorless from the still, but they can still have a lot of flavor — sometimes with a natural but unpleasant "bite" that makes your mouth pucker (sort of like biting into a lemon). Allowing the distillates to rest and age with others in a finished blend or alone for a while in wooden barrels and casks smoothes away the bite caused by excessive tannins (bitter flavor compounds found in plants). Because of the intimacy among the spirits in the barrel, it's called *marrying.* Rarely is a divorce necessary.

 Aging in a wooden barrel or cask is a legal requirement for any dark spirit such as whiskey or rum. A little aging — enough to smooth the bite but not to add flavor, aroma, or color — may also benefit vodka, but it isn't a legal requirement.

As the spirits age in the barrels, some alcohol and water evaporates; distillers commonly call the alcohol lost to evaporation the "angels' share."

Oxygen flowing through the porous barrel triggers chemical reactions that promote the formation of flavor and aroma. The spirits absorb specific flavor, aroma, and color compounds from the wood itself or from the previous contents of the barrel. For example, whiskeys aged in casks that once held sherry or port absorb some of the sweetness of these wines.

This absorption of some flavors and aromas occurs immediately in the barrel. But other compound extractions and oxidation take place at various times, some early "in the wood," and others later. In the first two years of aging, the changes in the spirit depend to a large extent on how much color, flavor, and aroma are in the wood itself.

In the end, what goes into the barrels as a relatively sharp-tasting, clear liquid emerges smooth, flavorful, and glowing amber to rich dark brown in color.

The classic oak barrel

Distillers use different kinds of wood to form the barrels in which they age their spirits. For example, in Japan, sake is sometimes aged in cedar barrels to give the products an unusual piney flavor. But the favorite wood by far is the noble oak — that is, the American oak in the United States, Spanish oak (sherry) casks, and Limousin oak from France.

No one knows for sure exactly why the Romans chose oak wood to make the first spirit aging barrels or why early distillers decided to think that was the only way to go. Maybe oak trees were the most abundant and thus the best renewable source of wood. Maybe oak was the easiest wood to work into barrels — flexible, strong, and resilient. Or maybe someone noticed strictly by accident that spirits aged in plain oak barrels just plain tasted better.

Fancy oak is good, too. For making American whiskeys, the law dictates that the inside of the barrel must be charred before use. The depth of the char depends on the desired flavor profile. As you might expect, the charred wood yields more flavor, aroma, and color than bare wood does.

Other distillers, notably the Scots, age their spirits in barrels once used for sherry or American oak once used to age Bourbon. Aha, you may say, the thrifty Scots are minding their pennies by reusing the barrels. Well, yes. But as I note in the previous section — and explain more fully in Chapter 5 — the sherry-impregnated barrels also lend a certain flavor distinction to the new spirits.

In addition to contributing to flavor and smoothness, the distiller must decide what kind of wood to use in light of its *porosity* (allowing oxygen to join in the ceremony). Several other economic and technical factors keep the interaction between barrel and its contents active for a specific period of time.

Is getting older always better?

Is getting older always better? To a point. A touch of aging benefits most spirits, including clear spirits such as vodka, by reducing the original bite. But aging a vodka is a distiller's choice. Aging a whiskey is mandatory. For example, in the U.S., Bourbon must be aged for at least four years before it can be bottled. Scotch whisky's minimum aging is three years; however, tradition says that the longer it rests in the barrel, the tastier it will be. Many Scotch whisky distillers disagree. The common wisdom seems to be that after 21 years, the whisky begins to lose some flavor notes. If that supposition is true, then why is it that older whiskies have a greater value in the marketplace? There's a lesson there.

Blending Science with Art

The road to perfection in making a spirit product is long and sometimes difficult. Establishing a flavor profile is just the beginning. Choices must be made all along the way, from the mash used to the yeasts used to when to end the distillation to the type of barrel used and then to the final taste in the bottle. With so many decisions, it's possible that tasting the spirit when it's aging in the barrel may convince a tasting panel that something is missing. Whereas a chef may be asked to add a pinch of salt, in the case of spirits, the suggestion is most likely to be, "How about adding something from Barrel 1,234?"

Agreement is reached, and the product in one barrel is enhanced by adding some of the contents of another barrel laid down on the aging warehouse shelf in a different year, at a different time of year, in different barrel wood, and even with a different still master temperament that day.

After the blend is decided on, the spirit is once again married to make certain that the flavor is truly blended. And that's the art connected with the science of distillation.

Samuel Bronfman (1889–1971) is the man who created and built The Seagram Company, Limited, which was once the world's largest maker and marketer of distilled spirits. Bronfman was widely respected for introducing blended whiskeys to North America after the repeal of National Prohibition in the United States (for more on blending and other facets of a revolutionary whiskey, turn to Chapter 7).

It wasn't an accident. Bronfman's mantra, repeated to every new (and old) member of the Seagram team, was simple: "Distilling is a science. Blending is an art."

Even today, some still masters would disagree. They hold that the only "artistic" spirit is unblended; that the real art is to create a high quality spirit that needs no other spirit, color, or flavor to make it consistent and to make it good. You decide who's right.

Straight spirits

When the still master pumps his distillates into barrels for aging, he pumps in one distillate from several runs of the still into each barrel. If this distillate (plus water to lower the alcohol content) is left to age on its own and is then bottled on its own, the product is a *straight spirit* (by U.S. standards).

Straight spirits are products whose flavor and aroma may vary subtly from batch to batch, depending on such variables as

- The grain from which the spirit was distilled
- The exact moment the distillates came off the still
- The barrel in which the spirit was aged

As a result, straight spirits from a reputable distiller can be an exciting taste experience for those who appreciate trying something new and unusual, rather like tasting vintage wines. Blended spirits are more consistent in flavor because they adhere to a set recipe.

Blended spirits

The alternative to a straight spirit is a *blended spirit,* such as a blended whiskey.

Proving the point

No alcohol comes off any still totally free of water, and all alcohol beverages are alcohol plus water; wine and beer also contain some residue of the foods from which they were made.

The label on every bottle of wine and spirits describes the alcohol content of the liquid inside with the term *alcohol by volume* (ABV). (For reasons too complicated to discuss in fewer than, say, 50 pages, beer containers may carry this information, but U.S. law doesn't require that they do.)

ABV measures the amount of alcohol as a percentage of all the liquid in the container. For example, if the container holds 10 ounces of liquid and 1 ounce of that is alcohol, the product is 10% ABV — the alcohol content (1 ounce) divided by the total amount of liquid (10 ounces).

An older term for describing alcohol content is *proof,* which is a measurement equal to two times ABV. For example, an alcohol beverage that's 10 percent ABV is 20 proof.

The word *proof* (in regard to alcohol beverages) derives from a series of experiments sometimes credited to an unknown 17th or 18th century British naval officer desirous of making sure British sailors got the full measure of alcohol in their daily tot of rum. The officer, or maybe someone more scientifically credentialed, tried dampening gunpowder with the beverage and then setting the stuff on fire. After much trial and error (and several scorched walls), the naval officer or his scientific alter ego determined that no flame meant no alcohol in the bottle, while a slow-burning flame showed that the spirits were "at proof" (50 percent alcohol in the liquid). If the flame sort of sputtered and died, the alcohol beverage was deemed underproof; a bright yellow flame signified overproof.

That eyeballing way to measure alcohol content went out in the 19th century with the invention of scientific instruments to measure the specific gravity of liquids. Appearance of ABV on bottle labels is a recent innovation, with producers given the option of using either proof, proof and ABV, or ABV alone for a few years until 2003 when ABV was made the totally official, absolutely standard label term. Of course, distillers are allowed to also show the level of alcohol in the bottle in terms of proof if they so desire.

To make a blended whiskey, the still master mixes together in one barrel distillates from several runs of the still, several different barrels, or even barrels from other distilleries and allows them to age together.

Blended spirits are designed to maintain a brand's distinctive character by delivering the same flavor and aroma characteristics batch after batch after batch.

The recipe the still master uses to create blended whiskey is (as you might expect) a very closed industrial secret, guarded with the still master's life. Or at least with serious discretion.

Bottle, Bottle, Who's Got the Bottle?

The last step in the production of spirits is bottling.

Choosing a model bottle

According to the Food Marketing Institute, a trade organization for the nation's food markets, in 2005 the average American supermarket carried 45,000 different products.

The average liquor store has fewer bottles than that, but you still see plenty of brands in all different sized bottles vying for your attention whenever you step into the spirits section. As a result, the distiller's job is to make sure his product yells "buy me" louder than the next one on the shelf. And that means making his bottles as attractive as possible.

To that end, a designer makes a clay model of the bottle for any new product (older products are presumably as attractive as they can be). If the distiller approves it, the designer makes a mold from the model and produces test bottles. If the distiller approves again, the designer sends the mold off to the glass factory to be manufactured. The bottles come back and, at last, the end of the distilling process is really in sight. Sometimes the bottle may even be tested on a random sample of consumers called a focus group. The winning bottle shows up down there at the end of the bottling line.

The bottling line

Pay attention, watch your fingers, and keep your eye on the moving bottles. This part of the distillery-to-you process really zips along.

First, cases of empty bottles are delivered to the distillery. The cases are opened and placed upside down on a conveyor belt so that the bottles slip out (still upside down) while the cases go off to wait for the filled bottles.

PET project

Glass is still the most popular material for spirits bottles, but within the last 20 years, the U.S. government has also approved the use of bottles made of PET (polyethylene terephthalte). This is a plastic that doesn't affect the flavor or quality of the spirit inside, weighs less than glass, is less easily broken, and can be colored or frosted or have the label printed right on the surface of the bottle.

Of course, governments being what they are, they didn't just say "go for it" on PET. In fact, they wrote strict regulations. According to *Title 27 of the Code of Federal Regulations, Alcohol, Tobacco Products, and Firearms,* PET used for spirits bottles in the U.S. must

✔ Be a molded rigid or semi-rigid material

✔ Have uniformly thick walls

✔ Be made in an approved process

✔ Meet U.S. Food and Drug Administration health and safety standards

✔ Permit the evaporation of no more than 0.25 percent alcohol by volume (ABV) during bottling for spirits sold in 50 ml and 100 ml bottles

✔ Permit the evaporation of no more than 0.15 percent alcohol by volume (ABV) during bottling for all other spirits

Next, the upside-down bottles ride along the conveyor belt to be cleaned and sanitized with a compressed air/vacuum/suction device that swooshes out any stray particles.

After that, the cleaned bottles, now right side up, move along to the part of the conveyor belt where jets above the conveyor belt squirt spirits into the bottles, filling them to precisely the right level. No muss, no fuss, no expensive waste.

Now the bottles move on to the capper, which is exactly what it sounds like: the device that either corks the bottle, or, more likely, screws on the top.

After they're sealed, the bottles continue along to the label station, where paper labels are applied with glue. (Sometimes a label is already etched or silk screened onto the glass and this step is skipped.) If the labels are glued on, the next step is a pass through a machine that's something like a carwash, where pads press the label in place and swinging brushes clear away any excess glue.

Size matters

Old timers may still ask for a *fifth* or a *quart* or a *mini* — terms for spirit bottle sizes used in the United States from Prohibition Repeal until the 1980s. At that time, the Americans decided to join their British and Continental fellows in measuring their foods and beverage products in metric terms.

Most food products continued to be sold in the familiar ounces, pounds, and quarts, but in 1982 the Treasury Department's Bureau of Alcohol, Tobacco, and Firearms (BATF), now called the Tax and Trade Bureau (TTB), specifically required distillers to repackage their products in bottles conforming to metric sizes.

In 1994, the Food and Drug Administration amended the Fair Packaging and Labeling Act to require dual units — ounces, pounds, or quarts plus metric — on all consumer products. But distillers are still the only ones who absolutely have to use metric.

Some consumers, believing that metric measures gave them less product for the buck, were unhappy. Complaints to distillers rose for a while, but as the new measures settled into the national consciousness, the furor abated and a liter became as cozy a term as a quart had been.

And surprisingly enough, consumers got an even better bargain, monetarily speaking, because a liter is actually larger than a quart. Who knew?

The following table shows the comparisons.

New Sizes (Metric)	Old Sizes (Standard U.S.)
1.75 liters	None
1 liter (1,000 ml/33.33 ounces)	Quart (32 ounces)
750 ml (25 ounces)	Fifth (25.6 ounces)
500 ml (16.67 ounces)	Pint (16 ounces)
375 ml (12.5 ounces)	Half pint (8 ounces)
50 ml (1.67 ounces)	Miniature (1.7 ounces)

From there, it's a short trip to the case-packer, where the appropriate number of bottles (varying by size, of course) is packed into the appropriate cases (varying by size, of course).

And that's it. Distilling's done.

Chapter 3

Enjoying Spirits

- -

In This Chapter

▶ Preparing for a tasting

▶ Discovering the rules of tasting

▶ Understanding your senses

▶ Evaluating distilled spirits

- -

*T*he basic rules for tasting spirits are pretty much the same as those for tasting any food or drink: Choose your samples, taste them, and decide which you like best.

Fine distilled spirits are a pleasure to the senses. To enjoy them, you need to bring to the tasting table a set of tools — the product you plan to sample; the perfect tasting glass; and, of course, your body with its incredible sensory organs.

Novice or expert, this chapter lays out the "Rules of the Ritual" for you to enjoy. These rituals include choosing spirits, picking glasses, and creating a tasting sheet to record your impressions of each product you sample.

Assembling the Accoutrements

Yes, *assembling the accoutrements* is a fancy French way of saying "What follows is a list of the equipment you need to run a success-ful tasting." You need to select the spirits for tasting and present them in an organized way to maximize your guests' enjoyment. In this section, I tell you what accoutrements you need and give you tips on setting up a tasting to remember.

Choosing your spirit

Clearly, you're the best authority on which spirit to feature at your tasting. After you make that decision, the question is how many different types you want to try. That decision depends on the spirit you're tasting and the type of tasting you plan to run.

Selecting spirits by type

Tasting Irish whiskeys? Then you probably want one from each of Ireland's three major distilleries: Midleton, Bushmills, and Cooley (for more on each, check out Chapter 4).

Aiming for Scotch? Clearly, you want at least one single malt whisky and one blended whisky. More ambitious tasters may want five single malts, one from each of the Scotch whisky-making regions listed in Chapter 5, plus at least one blended Scotch. Or, you may just want to compare blends of Scotch.

Similar rules apply to your choice of other types of distilled spirits; for the details, check out the appropriate chapters.

 When choosing spirits for your tasting, less may well be more. In other words, pick three — or, at the most, five — rather than 30. Your sense of smell and taste operate more efficiently when you have fewer choices (I give you more details later in this chapter). Save the others for your next tasting. And the one after that.

Selecting spirits by the type of tasting

Experts describe the tasting ritual as either a *vertical tasting* or a *horizontal tasting.* No, a vertical tasting is *not* a tasting you do while standing up. It's a tasting that compares different products from the same distillery. For example, Powers and Jameson are Irish whiskeys from the Midleton distillery. But each has its own distinctive character; comparing the two shows how one distiller can vary his style.

A horizontal tasting, on the other hand, compares similar products, such as vodkas or single malt whiskeys, from different distillers. Once again using Irish whiskeys as an example, your choice of unblended whiskeys may include Midleton (Midleton), Bushmills Single Malt (Bushmills), and Connemara (Cooley). Comparing these three whiskeys shows different styles from different distilleries.

Tasting the very special stuff

Few whiskey aficionados have the pocket change required to plan a tasting around unusual bottlings like these:

- ✔ **The Macallan Fine and Rare Collection,** 1926, 60 years old. *Forbes* magazine pegged this Scotch at $38,000 a bottle in 2004.

- ✔ **Chivas Regal Royal Salute,** 50 years old. At $10,000, this Scotch costs less than a third of the price of the Macallan, but it may still be out of your price range.

- ✔ **Springbank,** 32 years old. A bottle of this Campbletown single malt Scotch has a three-digit price tag of $750.

Even if you decide that these whiskies are worth saving your pennies, good luck finding a bottle.

But the hefty price tag of these bottles doesn't mean that you can't taste some very special whiskeys at your favorite swanky bar or plain old neighborhood tavern.

Walk in. Study the line-up of bottles on the back bar. Accept the fact that you may not know which of them is the finest and ask the barkeep to suggest, say, three for tasting. And be real about it: If the whiskeys are very, very expensive — even by the drink — settle for two. Then taste, savor, and dream of the day when you, too, are a cyber-billionaire with all these very, very expensive bottles lined up in your very own living room.

Setting the tasting table

You wouldn't sit guests down to dinner without plates, flatware, and glasses, would you? Same thing goes for a tasting. Before your tasting begins, put the following items in the center of the table where everyone can reach them:

- ✔ **The spirits bottles.** Open each bottle, and remove the cork or closure to allow the spirit to air out, or more correctly, to allow air in for a while before you start the tasting. The air enables the spirits to open, which is tasting talk for "the molecules mix with air and bounce about, intensifying both the flavor and aroma."

For a really sophisticated tasting — experts only need apply — cover the original labels with stick-on labels numbered 1, 2, 3, and so on, and then challenge the tasters to identify the products.

✔ **Pitcher of fresh, cold water.** The water, used for diluting the spirits during the tasting, should be still (no bubbly, please) and as mineral-free as possible to avoid compromising the flavor of the spirits.

✔ **Unflavored crackers.** Plain Melba toast nicely cleanses your palate — that is, it gets rid of the taste of one spirits sample before you move on to the next.

✔ **Spit bucket.** An empty paper ice bucket is fine.

The communal spit bucket and crackers are okay; a small individual spit bucket and stack of crackers at each place setting is classy.

To continue setting the table for your tasting, put the following at each place setting:

✔ **A shot glass.** Use this 1- to 1.5-ounce glass to measure the spirits for tasting. No shot glass? Use your kitchen measuring cup, which may be even more precise.

✔ **A tasting glass.** The ideal tasting glass is a *snifter,* a glass that narrows toward the top, collecting the aroma molecules so that you get a really good sample when you stick your nose into the glass.

On the other hand, perfection sometimes must bow to reality: If you don't have snifters, 12-ounce lowball glasses (see the "Avoiding glass warfare" section later in this chapter) will do. But no plastic and no paper cups; these materials add aromas and flavors of their own, compromising those of the spirits.

Note: Ordinarily, the taster rinses the glass between samples. Lots of glasses make things easier.

✔ **Napkins.** For the inevitable spill or dribble, of course.

Creating the tasting sheet

The *tasting sheet* is a record of your personal evaluation of each spirit you taste. Table 3-1 shows a sample tasting sheet that you can copy or adapt as you see fit. The section "Getting to the Good Part" delves into the elements you evaluate on the tasting sheet.

Table 3-1		Spirits Tasting Sheet			
Spirit	*Color*	*Legs*	*Aroma*	*Flavor*	*Comments*
#1					
#2					
#3					
#4					
#5					

Getting to the Good Part

At least three of your five senses — sight, smell, and taste — play an important role in your evaluation of the spirits. Some people say that touch also plays a role, as in the pleasure of holding a well-made crystal glass, and that the sound of the spirit flowing or splashing into the glass may also set your senses a-jangle. Could be. But, in truth, the eyes, nose, and tongue do most of the work.

Let the tasting begin!

Enjoying the view: Color and legs

Begin by pouring 1 ounce of one of the spirits into the tasting glass. Let the glass sit quietly for a few minutes, once again to allow the spirits to open (see the earlier section, "Setting the tasting table," for more information on letting the spirits open).

While you wait, observe the liquid. Your eyes may be the windows to the soul, but they're also the gateway to the stomach: If food doesn't look good, the body says, "Who me? Eat that? No way." For example, imagine a dish of creamy mashed potatoes, topped with a dollop of butter. Yummy. Now imagine those potatoes colored dark green. Yuck. Or, more on point, imagine a glass of warm, amber whiskey. Lovely. Now imagine *that* dark green. Not!

In fact, various experiments with truly tolerant volunteers have shown that simply seeing something that looks yummy can send sensory messages to your brain that trigger the transmission of similar messages to other parts of your body. Message to the salivary glands: Start secreting saliva to dissolve the food or dilute the drink. Message to the stomach: Start secreting gastric juices to digest what's coming.

In short, the first step toward tasting isn't putting something into your mouth: It's *seeing* something you want to put into your mouth.

In distilled spirits, color is a guide to how long the product has been aged. Most gins, rums, and vodkas are perfectly clear. The exceptions are slightly aged gins, aged rums, and vodkas with added flavor/coloring.

On the other hand, the color of whiskey ranges from warm gold to amber to the dark brown the Yanks call *molasses* and the Brits call *treacle*. As a general rule, the darker the color, the longer the whiskey has aged in the barrel and the greater the malted grain content of the mash from which the whiskey was distilled.

Note the color of the spirit on your tasting sheet (check out Figure 3-1 for an example of a tasting sheet), and move on to the second sight criterion: *legs*.

Body is defined as the consistency of the spirit. The best way to evaluate body is to put the glass flat on the table and swirl it so that the spirit spirals up the inside surface of the glass and then slides down again, leaving a trail (known in the trade as *legs*) as it goes.

Watch how fast the liquid runs down the side of the glass to pool again at the bottom. A spirit that runs down slowly is more *viscous* (thicker) than one that runs down quickly. Viscosity is a product of aging, so the slower the spirit runs down the sides of your glass, the older it is.

I cover more about body in the upcoming section on how the spirits feel in your mouth.

The nose knows

When it comes to tasting, your nose is right up there with your eyes. Simply inhaling the lovely aromas of food and drink sends sensory messages to your brain to alert the rest of you that something good is coming.

The proof of the pudding, sorry, the tasting, is that when you can't smell, you can't really taste. As anyone who's ever had a cold knows, when your nose is stuffed and your sense of smell is deadened, almost everything tastes like plain cotton. Even if your taste buds are working like gangbusters.

So go ahead, stick your nose right into the glass and take a deep breath to inhale the aromas.

With the exception of most vodkas, whose claim to fame is no aroma at all, good spirits smell, well, good. Each spirit has characteristic aromas of its own. Take your time. With patience and practice, you can learn to identify the characteristics of each type of spirit. (For a guide to the aromas associated with each spirit, check out the appropriate chapter.)

Actually inhaling the liquid into your nose is a serious breach of tasting etiquette — and it's also physically unpleasant.

Budding tastes

Taste buds are tiny bumps on the surface of your tongue, sensory organs that enable you to perceive different flavors in food — in other words, to taste the food and beverages you eat and drink.

Each taste bud contains groups of receptor cells that anchor an antenna-like structure called a *microvillus,* which projects up through a gap in the center of the taste bud, sort of like a thread sticking through the hole in a Lifesaver candy.

The microvilli in your taste buds transmit flavor signals from food along nerve fibers to your brain. Then those nerve fibers translate the signals into perceptions: "Oh, wow, that's good," or "Man, that's awful."

Taste buds recognize four basic flavors: sweet, sour, bitter, and salty. Some people add a fifth basic flavor to this list: *umami,* a Japanese word used to describe richness or a savory flavor associated with soy products such as tofu.

Early on, scientists thought that everyone had specific taste buds for specific flavors: sweet taste buds for sweets, sour taste buds for sour, and so on. Today, the prevailing theory is that groups of taste buds work together so that flavor chemicals in food link up with chemical bonds in taste buds to create patterns you recognize as sweet, salty, bitter, sour, and umami. The technical term for this process is *a cross fiber pattern theory of gustatory coding.*

Combining foods can short-circuit your taste buds' ability to identify flavors correctly. For example, sip a brandy, Bourbon, Scotch, vodka, whatever, even an apparently smooth and silky one, and your taste buds say, "Hey, that alcohol's sharp." But take a bite of cheese first, and the spirits will taste smoother (less acidic) because the cheese's fat molecules coat the receptor cells in your taste buds so that the acidic alcohol molecules can't connect.

A similar phenomenon occurs in serial spirits tastings (tasting many spirits, one after another). Try two equally acidic spirits and the second will seem mellower because acid molecules from the first one have filled the space on the chemical bonds that perceive acidity.

Here's another way to fool your taste buds: Eat a globe artichoke. The "meat" at the base of the artichoke leaves contains cynarin, a sweet-tasting chemical that dissolves in water, including your saliva. Any food you taste after the artichoke will taste sweeter. Try it. You may like it.

The tasting technique

At last! You set up your tasting, poured your first spirit, and took note of its color, legs, and aroma. Now it's time to check out the flavor. Take a small sip of the first spirit plus a little air. The best way do this is the classic *slurp* — a sort of sip-plus-inhale. And, yes, the strange sounds you make while slurping are acceptable at tastings.

After you evaluate the spirit, spit it out in the provided spit bucket.

After spitting out the first taste, take a cracker, and move on to tasting the spirits with water. Make note of the differences in flavors between the plain spirits and the spirits-plus-water, and decide which pleases your palate. Remember, there is no "correct" decision — just your own personal preference. Not quite sure what words to use? Table 3-2 is an expert's guide.

When you're done with spirits #1 and spirits #1-plus-water, take a plain cracker and a sip of plain water to cleanse your palate and move on to sample #2.

Sip. Evaluate. Spit. Note. Sip. Evaluate. Spit. Note . . . and so on.

Describing what you're tasting

The taste of the spirit comprises two distinct characteristics, mouthfeel and flavor. *Mouthfeel* is the texture of the liquid in your mouth, an attribute similar to *body* (for more info on this quality, refer to the "Enjoying the view: Color and legs" section, earlier in this chapter).

Your taste buds and your health

Your health (or lack thereof) may alter your sense of taste, causing partial or total *ageusia*, the medical term for loss of taste. Or you may experience *flavor confusion* — meaning that you mix up flavors, translating sour as bitter, or sweet as salty, or vice versa.

The following factors may contribute to alterations in your sense of taste:

✔ A bacterial or viral infection of the tongue may produce secretions that block your taste buds.

✔ An injury or radiation therapy affecting the nose, mouth, or throat may damage nerves that transmit flavor and aroma signals.

✔ Dentures may cover (and block) taste buds.

✔ Some medicines block your ability to taste or change your perception of flavors. The pharmacological miscreants include drugs to lower blood pressure, anti-fungal products, some psychotropic medications, and some drugs used to treat infectious illnesses such as tuberculosis.

The textures that you're most likely to experience in tasting spirits are

- ✓ Smooth and "thick"
- ✓ Airy, or vaporous, with fog-like tendrils of flavor
- ✓ Astringent, also known as dry

Evaluate the flavor by letting the aerated whiskey rest in your mouth for a second or two — one-one-thousand, two-one-thousand. Now swirl it around your mouth and let a little bit drip down the back of your mouth and into your throat. Notice the following:

- ✓ **The overall impression.** The first time you go through this ritual, you may get an overall impression of the spirits, but not be able to identify individual flavors. Take your time. Try again. With practice, you may be able to pinpoint several different flavors.

- ✓ **The special flavors.** With the exception of vodka, which made its marketing bones by having no flavor at all, the different spirits do taste different from each other. The exact flavors you find in spirits depend on the food from which the spirits are made, the way the product is distilled, and — most importantly — the aging process. The longer the aging, the more complex the flavors are likely to be.

 I tell you about the distinct flavors found in individual spirits in the chapters on each spirit. Eventually, with practice, you may be able to identify sweet flavors and bitter (dry) ones. Some spirits, such as Scotch whiskies, may have a salty or sour tang, but salty and sour are far less common than sweet and bitter.

- ✓ **The finish.** How intense is the flavor you taste? What about the finish (the length of time the flavor of the spirits remains in your mouth; the longer the finish, the longer the aging)? Does it linger in your mouth or disappear as soon as you spit? Is there an aftertaste? If so, is it pleasant or not?

- ✓ **The flavor with water.** Note that the flavor is milder when the spirit is mixed with water than when straight. But you guessed that, didn't you?

Table 3-2	Tasting Terms
Term	*Definition*
Clean	No unpleasant flavors
Dry	Not sweet, crisp

Term	Definition
Green	Flavor of grass or other greens (herbs)
Heavy	Strong aromas and flavors
Light	Clear but not overwhelming flavor and aroma
Mellow	Warm, aged
Rich	Strong, slightly sweet flavor
Round	Balanced flavor and aroma
Sharp	A prickling sensation, similar to that of the bubbles in a carbonated beverage

Source: Adapted from Scotch Whisky Association, www.scotchwhisky.com.

Serving Spirits Day to Day

Tastings are special events. Enjoying fine spirits is an everyday pleasure: Select a product and serve it well, in moderation. When you've chosen the type of spirits you want, the question is how to differentiate among the apparently thousands of bottles on the shelves. First, find a liquor store you trust. Second, learn how to read a label. And after you make your purchases, store your precious spirits properly, and serve them in the right glasses. The following sections walk you through the process.

Choosing a liquor store

As you know, the best liquor store has (a) a really good selection of products, and (b) salespeople whose suggestions pan out time after time.

The store doesn't have to be enormous to qualify. All you need is a reasonably varied selection of types and products. To verify this, do something radical: Walk down the aisles and look at the bottles. If you find at least ten brands (in a variety of sizes) for the major spirit types, the store makes the grade.

Finding a salesperson who consistently gives you good suggestions is a bit trickier. It requires an investment of time and money. To start, ask a trustworthy salesperson for a specific product (say, single malt Scotch whisky); he or she should do the following:

> ✔ Recommend at least five brands
>
> ✔ Be able to tell you exactly what makes each one unique
>
> ✔ Meet your price requirements, perhaps suggesting that you try small bottles (0.50 ml/miniatures, or 375 ml bottles) first

When you go back to the store and tell your salesperson which brands you liked best, he or she may repeat the process until you get exactly what you're seeking.

Surfing the Net

Can you buy spirits on the Internet? Yes. Do you want to? Maybe.

Keep in mind that you can run into a couple of problems when you buy on the Internet. It's necessary to be informed and work through the following issues:

> ✔ Find out whether shipping to your home is legal in your state.
>
> ✔ If shipping spirits to your home isn't legal, the online retailer may have to first deliver your order to a nearby retailer (or have a local distributor do that), and then you have to either pick it up or arrange for delivery.
>
> ✔ If shipping spirits to your home is legal, the law says an adult must be available to accept delivery. This can be a hassle if you and your housemates work during the day.
>
> ✔ Evaluate the price. The initial price quoted on a Web site may be lower than the price at your local retailer. True, the Internet price is usually free of the federal, state, and local taxes that can account for up to 50 percent of the local cost. However, shipping and handling charges may actually bring the real price right up to what you pay when buying locally.
>
> ✔ Because the Internet is global, be certain that the supplier is located in the United States and therefore is licensed by all the laws governing quality assurance.

If you do decide to try the Net, stick with nationally advertised brands, at least until you establish that you're dealing with a reputable company that accepts the need to obey the laws governing products and sale of all alcohol products.

Reading a spirits label

The multiple labels on a bottle of spirits sold in the United States serve up multiple factoids about the product: the type of spirits, where it was made, who bottled or imported it, the amount of alcohol in the spirits, whether the spirit has any added coloring or flavoring agents, whether the spirit has any major allergens (including sulfites), and, for those who want still more bottle reading, a warning about who shouldn't drink the spirit.

All this info — which may be more than you ever wanted to know — must be stated in English. Exceptions: The brand name can be in any language, and spirits bottled for sale only in Puerto Rico can print everything in Spanish except the word "imitation" and the net contents (exactly how much is in the bottle).

Figure 3-1 shows a typical set of labels on a typical bottle of spirits sold in the United States.

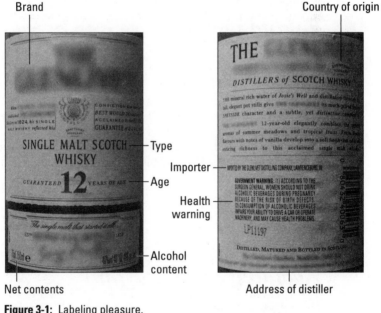

Figure 3-1: Labeling pleasure.

Protecting your investment

Do you plan to reserve a bottle of very expensive Scotch or Cognac for a special occasion — or a special tasting? Protect your investment with tender loving care by following these steps:

✔ Store the bottles in a cool, dry location. The traditional cellar is fine; so is a cool room, preferably on a standard bottle rack.

✔ Check the bottles from time to time. Be sure the top is still tightly sealed. Some people suggest that if the bottle's leaking, you can reseal it with melted candle wax, but any leakage means that air's gotten in and the alcohol inside may be evaporating out. Best to drink it sooner rather than later.

✔ Turn each intact bottle slightly to keep the cork inside moist. Dry corks crack, allowing air to enter and alcohol to escape. And dust the bottle to keep it looking nice.

✔ Keep a notebook listing any rare (or very expensive) bottles. Jot down the date of purchase and the cost to remind you what's awaiting your attention. And when the bottle is emptied, soak off the label and put it in a scrapbook, adding the occasion on which you finished it and what particular quality you enjoyed the most.

Taking temperature into account

To chill or not to chill? Actually, that should be to warm or not to warm?

Most dark spirits do well at room temperature; the temperature of the tasting rooms at most Scotch distilleries is about 60 degrees Fahrenheit (15 degrees Celsius). Whiskeys and brandies exude stronger aromas and release deeper flavors when you warm them by holding the glass in your hands before drinking.

The serious exception to warming is vodka. Warm, unflavored vodka can smell like — how to put this delicately — gasoline. Always serve vodka chilled. Maybe even straight from the freezer. No kidding.

Avoiding glass warfare

Is a Martini a Martini if it's not served in a Martini glass? The head says yes, but the heart says no.

Serving spirits in the proper glasses often makes a drink look better — imagine whiskey and soda in a cocktail glass rather than a rocks glass. In addition, the physical shape and size of a specific glass may actually enhance the flavor and aroma of the spirits.

The glasses commonly used to serve spirits are:

✔ **Shot glass:** Holds exactly one serving of spirits, defined by the United States Department of Agriculture/Health and Human Services (USDA/HHS) Dietary Guidelines for Americans as 1.5 ounces. Perfect for whiskey taken *neat* (straight, no mixer); also useful as a measuring cup.

✔ **Lowball, rocks, or old-fashioned glass:** This blocky, usually straight-sided glass commonly holds 12 ounces. Used for serving spirits with a splash of water, with or without ice, or some spirits cocktails, such as a whiskey sour over ice.

✔ **Highball glass:** Tall version of the lowball glass, used for spirits served with appreciable amounts of mixer — think Bourbon and branch water — with or without ice.

✔ **Snifter, brandy snifter:** Rounded, stemmed glass, broader at the bottom than at the top. Used for serving brandy, which is commonly warmed by holding the glass with your hands cupped around the rounded bottom.

✔ **Cocktail or Martini glass:** Shaped like an upside-down umbrella on a stem; holds 3 to 6 ounces of a spirits cocktail.

✔ **Cordial glass:** Jazzier version of the shot glass; 1- to 1.5-ounce capacity, stemmed or not, as you prefer.

Figure 3-2 is a visual guide to the types of spirits glasses.

Figure 3-2: Spirits glasses.

Distilled wisdom

Moderation is the key to enjoying spirits.

Fine spirits deserve respect. Each sip should be a reward, not the warning of a miserable morrow. In other words, "Cheers. Not tears."

The morning after isn't fiction. It's miserable physical fact caused by carelessly taking in more alcohol than your body can comfortably metabolize (digest) and flush away.

Drink a glass of beer, wine, or spirits, and its alcohol flows down your gullet to your stomach and small intestine and from there to your liver. In your stomach, an enzyme called gastric alcohol dehydrogenase (GADH) begins to digest the alcohol, but the heavy lifting occurs in the liver where a similar enzyme (liver alcohol dehydrogenase) completes the job.

Men generally produce more ADH than women do, and Caucasians produce more than Asians and Native Americans, but every single body has its limits. Regardless of your gender or ethnicity, if you take in more alcohol than you can metabolize in one pass through the stomach and liver, the leftover unmetabolized alcohol continues to circulate through your bloodstream, making trouble everywhere it goes.

For example, alcohol is a diuretic, so you urinate a lot, losing fluids and vital minerals while piling up irritating uric acid. Alcohol dilates blood vessels, including those in your head, so your head hurts. Alcohol irritates the lining of the stomach, causing it to secrete extra gastric acid, so your stomach aches and you feel queasy. Finally, alcohol slows the exchange of electrical impulses among nerve cells in the brain: Thinking slows, judgment slides away, and the tongue twists.

No magic potion will cure these ills. No tomato juice, no prairie oysters, no combination of vitamins and minerals, no teensy whiffs of oxygen will relieve the misery. As for the hair of the dog: Put a leash on it. Yes, alcohol is an anesthetic, so a sip may temporarily calm jangling nerves. But the additional sip must also be metabolized, which means more time until recovery.

In truth, the only cure for overindulgence is time. As it passes, the body will whip up some more ADH, metabolize more alcohol, and eventually clear the alcohol from your blood, but not the memory of its effects from your mind.

The next time around, all that went before should convince any rational person that enjoying alcohol in moderation is the only reasonable way to go. Cheers.

Part II
Whiskeys from Around the World

The 5th Wave   By Rich Tennant

©RICHTENNANT

"Well, I'm enough of a whiskey expert to know if the boat were sinking, there'd be several cases of this single-malt Scotch that would go into a lifeboat before you would."

In this part . . .

Whiskey is the prince of distilled spirits, and the cold dark reaches of the Northern British Isles is its ancestral home. From there, it set out to conquer the world. This part covers the first whiskeys, which came from Ireland and Scotland. Let the Irish and Scots argue about who invented whisk(e)y first. (More about that "e" in Chapter 5.) Then I examine what happened when Irish and Scotch whiskeys traveled west and came to North America with their emigrant distillers. I highlight those distinctly American whiskeys, Bourbon and Tennessee whiskey. If your personal preference veers to the north, I haven't left you out — Canadian whisky gets a chapter of its own. I also tell you about American blended whiskey and the whiskeys from fairly new markets, like Japan, India, and New Zealand. All you really need to worry about is how to enjoy all these wonderful spirits.

Chapter 4

Sipping the Irish Whiskeys

In This Chapter

▶ Tracking the origins of Irish whiskey

▶ Explaining what makes Irish whiskey unique

▶ Presenting a tasting guide to important Irish whiskeys

▶ Proposing a tour of Irish distilleries

*T*his chapter explains the origins and history of Irish whiskey and Scotch whisky (including why the Irish spell it with an "e"), notes the differences between the two, and tells why Irish whiskey (the world's first favorite whiskey) fell out of favor for a time and is now popular again.

You also get a tasting guide, a guide to enjoying the whiskeys, and, finally, the recipe and history for the original Irish coffee.

Entering the Emerald Isle

Ireland is truly special.

The warming Gulf Stream comes up from the tropics to kiss its Atlantic shore, bringing with it abundant rainfall that rarely turns to snow. On the other side of the island lies the wild Irish Sea, where 10 to 15 miles of water separate Ireland from England and Scotland.

Traveling along either coast, the visitor is dazzled by the rich green of the foliage framing a nearly tropical blue sea, thus earning Ireland the nickname the "Emerald Isle." Despite its situation on the northern part of the globe, Ireland is a fertile land with a temperate climate that supports abundant crops of grains, primarily barley, and low-lying mountains with clear mountain streams that provide more than enough unpolluted water for a unique whiskey.

Tracking the origins of Irish whiskey

You probably know that St. Patrick chased the snakes out of Ireland, but did you also know that he brought the "worm" in instead? At least that's the truth according to tales told over the bar in Irish pubs.

After the human race discovered distillation, many missionaries, commercial as well as religious, took the process with them as they traveled, introducing to the world the *worm,* the coils atop a still that condense alcohol vapors into neutral spirits, which is the first product of distillation. (Lost in the language? For a refreshing, sorry, refresher course in the distillation basics, bookmark this page, turn to Chapter 2, and then return to this very spot.)

St. Patrick, the gentle but determined fourth-century son of a Roman soldier and a British mother, was kidnapped as a child, sold as a slave in Ireland, and sent by his masters to study in a French monastery, where he was ordained and sent back to Ireland. In all likelihood, he took with him the product of monasterial distillation.

Patrick and his fellows, sent to "civilize" the Gaels, called their distilled spirits *aqua vitae,* Latin for *water of life.* In Gaelic, the Latin *aqua vitae* became *uisege beatha* (pronounced oosga *bee*-atha). Say that fast, with an Irish brogue, and it comes out close to *ushkey* — or at least, that's what it sounded like to British troops sent every now and then to conquer Ireland.

Well, to coin a phrase, how ya gonna keep 'em down on the farm once they've tasted *uisege beatha*? Naturally, the soldiers went home to tell friends and family about the wonderful — all together now! — ushkey, soon to be *whiskey.*

To "E" or not to "E": How come?

No etymologist (that's a word-derivation expert) knows exactly why the Irish spelled the wine of their country with an "e" and why their neighbors across the Irish Sea left the "e" out. It's often used as an indication that the Irish had the spirits first and because it sounded like a broad "e" in Gaelic, they started spelling whiskey with an "e." Under this theory, when the Scots started making aqua vitae, they wanted to point out the difference between theirs and the Irish. Hence, no "e." That's as good an explanation as any.

Sailing the Irish seas

The quickest way to stir up a fuss in an Irish pub is to suggest that the Scots were the first to make whiskey. In fact, the Scots and the Irish tied for first place in the distillation race. Sort of. Yes, the Scottish farmers may have started distilling earlier, but the Irish were the first to make the whiskey a commercial success.

Surrounded by the seas, the Irish were great sailors who had even designed a wood-frame hide or skin-covered waterborne vessel called a *curragh*. Julius Caesar first described the oval-shaped boats when he became one of the multitudinous invaders of Ireland and marveled at the craft's stability in choppy waters.

The curraghs, still in use long after the Romans left, made it easy for the Irish to cross the heaving Irish Sea to Scotland and deliver their whiskey to the populace. They were probably on one of those excursions to "civilize" the natives and increase Irish farmers' incomes.

As a matter of course, many of the seamen sailing from Ireland to Scotland saw the place as a land of new opportunity and settled right in, bringing with them their distilling techniques. In fact, so many made the trip east that modern genealogists may have a hard time locating a Scottish still master whose family tree isn't rooted in the old sod of Ireland. But that's a story for Chapter 5.

Beginning well: The early days of the Irish whiskey trade

What with the curraghs slipping back and forth through rain and sleet to deliver the goods to thirsty Europeans who used the whiskey not simply as a beverage but also as a purifier and flavoring agent for the local drinking water, everything was going swimmingly for the Irish.

That is, until 1608, 50 years after Henry VIII formed a Protestant state government in Ireland. That year, the British Crown issued the first license to an Irish distillery, Bushmills at Antrim in Northern Ireland.

Although the Irish had been making whiskey there for several hundred years, the new license served notice to the world — and the British treasury — that Irish whiskey was now a full fledged, legal member of world commerce.

And a cracking good time was had by all

One of the most popular Irish words is the Gaelic *craic* (pronounced crack). Nobody has an exact, original definition, but in modern language, *craic* means having a good time with other people by having fun, generally in a pub, with lots of conversation — and plenty of good Irish whiskey.

Then, in 1661, the British sat up and took notice of all the buying and selling back and forth, forthwith imposing a tax on all whiskey, a move translated by the Irish into: "The King is taxing Irish whiskey to benefit the Brits."

The new whiskey tax dramatically slowed the legal whiskey trade, encouraging the production of illegal *poitin* (pronounced po-*cheen*), or "little pot still," in honor of the type of stills used to make it. Still, Irish whiskey sailed off to Europe, carried by bootleggers and smugglers sailing under the British tax radar.

The higher prices didn't halt the British demand for good Irish whiskey, and the Irish beverage took a sudden leap forward in favor. Then, in the mid-18th century, a tiny insect called *Daktulosphaira vitifoliae* (common name: *phylloxera*) infested and decimated nearly all the wine grape vines in France. This decimation forced the thirsty French elite, who until then had looked on whiskey as a drink for the lower classes, to join the audience for Irish distillates.

Which left only the New World for the Irish to conquer.

Go west, young distiller

Crop failures are an unpleasant but familiar feature of farm life. For example, a widespread barley crop failure originally led Irish farmers to plant potatoes, a seemingly weatherproof and disease-resistant food brought back to Europe from the Americas. So adaptable was this multipurpose tuber that Irish farmers were soon labeled with the not-entirely-complimentary name of "potato eaters."

Potatoes, too, had been known to fall victim to a plant disease; over the years, limited crop failures had caused limited losses. But, the Great Hunger of 1845–1848 was a disaster of another magnitude entirely, a nationwide crop failure during which nearly 25 percent of the Irish people died from famine and more than 500,000 left for North America.

Those who stayed uprooted the potatoes and planted in their place grains to be used in distilling. The first whiskey they produced was less than perfect, but it was inexpensive and it sold well enough that soon an estimated 2,000 stills were in operation, making Irish whiskey again very available.

Across the Atlantic, as the Irish settled in the New World, they brought with them their distilling techniques and their special whiskey. Soon, the beverage was popular enough to convince American tavern owners to lay in a continuing stock, and once again, Irish whiskey began to gain favor with a new audience.

And then the Americans changed the rules.

Losing — and again finding — the luck of the Irish

As the 20th century began and Irish whiskey continued to make its popular way in the world, American voters decided to amend their Constitution to establish Prohibition, making it illegal to make, sell, or drink alcohol beverages (except for medical reasons, of course), thereby introducing millions of American and Canadian drinkers to smuggled whiskey — much of it Irish.

As if that weren't enough of a challenge, almost as soon as Prohibition was repealed via a second amendment to the Constitution, a very new American distilled spirit, blended whiskey, began to compete for the loyalty of drinkers who preferred the light flavor of the Irish variety.

As if *that* weren't trouble enough for Irish whiskey, during World War II, most American GIs stationed in Britain had their first taste of Scotch whisky and French wines, liked what they tasted, and brought their newly sophisticated palates home with them. Sales of the milder Irish (and American) whiskeys dropped to the point where it soon became difficult to find Irish whiskey on the shelves of many liquor stores.

Some Irish distillers tossed in the towel, cashed in their holdings, closed their distilleries, and retired to the South of France (just kidding on that last one). But the more faithful pulled up their distilling socks, so to speak, held on, and rode out the revolution much as they had the raids of Vikings and Goths.

Thanks to them, today's Irish whiskeys are back in force, with sales in the United States alone expected to cross the million case mark by 2010. It's been a hard road, but you can bet St. Patrick would be proud of his progeny.

The Uniqueness of Irish Whiskey

Virtually all Irish whiskeys are triple distilled (sent through a still three times), most often on pot stills (alembics), and aged a minimum of three years. Even those products that make no age claim on the label are likely to have aged in the barrel for between five and eight years.

Irish whiskeys may be

✔ Single malts (a single distillate from one distillery)

✔ Vatted (a blend of distillates and/or neutral spirits from one distillery or several distilleries)

✔ Vintage (a blend of whiskeys from a single year's production at one distillery)

✔ Limited bottling (single distillate or a blend from special aging casks that impart special flavor and aroma notes)

Regardless of the type, the distinctive character of Irish whiskey is determined chiefly by

✔ The grain (mostly barley)

✔ The water (mostly hard)

✔ The fire (coal or wood)

The following sections give you details on how grain, water, and fire come together to create the Irish whiskey you know and love.

Beginning with barley

Ireland's primary native grain crops are oats, wheat, and barley. The latter is a versatile product that can be used as food for human beings and animals, and as a base for fermented alcohol products, such as beer, and distilled spirits, such as whiskey.

As a general rule, distillers require 22 pounds of grain to produce a 600-liter cask of *mash* (the grain-plus-water base from which alcohol is ultimately distilled), which may be expected to yield 21 to 23 liters of grain whiskey.

But the amount of alcohol produced during distillation rises with the proportion of starch in the grain. A high-starch grain yields more alcohol than a low-starch grain.

Early on, Irish distillers used oats in their distilling, giving their spirits a recognizable "oaty" taste. Then some smart cookie in the distillery realized that barley has proportionately more starch than oats, while some food chemist discovered that barley also has lots of *diastase,* an enzyme that hastens yeast's conversion of the grain's starches to sugar, a vital step in controlled fermentation and distillation.

The smart cookie, having put one and one together, probably went straightaway to tell the smart cookie's boss to switch to the more efficient barley, making it the predominant grain for making Irish whiskey (and saving the company a bundle in the process).

Following the flow

The second component in the distinctive flavor of Irish whiskey is the water used in making the mash and turning the plain alcohol into a liquid that's no more than 100 proof (50 percent alcohol by volume). In other words, drinkable whiskey.

Most of the stream and spring water used in the distillation of Irish whiskey is naturally filtered through limestone in the Irish soil. As a result, the water is *hard* — that is, packed with minerals that lend a special flavor to the finished product.

Firing the spirit

Before the grains for whiskey can be made into mash, they must germinate (in other words, sprout). Heat speeds germination; in Ireland, the source of the heat is usually a wood or coal fire. Occasionally, the Irish may light their fire with *peat,* a compacted moss most commonly used in Scotland. (The Scots traditionally malt their whisky by spreading the barley on a floor, beneath which burns a hot peat fire. The smoke and flavoring agents from the peat fire are thrown into the grain. The Irish don't particularly go for that peaty taste and so burn theirs in bricks cut from the native peat beds, all fired up in an enclosed oven.)

The material burned in heating the grains can impart a flavor of its own; master distillers often have their own preferences in creating a special whiskey and use the malting process to help them out.

Cordially yours

Whiskeys are dandy but so are the candy, sorry, cordials made from Irish whiskeys.

The three Irish cordials best known and most generally available in the United States are Bailey's, a blend of Irish whiskey and fresh dairy cream; Bailey's Mint (ditto, plus mint flavor); and Irish Mist (whiskey plus honey and other flavors).

No, they don't go well with Irish potatoes or boiled cabbage, but as an after dinner treat? Terrific.

Fire also plays a role in developing the flavor of the whiskey in the barrel because Irish whiskeys, some of which are aged in barrels that once held Bourbon or sherry, are usually aged in charred barrels (for more about that, check out Chapter 2 where barreling and aging are discussed in complete detail).

The Leading Irish Whiskeys

Up until World War II, Ireland had dozens of distilleries, each producing its own style of whiskey. However, as drinking preferences changed and the demand for Irish whiskey fell, many of these facilities closed. The majority of the remaining ones merged to form the Irish Distillers Company, a conglomerate that held sway over the entire Irish whiskey industry up to and for some time after the war.

Within the past 20 years, a series of corporate sales and mergers ultimately brought almost all the Irish distilleries together under the corporate umbrella of the Pernod Ricard, a French company that is now the world's leading producer of Irish whiskey — and several other types of alcohol beverages.

The remaining distillers of Irish whiskey are

- Midleton
- Bushmills
- Cooley

You can see where they're located on the map in Figure 4-1.

Each has its own take on how a superior Irish whiskey should look and taste. Read on to quench your curiosity.

Figure 4-1: Ireland and its major distillers.

Midleton

Midleton is located in, well, Midleton, a town about 15 miles from the southeast Irish coastal city of Cork. One of the world's largest and most complex distilleries, the company has enormous continuous and pot stills capable of turning out 5.3 million gallons of whiskey every single day for Midleton's own brands and those of other distillers.

Midleton is also home to the world's largest pot still, constructed in 1825, a short time after the original Midleton Distillery was built. The "Big Still," no longer in use, could accommodate more than 40 gallons of mash at a time, a big deal in its day. The still was shut down after construction of the new Midleton plant in 1975.

Midleton's leading export brands are Jameson, Powers, and Redbreast.

Jameson

Jameson (80 proof/40 percent ABV — alcohol by volume) was originally made at the Jameson Distillery in Dublin (founded in 1780). Its popularity increased until it became the world's leading Irish whiskey. At that time, Jameson production was moved to Midleton, and its original Dublin plant was converted to a must-see visitor's center.

The pale gold whiskey is a blend of about 50 percent pot still spirits plus malted spirits from continuous stills, aged in sherry casks. Its light, sweet taste not only makes it easy to drink neat but also makes it a superb base for the cocktails Americans love.

You can find Jameson and Jameson 12 Year Old around the world. Jameson Gold 18 Year Old may be harder to find.

Midleton

The Midleton offerings (80 proof/40 percent ABV) are most often special bottlings, such as Midleton Very Rare 1994, and several very costly single cask-aged whiskeys, each with a slightly different and smoother flavor.

These are top of the line whiskeys, and the variety of flavor hints provided by the different barrels make them exciting to track down.

Powers

Powers (80 proof/40 percent ABV) is another famous Dublin whiskey, first made in 1791, whose original recipe has been faithfully preserved at Midleton.

Powers Gold Label carries no age statement, but like other Irish whiskeys, it's aged for a minimum of three years. Powers 12 Year Old Millennium, with a higher percentage of malt spirits, is more deeply flavored. The regular Powers is really designed as a mixing whiskey and is most often the Irish whiskey used in taverns for that purpose.

Redbreast

Redbreast (80 proof/40 percent ABV), an old-style pot still whiskey in the Jameson line, is brighter in color than the traditional Jameson. It has a deep body and a flavor that lingers on the palate, leading some tasting experts to insist that "one can always identify Redbreast, even in a blind comparison tasting."

The whiskey, originally available primarily in Ireland, is now being distilled at Middleton so that more is available for export.

Bushmills

Bushmills, the world's oldest licensed distillery (1608), is located in Antrim, Northern Ireland, near the famed Giant's Causeway — a spread of natural granite pillars in the sea that some consider the ruins of a natural bridge to Scotland, less than 25 miles away. Legend has it that the Irish giant Fingal ("Finn McCool") walked across the bridge to carry distillation from Ireland to Scotland. Frankly, as Julius Caesar noted, the carraghs seem a better bet.

A fire destroyed the original Bushmills building in 1885; the "new" distillery uses only pot stills to turn out several well-known blended light whiskeys.

Bushmills Original

Bushmills Original (80 proof/40 percent ABV) has a distinct malty flavor and an aroma reminiscent of toast or baking bread. This blend of grain neutral spirits and whiskeys is distilled and aged for up to seven years on the Bushmills grounds in eight "cellars" large enough to hold a total of 175,000 quietly aging barrels.

Black Bush

Despite its name, Black Bush (80 proof/40 percent ABV) is a brilliant deep gold. The whiskey has an intense malt flavor and is a favorite with those who prefer a stronger flavor than Bushmills Original. Black Bush costs more; however, its fans say the price reflects the quality and the heritage which in itself is worth the money.

Bushmills Single Malts

This unusual group of whiskeys — the Bushmills Single Malts (80 proof/40 percent ABV) — includes 1608 Special Reserve 10 Year Old, Bushmills 12 Year Old, and Bushmills 16 Year Old Madeira Cask Aged.

Each has the characteristic Bushmills toasty flavor and aroma, but the 16 Year Old is notable for its age-related smoothness and the subtle flavor tones imparted by the casks that once held Madeira wine (and if you've ever tasted an aged Madeira you won't ever forget it).

Cooley

Cooley, near the Cooley Mountains that span the northern side of the border between Eire (The Irish Republic) and Northern Ireland (Great Britain), is a rarity among Irish distillers.

The company isn't centuries old. In fact, it's not even one century old, having been established in 1987 by an investment group that decided to reactivate Cooley's existing plant. The plant had been distilling ethanol to export in bulk to whiskey makers in other countries or to ship off to people making *gasohol,* the lowered emission auto fuel.

Despite powerful competition from the Irish Distillers Group, the Cooley guys were cool enough to think they could fill a niche by producing special Irish whiskeys made solely on pot stills and distilled only two times rather than three times, like other Irish whiskeys.

Originally, Cooley resurrected Irish whiskey names no longer available and marketed them mostly in Great Britain, often as private labels (or as the British call them, "store owned"), but as the distillery's reputation grew, the company began to produce its own branded products for the global market. Today, a few Cooley whiskeys are available in the United States, but some are in limited supplies, so be prepared to hunt them down.

Connemara

Connemara (112 proof/59.6 percent ABV) is the only non-blended, peated malt whiskey made in Ireland. Needless to say, it makes a potent mouthful but also a very robust, tasty one. The best way to try this is with water and slow sipping.

Connemara is also available in the more common 80 proof (40 percent ABV) version. Connemara has created a buzz because the peat fired under the still in Scotch-whisky-style lends it a flavor different from that of the usual, lighter Irish whiskeys.

Yes, this chapter is about Irish whiskeys. Yes, peat firing is usually reserved for Scotch whiskies. So here's a thought: How about comparing the flavor of Connemara (if you can find it) with your favorite Scotch whisky and a more traditional Irish whiskey, such as Bushmills?

Tyroconnel

The single malt Irish whiskey Tyroconnel (80 proof/40 percent ABV) is aged in charred and recharred Bourbon barrels, which gives it an interesting flavor that's unlike the flavor of other Irish whiskeys. It's sweeter but not smoother, and it could make nice a change for Bourbon fanciers.

By the by, the whiskey is named for a 19th century racehorse who won the Irish Classic and paid 100 to 1. The event is memorialized on the Tyroconnel bottle label.

Tasting Irish Whiskey

Time for the best part, a grand *craic,* and have a grand time tasting whiskeys from Ireland.

Virtually all the whiskeys you'll taste are

- ✓ 80 proof (40 percent ABV)
- ✓ Blends of various malt whiskeys and grain neutral spirits
- ✓ Aged in a variety of wooden barrels or casks

Creating the tasting sheet

Before you start to put your tasting together, set up your tasting sheet, a piece of paper on which you can record your very own personal evaluation of each whiskey that you try.

In Chapter 3, you can find a sample tasting sheet that you can copy or adapt as you see fit.

Setting up the tasting

The basic rules for setting up a tasting of Irish whiskeys are pretty much the same as those for tasting any food or drink: Choose your samples, smell and taste them, and decide which you like best.

Chapter 3 spells out the details of a general tasting, along with an explanation of how your nose and palate transmit signals that your brain interprets as, "Oh, boy that's good," or "Eeeeew. Take that stuff away."

To apply these details to a tasting of Irish whiskey, choose a minimum of three whiskeys or a maximum of five, and then let the tasting begin.

Observing and tasting the whiskeys

As you go through the following steps, note your reactions on your tasting sheet so that you can review them later:

1. **Consider the color.**

   Pick up the glass of plain, unadulterated whiskey #1. With a blank white sheet of paper behind it, hold the glass up to the light and study the color. Irish whiskey color ranges from light golden to rich brown, reflecting age and the grains used to make the whiskey. As a general rule, the darker the color, the older the whiskey and the higher the malted grain content of the mash from which the whiskey was distilled.

2. Look for the "legs."

Put the glass down on the table and swirl it clockwise so that the liquid runs up the inside of the glass and then slides down again, leaving a trail (legs) as it goes.

The legs indicate how long the whiskey was aged. Older whiskeys are more viscous (thicker), so they slide down more slowly than younger whiskeys. The slower the whiskey runs down your glass, the older it is.

3. Use your nose.

Go ahead and stick your nose right into the glass and take a deep breath to inhale the aromas. Good whiskey smells good. And each whiskey has characteristic aromas of its own. Take your time. With patience and practice, you'll be able to identify those characteristics of Irish whiskey. For a guide to what's in the glass, check out Table 4-1.

4. Taste.

At last! Take a small sip of whiskey plus air. Yes, you have permission to *slurp* at the tasting table. Let the whiskey/air combo rest in your mouth for a second or two, and then swirl it around your mouth, letting a little drip down your throat. Performing these maneuvers makes it possible, with practice, to perceive specific flavors, such as those I list in Table 4-1.

5. Spit.

Chapter 3 tells you to have a spit bucket ready for your tasting. Now's your chance to use it. Spit out plain whiskey #1.

6. Taste with water.

Add water to the whiskey left in your tasting glass (about as much water as there is whiskey). Repeat the aroma and flavor tests to see whether the flavors hold up when the whiskey is diluted.

7. Take notes and cleanse.

Note your experiences on your tasting sheet, and munch on a cracker to cleanse your palate. Move on to whiskey #2. Repeat all the steps for each whiskey.

Table 4-1	Flavors and Aromas in Irish Whiskey	
Sweet Flavors/Aromas	*Spicy Flavors/Aromas*	*Hearty Flavors/Aromas*
Apricots	Ginger	Oats
Caramel	Leafy	Toasted almonds
Prunes	Mint	

Brewing a special cuppa

Prop planes crossing the Atlantic in the years just before and after World War II couldn't make the trip in one hop; they needed to stop to refuel.

So did the passengers.

To accommodate both, the airlines said to the Irish, "Build an airport and we will come." And that's how Shannon, a gateway to Europe at the western edge of Ireland, was born.

In keeping with Irish hospitality, Shannon barkeeps earned a place in food history by creating Irish coffee to welcome travelers into Ireland or send them off satisfied on the trip home. Eventually, of course, the coffee crossed the Atlantic — and the rest of the world's oceans — and arrived in San Francisco where it became a celebrity and tourist favorite. Ultimately, Irish coffee has become a staple wherever fine drink is served.

Without further ado, I present to you the original recipe:

Classic Irish Coffee

Warm a stemmed glass.

Add a generous serving of Irish whiskey (1.5 to 2 ounces).

Add strong, black coffee and sugar to taste; stir well.

Place a spoon upside down over the edge of the glass, just above the coffee, and pour fresh whipping cream slowly over the spoon so that the cream lies atop the coffee.

Or, for pure decadence, top the coffee with fresh whipped cream.

Then sip slowly while singing the praises of the Irish.

Planning a Blended Meal

Irish whiskey is light, so most devotees prefer to take it straight, over ice, or with a splash of still or sparkling water as an *aperitif* (if you're talking like an expert, you may as well speak French), which is a before-dinner drink intended to stimulate the appetite.

Sweet, light blended Irish whiskey is also perfect in most cocktails, such as a classic Manhattan (sweet vermouth, bitters, a maraschino cherry, a twist of orange, and some whiskey — in this case, the Irish).

During dinner, Irish whiskey mixed with water, club soda, or bitter lemon in a tall highball glass complements the sometimes salty traditional Irish dishes, such as grilled salmon, corned beef and cabbage, or a traditional Irish (read: lamb) stew.

Skip the Irish whiskey if you're serving spicy food, such as some Asian dishes. The strong flavors of the food may leave the mild whiskey flavorless. Well, nothing's perfect.

After dinner, try an Irish cordial or an Irish coffee, the perfect end to an Irish whiskey dining experience.

Touring the Source

Modern Ireland definitely isn't the bucolic Eire of literature, art, and music. Today, the country is known far and wide as the "Celtic Tiger," a land powered by a booming economy powered by an equally booming rush of immigrants who lend Ireland a truly international character.

To plan your trip to Ireland, start with a copy of *Ireland For Dummies,* 4th Edition, by Elizabeth Albertson (Wiley).

Hit the high spots like Dublin and Cork, of course, but after you hang upside down by your heels to kiss the Blarney Stone, take time to visit one or more of the three major operating Irish distilleries and/or one of the two well-maintained Irish distillery museums: Old Jameson's on the site of the original Jameson's distillery in Dublin, and Locke's in the countryside of County Cork. Table 4-2 has the necessary contact information.

Table 4-2	The Irish Distilleries	
Facility	*Web site*	*Information for Reservations*
Bushmills Distillery	www.bushmills.com	Phone: +44 (0) 28 207 33218 E-mail: Form on Web site
Cooley Distillery	www.cooleywhiskey. com	Phone: 00-353-(0) 42-9376102 Fax: 00-353-(0) 42-9376484 E-mail: info@cooley-whiskey.com
Midleton Distillery	www.jamesonwhiskey. com/omd/	Phone: 021-461 3594 Fax: 021-461 3704 E-mail: bookings@omd.ie
Locke's Distillery Museum	www.lockesdistillery museum.com	Phone: 0506-32134 Fax: 0506-32134 E-mail: lockes museum@iol.ie
Old Jameson Museum	www.whiskeytours.ie	Phone: +353 (0) 1 807-2355 Fax: +353 (0) 1 807-2369

How the Irish say good job, congrats, bye-bye, and fare-thee-well

Common wisdom has it that the first to lift a glass to salute a fellow drinker were the Danes, who are said to have hoisted a brew-filled bull's horn to bid farewell to a traveler or a lost comrade.

Several centuries later, the Brits made the ritual a bit more complex by dipping a piece of toasted bread into the drink to lend a maltier flavor. Does it suggest a certain lack of originality to note that they called the ritual "toasting"? No matter: Soon everybody and his brother used the term to describe a liquid salute.

Naturally, the poetic Irish turned the everyday toast ("Here's to ya") into memorable poetry. Consider the toasts that follow:

✔ Here's to the maiden of bashful fifteen,
Here's to the widow of fifty.
Here's to the flaunting extravagant queen,
And here's to the housewife that's thrifty.
I'll warrant she'll prove an excuse for the glass.

✔ May the road rise to meet you.
May the wind be always at your back.
May the sun shine warm on your face,
And rains fall softly on your fields.
And until we meet again
May God hold you in the hollow of His hand.
(And never close His fist too tight.)

You can add that last line from a similar toast.

✔ May your coffin have six handles of the finest silver.
May your coffin be carried by six young maidens.
And may your coffin be made of the finest wood
From 100-year-old trees
That I'm going to plant tomorrow.

✔ I used to know a clever toast.
But now I cannot think it.
So fill your glass to anything
And damn your souls, I'll drink it.

After toasts like these, the only thing left to say is *Slan* (pronounced slawn), which is the good Gaelic word for *farewell*.

Chapter 5

Saluting the Scots

In This Chapter

▶ Listing the grains used to make Scotch whisky

▶ Explaining the difference between straight and blended Scotches

▶ Describing the whisky-making regions of Scotland

▶ Visiting Scotland and its distilleries

*A*s the old saying goes, "If it's been around this long, it must be good." The Scots were among the world's earliest distillers and have had centuries to develop the flavors of whisky, grains to make the flavors, and methods of bringing the essences of those grains into liquid, otherwise called "distillation."

It's why Scotch whisky went from being the best in Northern Europe to being synonymous with the word "whisky" throughout the world. It's also why after a few years of being ignored by the elites of the United States, Scotch whisky is gaining in popularity every year.

This chapter relays the history, production, and special pleasures of the various types of Scotch whisky. I also explain the differences between straight, blended, and "vatted" whiskies, and I present a tasting plan guide to enable you to sample the differences. And I say, as they do in Scotland, *Slainte Mhath* (pronounced slawncha' va) — Good health!

Which Came First: Whiskey or Whisky?

Who made whisk(e)y first — the Irish or the Scots?

Patriotic pride aside, the facts say that either (a) the Irish sailors carried their whiskey with them when they sailed across the Irish Sea to trade in Scotland, or (b) the Scots — who christened their beverage whisky without the "e" — learned the art of distilling from Christian missionaries who brought distilling to Scotland just as St. Patrick had brought it to Ireland.

In other words, anyone who speaks with an Irish brogue or a Scottish burr can stake a claim to have been first with the whiskey, er, whisky. Just so long as he doesn't do it on the other person's turf.

From monastery to market

The first recorded indication of distilling in Scotland is an entry in the Exchequer Records of 1494 showing that eight *bolls* (from bowls) of malt were purchased by one Friar John Cor "to make aquavitae."

Eight bolls, the equivalent of three bushels of grain, can be distilled to produce about 1,500 bottles of whisky. So it may be deduced either that the monks had a great thirst or that Father Cor had developed an extensive market for his whisky. Which conclusion is true remains an historical mystery.

What is known, however, is that small "cottage" distilleries were the norm in Scotland until 1644 when, noting the large quantities of whisky (and profits) being made up north, the British Parliament decreed an excise tax of approximately two shillings per gallon on all whisky made in the United Kingdom.

Over the next few hundred years, the excise tax was regularly adjusted up or down depending on the price of the grain used to make the whisky.

But in the process, a funny thing happened in Scotland. With the government unwilling or unable to make up its mind on how high or low the whisky tax should be, the Scots took things into their own hands and hid their distilleries from the tax collectors.

Thus, the finest of the Scottish whisky distilleries came to be located in secluded hidden valleys (glens), primarily in a section of Northeast Scotland known as The Highlands.

The local farmers tucked their distilling equipment away, out of sight of the revenue agents. These agents were known as *gaugers* because their job was to check the gauges on the stills to make sure that the government knew exactly how much alcohol was being distilled and could tax it appropriately.

But as the business grew, distillers became creatively adept at hiding their whisky-making apparatus. For example, one popular legend tells of a smuggler (which is what the gaugers called the distillers) who disguised his still as a bagpipe. (But maybe that's just a legend.)

The "smugglers" take to the high seas

The hidden Highland glens, dotted with hidden distilleries, became centers for merchants who bought the whisky and sold it in the surrounding towns and cities. Soon, the Highlanders were looking for markets elsewhere in the world.

Surrounded as they are by water, the Scots — like the Irish — are shipbuilders and sailors, so they quickly took to exporting their whisky by sea. They set sail from cities on the eastern coast of Scotland, such as Dundee, which soon became known as smuggler's ports. The British authorities could do little to stop the practice.

This kind of Wild West behavior continued until 1823 when the British Parliament — learning of the tens of thousands of hidden stills and salivating at the thought of the taxes lost to the secret distillers — passed yet another Excise Act.

This time, the British Parliament took two steps forward by

- ✔ Licensing distillers so as to regulate production
- ✔ Lowering the taxes while streamlining tax collection

In other words, the legislators made distilling a legal business.

Initially, the Scots resisted, thinking that the Brits were about to turn gauging into (forgive the pun) gouging. But the first distillery license was issued in 1824 to a highly respected Scottish landlord, George Smith, on a farm owned by the Duke of Richmond and Gordon. Smith named his distillery Glenlivet for the Livet River on whose banks it sat, and he called his whisky *The Glenlivet* to distinguish it from all the others in the area.

He also carried two guns whenever he left home to take the product to market. He made it through the early times well enough to see his sons take over the distillery, which they in turn passed on to their descendants.

As the distillers prospered, so did their reputation, especially in the lands of the British Empire on which "the sun never set." In taverns from New Zealand to the Caribbean, those who requested whisky were handed one of the many Scotch varieties. And so it continues until this very day.

Making Scotch Whisky

Geologically, Scotland is a fascinating and complex land mass.

- ✔ Some of the earth's oldest rock formations jut up through the rich top soil of Islay off the southwest coast.
- ✔ Twelve percent of the country's total land area is composed of peat-rich bogs.
- ✔ The country is surrounded by the sea on three sides — east, west, and north; and the land itself glistens with clear deep lakes and rushing streams left by melting glaciers.

As for the climate, Scotland experiences not only the Arctic chill but also the Gulf Stream's temperate breezes. John O'Groats, the northernmost town on the Scottish mainland, lies within a shout of the Arctic Circle. And those Gulf Stream breezes blow across the southwest coast, carrying invisible microorganisms that feed the flavor and aroma of Scotland's grains while distributing the heathery particles that enhance its water.

Together, these elements of geology and climate combine to produce the characteristic Scotch whisky flavor: heathery and slightly briny with an occasional medicinal (actually mineral) tang.

The Scottish difference

Like all whisky, Scotch is a product of grains and water. In this case, the predominant grain is Scottish barley, sometimes with an added dash of Scottish oats. The water may come from a stream rushing down from a granite hilltop, a quiet river, a deep well, or a pond or loch (preferably one without a hidden monster). Each has

What's in a name? Plenty

This chapter makes liberal use of the words *Scots, Scotsmen, Scottish,* and *Scotch.* Although they seem similar, they really do have different meanings.

As any Scotsman will tell the visitor who accidentally calls him Scotch, "Laddy, Scotch is what you're drinking. We are the Scots who make it right here in Scotland."

To which the visitor may graciously reply: "Aye, *Scotch* is made only in *Scotland* by *Scots,* which makes it *Scottish* in origin."

its own specific combination of minerals (or lack thereof), and each carries a hint of one or more of the three indigenous species of Scottish heather, each with its own flavor and aroma notes.

As you can read in Chapter 2, in most cases, when grain arrives at a distillery, it's stripped of its outer covering, cleaned, and sent on to be mixed with water into the mash from which whisky is distilled.

The Scots, however, add a step or two of their own design: First, they *malt* the barley. Then they dry it over heat from fires fueled by *peat*. And that makes all the difference.

Malting

In a Scottish distillery, after the barley is cleaned and soaked in water, the damp grain is spread out on a large surface in a *malt barn* to germinate (sprout). Originally, the distillery floor served this purpose.

The germinating mass is stirred regularly, traditionally by men with shovels who toss the stuff into the air to turn the grain and prevent it from overheating. As the grain germinates, enzymes in the grains are activated to convert its starches to sugars, making it easier for the yeasts introduced later in the game to ferment the mash.

After a week of germinating, the malted barley is dried by a heat source operating at a temperature of about 158 degrees Fahrenheit (70 degrees Celsius). That temperature is warm enough to stop the fermentation and dry the grain but low enough not to interfere with the activated enzymes.

Perfect peat

In traditional Scottish distilling, the fuel that fires the heat is *peat*. Peat is a natural material found in swamps or bogs where minerals leached from decomposing plant matter over several thousand years form a solid layer that prevents decomposing plants from sinking into the muck.

The plant matter builds up layer after layer to create the high-carbon peat. (How high is the carbon? Here's a hint: Heat it under pressure, boil away the liquid, and you get coal.)

Most peat is found in northern latitudes where it may cover as much as 5 percent of the land. Many people have been smart enough to use peat as fuel, but only in Scotland has peat assumed a leading role in the production of whisky.

Each year, from April to September, the Scots harvest their peat, which is to say they

1. Pull on their hip boots.

2. Go into the bogs.

3. Cut into the peat to a specified depth.

4. Lift out the peat.

5. Compress the peat into "bricks" that are approximately 24-x-6 inches.

After they harvest the peat, they bundle the bricks, label the bundle with the name of the bog from which it came, and ship the stuff off to various distillers. Each of those distillers has his own requirements for the peat used to make his whisky. For example, one may prefer peat from Glen Machrie, a bog in Islay noted for its salt air tang, whereas another likes one from Scotch's leading home near the River Spey.

The peat used to fuel the fires that dry malted barley imparts its own flavors and aroma. Like some wine enthusiasts who can taste a wine and then identify the place where the grapes were grown, some Scotch drinkers swear they can taste a Scotch and tell you where the peat that heated the mash that made the spirit came from.

In any event, after the malted barley is dry, it goes off to be distilled, a process that, in Scotland, is pretty much the same as everywhere else whisky is made.

Distilling the whisky

After the grain is dried, it's ground into coarse flour and mixed with water to make a mash. The mash is heated to set those enzymes humming to convert the grain starches to sugars so that when yeasts are added, they can easily ferment the mash.

As Chapter 2 explains in excruciating detail, spirits are produced in two kinds of stills: the pot still and the column still.

The chief virtue of the pot still is, surprisingly, its limited capacity, which makes it possible for the still master to exercise tight control over the specific flavor and aroma composition of his spirits.

The column still, on the other hand, dramatically increases the amount of spirits a single distiller can produce. At the same time, the column still allows a still master to capture distillates with specific levels of flavor and aroma compounds.

By a happy accident of history, the column still appeared just as the population of Scotland grew and many of the local Scottish *crofts* (farms) began to disappear. Those crofts had been growing the barley used in Scottish distilleries, so their disappearance required distillers to buy their grain from new vendors.

Using the new still made it possible for the distiller to minimize the flavor and aroma discrepancies caused by using grains grown in different soils. Individual single malt whiskies may not taste exactly the same as they did when the distiller made them from the same local grain time after time. But a skilled distiller could blend single malt whiskies to produce a beverage whose quality remained consistent time after time after time.

Stop! If your reaction to the preceding paragraph was, "Say what?" do not pass go, and do not wait one minute more before turning to Chapter 2. That chapter explains every single sentence you've just read and everything else you need to know about distillation. Then come back here to find out how Scotch whisky also benefits from a classic selection of grains and water from which the initial mash is made and the special fuel most often used to heat the mash.

To find out what's in that Scottish glass, read on.

The Styles of Scotch Whisky

The Scots produce two broad categories of whisky: single malt whiskies (one whisky from a single distillery) and blended whiskies (a mixture of two or more whiskies from two or more distilleries).

The Scotch Whisky Association (SWA) is the trade organization representing the people who distill, blend, and export Scotch whisky. In 2005, the SWA issued a new set of names for five styles of Scotch whiskies. According to the SWA:

- ✔ **Single malt whisky** is one whisky from one distillery, distilled from 100 percent malted barley.

- ✔ **Single grain whisky** is one whisky from one distillery, distilled from one grain or a mixture of grains, commonly up to 20 percent malted barley and up to 80 percent other grains, such as wheat or corn.

- ✔ **Vatted or blended malt whisky** is the traditional Scottish blended whisky, consisting only of single malt whiskies, which may come from more than one distillery.

✔ **Blended grain whisky** is made of a mixture of grain whiskies from more than one distillery.

✔ **Blended Scotch whisky,** a more recent innovation, is a blend of whiskies, commonly made of 20 to 40 percent single malt whisky plus 60 to 80 percent grain whisky, usually from several distilleries.

Although these categories are technically correct and so important for distillers, most Scotch drinkers are just fine dividing their favorite whisky into two broad groups: straight (single) malt whiskies and blended whiskies.

Regardless of type, by law, Scotch whisky must be aged for three years. However, many distillers age their whiskies for longer periods of time to continue the smoothing process that adds flavor and color to the product. For example, most single malts are aged from 8 to 15 years. Some special products may be aged as long as 21 years — old enough to be able to order a drink themselves at any American tavern, bar, or watering hole.

The milder blended whiskies have become increasingly popular, accounting for more than 90 percent of the Scotch whisky sold worldwide. But the Scottish single malts remain distinctive products, valued by connoisseurs who recognize each as an individual product of a specific whisky-making region in Scotland.

The whisky-making regions of Scotland: Where the single malts come from and the blends are born

Early on, the Scots realized that the whiskies made in one distillery in one glen differed in flavor and aroma from whiskies made even in a neighboring distillery in the next glen.

As each distiller gathered a coterie of fans for his production, he learned to keep his recipe of grains, water, yeast, and peat a closely guarded secret. Considering the combative nature of the early Scots, that was probably a good idea.

In 1784, the British tax collectors made the first stab at differentiating the Scottish whisky-making regions by drawing an imaginary line through Scotland from near Dundee in the east to Greenock in the west. Distilleries south of the line were said to be in The Lowlands; those north of the line were in The Highlands.

Eventually, to lower the tension and, more importantly, to identify relatively similar products, the Scots themselves divided the country into five specific regions, a version of the "appellations" by which the French first characterized their wines.

The whisky-making regions of Scotland are five broad geographic areas: The Lowlands, The Highlands, Campbeltown, Islay, and Speyside. Figure 5-1 is a map of Scotland showing these regions.

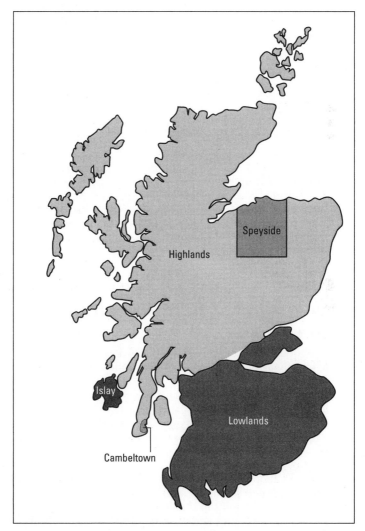

Figure 5-1: Where the Scots make their whisky.

Eventually, the SWA may (or may not) grant an appellation to a sixth area, known as The Islands. This area includes locations such as the Orkneys off the northern tip of Scotland, and Arran, Jura, Mull, and the Isle of Skye off the west coast.

Table 5-1 shows which single malt whiskies are produced in the different Scottish whisky-making regions; you can find more than 100 distilleries in Scotland, so this list is only a sample of those most likely to be readily available in U.S. liquor stores and bars. For a longer list, get on the plane to Glasgow!

Table 5-1	Locating the Single Malts
This Region . . .	*. . . Is Home to This Whisky*
The Highlands	Dalmore, Glenmorangie
Campbeltown	Campbeltown Loch, Hazelburn, Springbank
Islay	Bowmore, Bunnahabhain (pronounced bu-na-ha-venn), Lagavulin, Laphroaig
Speyside	Aberlour, Cardhu, Dalwhinnie, Glen Grant, Glen Spey, Glenfiddich, The Glenlivet, Knockando, Macallan, Strathisla (the distillery for Chivas Regal)
The Lowlands	Auchentoshan
The Islands	Arran, Highland Park, Talisker

The Lowlands

The identifying characteristic of Lowlands whiskies — which are primarily grain whiskies — is their mild, pleasing flavor.

Originally, Lowlands whiskies were used primarily for blending with the more robust whiskies from The Highlands. Today, the few remaining brands of Lowlands single malts are a fine entry level beverage for folks just beginning to taste Scotch whiskies.

The Highlands

Highland whiskies are made as far north as the Orkney Islands (the most northern point in the British Isles), as far south as the country around Glasgow, and in some of the islands off the west coast of Scotland. If even one constituent of the whisky comes from The Highlands, the whisky is a Highland whisky. For example, Glengoyne is considered a Highland whisky because the water used to distill it comes down from the north.

The size of the area is so large that some experts divide it into the northern Highlands, the central Highlands, and the southern Highlands. So, it isn't surprising that when most people say "Scotch whisky," what they mean is the whisky from The Highlands, known for its peaty flavor and the briny hints of seawater.

The single malts of The Highlands remain popular with connoisseurs, but as consumers came to prefer milder whiskies, many of the Highland distillers closed. Today, most whiskies from The Highlands are used to lend strong flavors to blends made with milder whiskies from other regions.

Campbeltown

One school of thought says that Campbeltown is the site of the first distillation of Scotch whisky. In any event, at one point, more than 30 licensed distilleries were working there; today only one — Springbank — still makes and markets single malt whisky. The rest of the Campbeltown production goes for blending.

Islay

Islay (pronounced eye-lay) is the most important of the coastal islands. Several well-known brands of Scotch whisky are made here, and Islay is historically significant for its contribution to the flavor and aroma of classic Scotch whisky.

Islay whiskies are quintessentially Scottish, briny with the sea breezes and heavily peaty because the island is virtually one big peat bog. Modern Islay still makes distinguished single malts, such as Laphroaig, but most Islay whiskies, like those from The Highlands, go into blends.

Speyside

Speyside rightly bills itself as the distilling capital of the world. No other Scottish region is as well known; more to the point, more than half of all the malt whiskies distilled in the world are made in this region. It stretches between Inverness on the west and Aberdeen on the east, around the watershed of the Spey (Great Britain's longest river) and the legendary Livet.

Blended Scotch whiskies

In 1853, the Scots enacted a law making it permissible to *vat* (blend) whiskies. The idea was to give small local distillers a way to compete with the new, large distilleries. The smaller distilleries were using pot stills to create relatively small quantities of single malt whiskies. The large distilleries, on the other hand, were using their new column stills to turn out humongous quantities of spirits that could be blended to match the quality of the single malts.

Vatted whiskies produced by individual distillers are as distinctive as single malts. As the popularity of the vatted whiskies grew, fans of the new and unusual blends began to demand that their local whisky merchants offer similar products for sale.

The merchants complied with alacrity, ordering single malts from various distillers and blending them in unique combinations sometimes labeled with the merchant's own name — or the name of a very special customer who requested his own vatted blend.

The first of the locals to create a widely appreciated vatted brand was Andrew Usher, a stillmaster who created Old Vatted Glenlivet using whiskys from the Glenlivet distillery. By careful selection and blending, other independent distillers were soon making and selling vatted blends.

The individual "recipes" were a closely guarded secret passed down from generation to generation, sort of like the formula for that well-known cola. But to the educated whisky drinker's palate, the flavor of the vatted blends was more complex and challenging than the single malts, and that made them an increasing success.

To eliminate any confusion, the SWA is planning to add another category to its listing of permissible whisky types — blended grain whisky. This is a blend of grain whiskies from a number of different distilleries; the more selective vatted whisky is a blend of malt whiskies and grain whiskies.

Blended grain whiskies have a milder flavor and softer finish than single malts. They also offer another advantage: Because blended whiskies can be made in very large batches at very large distilleries, they're usually less costly to the distiller and less expensive for the consumer. As a result, vatted whiskies are now a disappearing specialty not widely available outside Scotland; blended whiskies have become the most recognized global Scotch whisky names.

However, in the 1990s, some major distillers of blended whiskies extended their offerings to include vatted malt whiskies. That makes an interesting way of comparing the two types.

Table 5-2 lists some of the better-known vatted malt whiskies and blended whiskies. In fact, the blended whiskies listed in Table 5-2 are the top ten most popular worldwide.

Table 5-2	Sampling the Blended Whiskies
Whisky Type	*Well-Known Examples*
Vatted Malt Whiskies	Bell's Special Reserve, Johnnie Walker Green Label, Ballantine's Pure, Famous Grouse Vintage Malt
Blended Whiskies	Johnnie Walker Red Label, J&B, Ballantine's Finest, William Grant, Johnnie Walker Black Label, Dewar's White Label, Chivas Regal 12 Year Old, The Famous Grouse, Bell's 8 Year Old, Cutty Sark

Tasting Scotch Whisky

No, you don't have to put on a kilt or even a clan scarf or tie. But if you want to taste Scotch whisky, you do have to be prepared for some pretty intense flavors and aromas.

The following sections lay out the qualities you should expect to find in a glass of good Scotch, along with guidelines for an intelligent evaluation of the whisky.

Can't wait? Don't want to read through all those directions?

Okay: Indulge yourself with a quick and simple comparison of two well-known, well-loved examples of the best Scotland has to offer. The Glenlivet is a quintessential single malt whisky with a clean, round flavor and aroma. Johnnie Walker Black holds the same status among the blends.

So here goes:

1. Pour an ounce of The Glenlivet into a glass.

2. Pour an ounce of Johnnie Walker Black into a second glass.

3. Let the whiskies sit for a few minutes to "open up."

4. Now sniff one. Taste one. Clean your palate with a piece of white bread. Sniff the other. Taste the other.

5. Note the differences.

In general, most people find that The Glenlivet offers a pleasing but less complex flavor and aroma than the Johnnie Walker Black. That really isn't surprising: The Glenlivet is a single whisky, and Johnnie Walker Black is a blend of several.

But what about the rest of the brands on the shelf? Has this simple comparison engaged your intellect as well as your sense of taste and smell? If your answer is "No," well, at least you've found two Scotch whiskies you enjoy. That's good. If your answer is "Yes," you've discovered the challenge in the Scotch. That's better, so read on.

Creating the tasting sheet

Slow down: Before you start to put your tasting together, set up your tasting sheet, a piece of paper on which you can record your very own personal evaluation of each whisky you try. The tasting sheet in Chapter 3 should suit your needs perfectly.

Choosing your samples

Blended Scotch whiskies may be the most popular worldwide, but the prevailing opinion among serious Scotch drinkers is that the only true Scotches are the single malts.

They have a point. After all, the single malts were the first Scotch whiskies, and they remain distinctly individual to this day.

But your personal tastes may not agree with the experts (some may call them "snobs"). To decide for yourself on which side of the Scotch divide you stand, sample some single malts, preferably one from each of the regions listed in Table 5-1. Then move on to the blends, choosing one relatively young brand with no age on the label (minimum is three years) and one older (aged more than ten years).

Sit down, pour your whisky, see what it looks like in the glass, swirl it around for a couple of seconds, watch the "legs," and then put your nose into the glass to inhale its heady aromas. Finally, taste its complex flavor profile while — between sniffs and sips — reciting this traditional Scottish toast:

> May the best ye've ivver seen be the worst ye'll ivver see.
>
> May the moose ne'er leave yer girnal wi a tear-drap in its ee.
>
> May ye aye keep hail an hertie till ye'r auld eneuch tae dee.
>
> May ye aye jist be sae happie as A wuss ye aye tae be.

For those of you who don't speak Scottish and are wondering what that moose is doing tramping around the tasting table, this toast translates to:

> May the best you have ever seen be the worst you will ever see.
>
> May the mouse never leave your grain store with a tear drop in its eye.
>
> May you always be hale and hearty until you are old enough to die.
>
> May you always be as happy as I always wish you to be.

Could na' ha' sayd it better meself.

Appreciating the appearance

The color of a single malt Scotch can range from perfectly clear as it comes off the still, through pale to warm gold as it ages in the barrel or cask, to the deep brown color of *treacle,* the British, sorry, Scottish word for a type of fancy molasses.

Aging also makes the whisky more viscous. If you swirl the glass so that the liquid runs up the sides and then slowly slides down again, the amount of time it takes for the whisky to puddle in the bottom of the glass gives a hint of how long it was aged: The longer the aging, the slower the slide.

Inhaling the aromas

Two groups of aromas are characteristic of Scotch whisky. The first group includes aromas associated with the distilling process: The choice of grain and water and, for malt whiskies, the use of peat to dry the grain. The second group includes aromas derived from the barrels in which the whisky is aged.

Aromas associated with grain, water, and distillation are often described as

- ✔ Leafy
- ✔ Flowery or floral
- ✔ Fruity or fragrant
- ✔ Grassy
- ✔ Leathery

✔ Tobacco scented

✔ Smoky (wood smoke, "peaty")

✔ Iodine and seaweed scented

Aromas associated with aging in wooden barrels include:

✔ Bourbon and sherry scented (from previously used casks)

✔ Buttery

✔ Honey scented

✔ Nutty

✔ Piney

✔ Resinous (from the resins in the wood)

✔ Vanilla scented

✔ Woody (an undesirable aroma in very old whisky)

Tasting the flavors

Like the aromas of Scotch whisky, the flavors originate either with the basic materials (grain and water) and the processing of the grain (malting with peat) or in the barrel.

Some of the flavors most frequently identified in Scotch whisky are

✔ **Fruity:** apple, citrus fruits, and dried fruits, such as apricots, prunes, and raisins

✔ **Malty:** cereal, grain

✔ **Nutty:** aniseed/licorice, walnuts

✔ **Peaty:** antiseptic, smoky

✔ **Sweet:** chocolate, treacle/molasses, vanilla

✔ **Spicy:** cinnamon, cloves, ginger, nutmeg

Don't be discouraged if at first you fail to identify each of these flavors and aromas in your glass.

The secret of expert tasting is practice. Sniff, sniff, sniff. Sip, sip, sip. Eventually, with time, without your noticing, you become — ta da! — an expert.

What could be more rewarding or delicious?

As the tasting guide in Chapter 3 explains, adding water to spirits changes the flavor (and the color, too, but you knew that). For a complete Scotch tasting experience, add water — equal to the amount of whisky in the glass — and go through the flavor tasting steps again. Note the differences.

Planning a Scotch-Friendly Meal

Scotch whiskies range from sweet and light to medicinal and really full and round (translation: strong stuff). Either variety is a fine introduction to dinner, either straight, with a mixer, or in a cocktail (such as a Whisky Sour, the recipe for which is in Chapter 15 along with nine other classic spirits cocktails).

The Scots serve hearty soups, such as Cock-a-leekie (chicken and leeks), followed by fine smoked salmon, good grouse, or other wild fowl, world-class Aberdeen Angus beef, lovely cheese, perfect scones, and heavily-buttered shortbreads.

But the absolutely, definitely, singularly Scottish dish is haggis, a mixture of minced sheep lungs, liver, and heart, plus oatmeal, onions, spices, suet (hard fat from around a cow or sheep's kidneys), and broth, stuffed into a sheep's stomach, which is then sewn up and boiled for many, many hours.

Haggis is traditionally served with neaps and tattles (mashed turnips and potatoes) on Burns Night, January 25, which marks the birthday of the most beloved Scottish poet Robert Burns; or on Hofmann (New Year's Eve); or whenever else the Scots want it during the year.

Considering how difficult it may be to scare up sheep innards outside of Scotland, people wishing to try haggis often order directly by mail from Scottish purveyors such as

- ✔ Scottish Food Overseas at `www.scottishfoodoverseas.com`
- ✔ Scottish Gourmet Food at `www.scottishgourmetfood.co.uk`

 When dinner's done, the perfect ending is a Scotch whisky liqueur, such as Drambuie. With just 165 calories, no fat, no cholesterol, no sodium, a delicious honey/Scotch taste, and only 13 grams of carbs, it sure beats a slice of chocolate cake.

Traveling through Distillery Land

As any travel brochure plainly shows, Scotland is definitely pictur-esque. Castles, including the one that inspired Shakespeare's Macbeth, stone bridges, woods, streams, rivers, and lush meadows glowing with heather abound. And every single one of them is wrapped in history and legend.

For specifics on traveling to Scotland, check out (what else?) *Scotland For Dummies,* 4th Edition, by Barry Shelby (Wiley). And, of course, the Scotland's National Tourist Board offers info on everything from travel to tastings at www.visitscotland.com.

Just be sure that after you trek through the classic tourist sites — What? You were thinking about *not* visiting Dunsinane Wood? — you make time for a tour of one of the famous distilleries.

Scotland is home to more than 100 distilleries — too many to list here. Many offer elaborate visitors' centers; some offer space for you to linger overnight. You can locate the one you want to visit by simply typing its name into your favorite search engine. Or you can take the easier route and let your travel agent make the arrangements.

Either way, despite the scurrilous rumors about Scottish stinginess and dour approach, probably circulated by Those People from The South (you know, the Sassenachs), wherever you go, you'll be met with warm hospitality.

And, although only 2 percent of all the Scots in Scotland speak Gaelic, most of them know and often use this phrase: Ceud Mille Failte (cay-*ut* mell-uh falsh-uh), which is Gaelic for "100,000 Welcomes."

To which one may honestly reply: "You, too."

Chapter 6

American Cousins: Bourbon and Tennessee Whiskey

In This Chapter

▶ Quashing the Whiskey Rebellion

▶ Discovering how Bourbon got its name

▶ Tracking the origins of Tennessee whiskey

▶ Enjoying the flavors

▶ Pairing the whiskeys with food

*O*ne sounds French, the other definitely Southern, but both are pure Americans, born in what President Lyndon Johnson used to call "the good ole' U.S. of A."

Bourbon and Tennessee, the whiskeys, owe their allegiance to their home country; to the early American hatred of "taxation without representation"; and to the entrepreneurial aims of frontier farmers looking to wring the highest profits from a surplus of very good corn, rye, and other grains.

For generations, these whiskeys gained little attention either at home or in foreign lands. Then the Japanese discovered their uniqueness and their global businessmen introduced Bourbon and Tennessee whiskey to more and more upscale drinkers around the world. Today, American whiskey sales outpace those of any other type. There must be some good reasons for that. Indeed there are, and this chapter deals with many of them.

Life, Liberty, and the Pursuit of . . . Whiskey?

In 1791, as the infant United States was creating itself, economic problems reared their ugly heads: The U.S. lacked the revenue necessary to implement a Westward expansion. So, Alexander Hamilton, the first U.S. Secretary of the Treasury, proposed to pay the cost of defending settlers against the Native Americans by instituting the country's very first "sin tax" — 25 percent on the value of the total output of every still in the country.

After all, who could complain about encouraging "temperance upon the human body and mind"? Dr. Benjamin Rush (1745–1813), the first Surgeon General of the United States, encouraged temperance, or moderation, in drinking. Rush also quelled a yellow fever epidemic in Philadelphia and said that alcohol could provide "nourishment, when taken only at meals and in moderate quantities." An excise tax could help promote that ideal by making whiskey more expensive and therefore driving it out of reach of the working class.

Because of the superb grain, soil, and climate in Pennsylvania, virtually all early American farmer-distillers were located in that state. As a result, Hamilton's tax fell most heavily on Pennsylvania farmers, particularly those in the least populous Western part of the state. Most of the farmer-distillers believed passionately — and probably correctly — that the new tariff would pretty much eliminate any chance of turning a profit by converting their surplus grains to their most valuable cash crop — whiskey.

In addition, the independent Pennsylvanians regarded a federal tax on local produce a usurpation of the Commonwealth's power to tax its own — just one more in an increasingly growing list of the federal government's interventions in their daily lives.

At first, the farmers simply grumbled, hoping that Congress would kill the tax plan. That didn't happen, and Congress accepted Hamilton's proposal. When it went into effect in 1793, federal marshals were sent to Western Pennsylvania to serve writs on every farmer in the region who operated a still. The writ was to be heard in the nearest court, which was located in Philadelphia, hundreds of miles away. It ordered each of them to pay a tax of at least $250 or be shut down.

Whether or not the tax was justified, the Feds had picked the wrong place to start.

Rumbling to rebellion

Early on, Western Pennsylvania — sometimes nicknamed Transylvania by its residents because it was the boundary between the well-settled East and the still-wild territories over the Appalachian Mountains — petitioned Congress to be recognized as the 14th colony. Congress said, "No way," and the Westerners never forgot the slight.

In 1794, a presently unknown federal marshal walked onto the Oliver Miller family farm in Allegheny County to serve his writ. Farmer Miller said, "No way," and told the law officer to take a hike.

The marshal stood his ground. Neighbors hearing the fuss came to Miller's aid. A shot was fired. The mob grew violent and the violence quickly spread to other areas. In a nearby county, the tax assessor's home was burned, and thus began the conflict that came to be known as The Whiskey Rebellion. This event made history as the first time federal troops were used to quell an "insurrection" in the new nation.

In due course, Oliver Miller, scheduled to be tried for dissing the federal marshal, was accidentally shot. The farmers got the idea that the government wasn't really heeding their grievance. Various town meetings were held, including one in Bradford, where a local voluntary militia formed to confront the attackers.

Back in Philadelphia, President Washington decided that, in order to protect the issue of Federalism versus state's rights, he had to put the rebellion down with a show of real force. He ordered the governor of Virginia to take charge of the federal troops. That governor was Revolutionary War hero, General "Lighthorse" Harry Lee; he was also the father of Robert E. Lee. To make the order to send Lee to Pennsylvania, Washington used the Militia Law of 1792 for the first time. This law still permits the president to "execute the laws of the union and suppress insurrections." Washington ordered militia from four states bordering Pennsylvania to restore order in the Western part of that state. Connecticut, New York, New Jersey, and Virginia all responded by sending troops to carry out a Constitutionally approved order.

One historical record reports that 13,000 troops (more than fought the British in any single battle of the American Revolution) moved into the Western Pennsylvania region. The rebellion ended swiftly with only two fatalities reported (Miller and another rebel). When it ended, two men were convicted of treason, but Washington pardoned them. Some farmer-distillers grudgingly accepted the tax and returned to making their rye whiskey.

But some of the more independent souls packed up and trekked over the Allegheny Mountains to a whole new, wide-open, whiskey-making region: the Ohio Territory. After all, the motto of their home state proclaimed "Virtue, Liberty, Independence." As far as they were concerned, the move backed up that motto fully.

Over the mountains

At the time, much of the present states of Illinois, Indiana, and Ohio were claimed by other states, such as Virginia and New York. In addition, the territory had been the Algonquin tribes' land until they signed treaties with the United States after the defeat of their French allies during the French and Indian Wars.

The new settlers from Pennsylvania discovered that their move to the "land beyond the mountains" was a way to escape what they perceived to be persecution by the federal government. It also turned out to be the answer to farmer-distiller dreams.

The land was beautiful: rolling hills and gentle valleys with deep, rich soil. In one direction, soft water streams and creeks flowed through de-mineralizing limestone into rivers rushing to the ocean. In the other direction was the Mississippi River and grass so green it was nearly blue. As for farming the grains needed for whiskey making, the weather was so perfect that all a farmer had to do was put the corn and rye seed in the ground and get out of the way.

Best of all, the existing connections to Eastern markets and shipping to other lands were remarkable. In Pennsylvania, farmers had to ship their whiskey to the East in 60-gallon casks carried by pack-horses — an inefficient and costly method. From the new territory, they could ship their casks in much greater numbers by barges. The barges traveled the Ohio River to Pittsburgh as well as down the Mississippi River to New Orleans.

In other words, the Pennsylvanians had found a happy home in what was to become Bourbon County, Kentucky.

Bourbon beginnings

Most people who know anything about Bourbon distilling know the story of the Baptist Minister Elijah Craig who established a distillery in Bourbon County, thus giving a name to his whiskey.

It's a good story, but it's not exactly true.

Yes, a Reverend Craig was chased out of Virginia for religious reasons, and he did move to Kentucky, where he set up a still. But this happened in 1780, and the place where he began turning out whiskey was called Fayette County. In 1788, Fayette County became Woodford County. In 1792, Woodford became Scott. However, it never metamorphosed into Bourbon County.

But, there *was* a Bourbon County for which a Kentucky whiskey was named. In 1780, as the Ohio Territory was cut into smaller and smaller units, the Virginians claimed a piece of it. They named it Bourbon County after the then-current French ruling family. They chose the name to honor the support of the French during the American Revolution. (French troops, naval vessels, and General Lafayette helped to blockade the British fleet at Yorktown, Virginia.)

Soon, dozens and then hundreds of small farmer-distillers were busily making whiskey in the region. In 1792, when Kentucky became a state, the really big Bourbon County was divided into 34 of the present existing Kentucky counties. One of which, of course, was Bourbon, with its famous whiskey.

The great schism: Bourbon gets its name, and Tennessee splits

For several decades, the still primarily rye whiskey made from the larger Bourbon County region was called "Old Bourbon," and served as the area's most important agricultural export.

Every barrel of whiskey shipped out of the area was marked on the barrelhead as "Old Bourbon." People in other parts of the country saw that designation on hundreds of barrelheads and assumed that the designation meant old (as in aged) whiskey. Of course, inside was Old Bourbon Whiskey that was, more and more, being made from corn. The acceptance of this designation was good for recognition and sales, so no one was going to tell customers that their assumption was wrong.

At some point around the mid-19th century, distillers stopped using the designation. This decision helped consumers avoid the confusion between the meaning of the name and what had become the common practice of aging the whiskey in barrels. But almost every corn-based whiskey made west of the Allegheny Mountains remained "Bourbon" to distinguish it from the "rye" whiskeys made east of the mountains. By the same token, even to this day there are people in the East who call all whiskey "rye."

Eventually, distillers in Tennessee sought to distinguish their spirits from Bourbon. They added a few methods to make their whiskey smoother and called it — no surprise — Tennessee whiskey.

Both whiskeys were well known for their sweet, smooth flavor. You could hardly say that about the men who made them. Check out the nearby sidebar, "The Bourbon and Tennessee whiskey boys," for the stories behind some of the early distillers.

The Bourbon and Tennessee whiskey boys

As a profession, distilling has always attracted entrepreneurs, rogues, and wise men. The hardy pioneers who produced whiskey in Kentucky and Tennessee all fit somewhere in that description. But no matter where they fall on the personality scale, they were hard-nosed, confident individuals dedicated to their choice of a way of life.

Here are just a few of the early distiller families who remain active in making Bourbon and Tennessee whiskey:

Colonel James Beauregard Beam (1864–1947) was the fourth generation of Kentucky distillers. Shortly after joining the business in 1882, "Jim" Beam and his brother-in-law Albert Hart built a new distillery that became famous for a brand they called "Old Tub" whiskey. After Prohibition, 70-year-old Jim Beam reopened the plant. The descendants of Jim Beam, his brother Park, and their uncle Joe are still working in it and with Beam's global operations. In the 20th century, the late Booker Noe, who married into the Beam family, introduced "small batch" Bourbons to the world.

R.B. Hayden built the original Old Grand-Dad distillery at the same time the Beam & Hart Distillery was built, about two miles down the railroad tracks. The grandson of a distiller who settled in Kentucky in 1796, R.B. named the brand after his grandfather and added the slogan "Handmade Sour Mash." During Prohibition, his plant was sold to the American Medicinal Spirits Company and was one of the few that remained in operation, selling whiskey for medicinal and religious purposes.

George A. Dickel (c.1818–1896) was born in Darmstadt, Germany. He immigrated to Tennessee and established a wholesale whiskey business in Nashville. In 1866, he opened a retail liquor store. In 1888, he purchased Cascade Distillery and founded the Dickel Company.

Jasper Newton "Jack" Daniel (1846–1911) was introduced to whiskey making as a boy. As an adult, he moved the family still to Cave Spring, which was near Lynchburg, Tennessee. Jack Daniel understood that if customers remembered him, they would remember his whiskey. Therefore, he cultivated a distinctive image for himself — he always wore a knee-length frock coat and a planter's hat, and he grew an elaborate mustache and goatee. Jack Daniel was active in the whiskey business

(continued)

(continued)

from the Civil War until his death in 1911. He never married, so his nephew Lem Motlow inherited the business.

Bill Samuels, Sr. was a sixth generation distiller who wanted to do things differently. To break with tradition, in 1943 he discarded his 1780 family recipe for distilling whiskey in order to create something new. In the next few years, using local corn and substituting winter wheat for rye, he developed Maker's Mark. His wife Margie created the bottle and the red wax seal. Bill, Jr. continues to run the company that created probably the earliest "premium" Bourbon.

James C. Crow (c. 1789–1856) was a Scottish physician who came to Kentucky in about 1825. He emphasized sanitation and the biochemistry of fermentation in his distilling. Oscar Pepper hired Crow as his master distiller, and their whiskeys (Old Crow and Old Pepper) became big hits. Crow died suddenly at work and left no heirs.

Evan Williams (?–1810) was, according to Heaven Hill (which makes Evan Williams Bourbon today), Kentucky's "first commercial distiller." Evan Williams established a distillery in Louisville in 1783. A few years later, he was indicted for making whiskey without a license. In 1797, he was elected to the town's first Board of Trustees. Despite (or because of) his presence, the Board's rules included a requirement that any "ardent or spirituous liquors" brought to meetings would be forfeited "for the use of the Board after adjournment."

The Pepper Family whiskey story started when Elijah Pepper came from Virginia to be a Kentucky distiller. In 1879, Oscar's son, James E. Pepper, moved to Lexington and built a new distillery. He made a Bourbon carrying his name and created the slogan "Born With The Republic" along with the trademark "Old 1776." After James died in 1908, the family sold the distillery and brands.

William LaRue Weller (?–1908) started a wholesale whiskey business in Louisville in 1849. His offices were on "Whiskey Row," a stretch of Main Street near the Ohio River. Many of the offices there had warehouses that led directly to the paddle-wheel steamboats that carried the whiskey to markets up and down the Ohio River. When Weller died in 1908, two of his young salesmen bought the company. One of those salesmen was Julian P. Van Winkle (1875–1963); during Prohibition, Van Winkle merged the Weller Company with the Stitzel Brothers Distillery and ran Stitzel-Weller until his death.

The Wathen Family patriarch was Henry Hudson Wathen, a distiller who came to Kentucky in 1787. His grandson, John Bernard (J.B.), ran the family distillery from 1863 until his death in 1919 — just months before Prohibition went into effect. In 1875, J.B. and his brother Nick had built a large distillery in Lebanon, Kentucky. In 1899, they bought the Old Grand-Dad distillery and placed their younger brother Nace in charge. They were all active in consolidating their existing whiskey inventories into the American Medicinal Spirits Company (AMS), which was permitted to produce spirits for "medicinal and religious purposes" during Prohibition. The last of the active "Whiskey Wathens" was J.B.'s son Richard. After Repeal, he became an executive with National Distillers, the successor to AMS.

Making Bourbon and Tennessee Whiskey

Like all whiskeys, Bourbon and Tennessee whiskey are distilled from grain and aged to perfection. By law, Bourbon whiskey must be

- Made in the United States
- Produced from a mash containing a minimum of 51 percent corn
- Distilled at less than 160 proof (80 percent ABV)
- Aged at least two years in new charred oak barrels (Most Bourbons are aged longer, and any Bourbon whiskey aged less than four years must list its age on the label.)

Tennessee whiskey must be

- Made in Tennessee
- Produced from a mash made of 51 percent corn
- Distilled at less than 160 proof (80 percent ABV)
- Filtered through a column of charcoal made from Tennessee sugar maple trees
- Aged for a minimum of two years in new charred barrels

Check out Figure 6-1 to see on the map where Bourbon and Tennessee whiskey are produced.

Selecting the grain and making the mash

The grain base for both Bourbon and Tennessee whiskey is primarily corn plus small quantities of malted barely (see Chapter 2 for more about malting), wheat, and perhaps some rye.

The grains are mixed with water, yeasts are added, and the mixture is heated to form a mash, which is transferred to the fermenting vat.

Bourbon County

Moore County

Figure 6-1: The homes of Bourbon and Tennessee whiskey.

Fermenting and producing distillate

Over a period of two to three days, the yeasts digest the sugars in the grain, producing an alcohol distillate called distiller's beer. The distillers use yeasts that are either from cultured strains, which can be many years old, or are "wild yeasts" that grow in the area and are blown about by the wind.

The mash left after distillation is either discarded or, more likely, made into nutritious animal feed. The acidic mash is believed to inhibit the growth of bacteria naturally present in the air that could possibly infect the animals.

As the yeasts do their work, they produce a watery alcohol liquid that rises to the top of the vat. The used-up mash sinks to the bottom and is transferred from the fermentation vat to the still for the next step in making Bourbon and Tennessee whiskey.

Distilling the whiskey

In the still (usually a continuous or column still; see Chapter 2 for more on these stills), the liquid is heated until the vapors rise to be collected, condensed, and transferred to a second still. In the second still, they're once again heated, and the vapors are collected and condensed a second time.

During the second distillation "run," the clear alcohol condenses at 120 to 130 proof (60 to 65 percent ABV). If necessary, distilled water is added to reduce the alcohol content to 125 proof (62.5 percent ABV) or less, depending on the amount of flavoring agents desired in the final whiskey. The more distillation, the fewer the flavoring agents (check out Chapter 10 for more details than you'll probably ever want on flavoring agents).

Changing the color and building the flavor: Aging

In the next distillation step, the distiller pumps the alcohol into newly charred American oak barrels for controlled storage. After the whiskey is deemed mature, and before bottling, it's sent through an activated charcoal (or similar substance) filter and can be called "charcoal filtered" on the label.

Charring turns the clear whiskey into to a new color. Depending on the length of time the raw whiskey absorbs flavoring sugars from the charred wood, the color can range from amber through

The story of the wood

The sole use of American oak in aging Bourbon and Tennessee whiskey isn't a matter of nativism. Every type of wood used in making the barrels has a specific hardness and porosity. In France, Limousin oak from the forests near Bordeaux is preferred for aging wines; in other countries, Hungarian or Spanish oak is preferred for locally made spirits.

Only the United States mandates charring the wood and the use of only new barrels. When emptied, these charred oak barrels are often in great demand because of the flavor constituents they can still impart to other whiskeys, such as Scotch. A busy and profitable market has grown up in sale of the once-used barrels, which can have a long second life. In order to get the perfect flavoring level, some of the old char is often carefully scraped down to a thinner layer.

gold to as dark as bronze. The depth of the char also helps create the final flavor because charring creates a layer of burnt wood and a layer of caramelized sugars brought out of the wood by the heat of burning.

Filtering

Although grain recipes may differ, the major difference between Bourbon and Tennessee whiskey has to do with filtration. By law, Bourbon must be charcoal filtered as described in the preceding section. However, the regulations apply only to whiskey made in Kentucky, allowing Tennessee distillers to come up with something different. In the middle of the 19th century, they commissioned the development of a different system of filtration. It was created by a distiller named Alfred Eaton, and it's called the Lincoln County Process in honor of the county in which he lived.

On the distillery grounds, stacks of Tennessee sugar maples are burned to charcoal. The charcoal is chopped into small pieces and placed at the bottom of a vat about ten feet deep. The whiskey is pumped from the second still into the vat, and it drips slowly over and through the charcoal into an aging barrel. The whiskey is further filtered in the usual manner just before bottling.

According to expert judges, the Tennessee whiskey gains a smokier, sweeter taste than Bourbon because of the Lincoln County Process.

The Types of Bourbon

Several different terms are used to classify the types of Bourbon. The following list cuts through the jargon:

- **Sour mash whiskey:** Bourbon and Tennessee whiskey aren't blended; they're classified as "straight whiskey." That makes maintaining a consistency of flavor — and often color — difficult from one distillation to another. Color control is maintained by the addition of caramel, which has nothing to do with the flavor. To maintain flavor consistency from year to year, however, a distiller "saves" some of the mash from one batch to use as a starter in the next batch. Like sourdough bread that's made with a starter from a previous batch of dough, all straight whiskey is made using this starter and can be called *sour mash whiskey*. The term is not an indicator of better or lesser quality, just that the flavor and color will be the same in one bottle as in another purchased weeks or months later.

✔ **Small batch Bourbons:** These small batches are a modern version of the old pot still method of making whiskey, akin to craft distilling. The term was introduced in the 1980s by the Jim Beam Company. A small batch Bourbon is bottled from a small group of specially selected barrels that are blended together in a manner similar to that of Reserve wines. These batches are said to be "the best of the best," but remember that every distiller has his own interpretation of what constitutes a "small batch."

✔ **Single barrel Bourbon:** A single barrel Bourbon is bottled from one specifically chosen cask. Obviously, the flavor depends on the distiller's ability to match the current preference in whiskey tastes. Each bottle from the barrel should state the barrel number on the label.

✔ **Vintage Bourbon:** The vintage is another means of modernizing Bourbon offerings. Similar to the small batch Bourbons, these whiskeys are older than the mandated four years. As with wines, vintage is a statement of superiority.

✔ **Bottled-in-Bond:** This method came into being in 1897 when the federal government permitted distillers to keep their barrels in government supervised warehouses for the four-year minimum aging period. More than anything else, this was a move to control taxation. After the minimum period, the distiller was allowed to remove his whiskey for bottling at 100 proof (50 percent ABV). Bottled-in-Bond came to be seen as a mark of superior quality whiskey. Actually, it's on the same level as any straight whiskey bottled at 100 proof with no age statement. Because of federal cost cutting, very few inspectors are around today, so the process and the term aren't often used.

Tasting Bourbons and Tennessee Whiskeys

Chapter 3 explains "The Rules" of a spirit tasting. You can skip back there for the details, or simply follow the simplified version shown here. You can also use the tasting sheet in Chapter 3 for Bourbons and Tennessee whiskeys.

Gentlemen, choose your whiskeys

You can find a large number of Bourbon whiskeys out there. When you're trying to select the one you prefer the most, pick out a few brands to taste and do comparison evaluating as you go. This is called a vertical tasting.

Another system to try is a horizontal tasting. Choose among the output of an individual distiller, such as Jim Beam or Heaven Hill, and compare offerings in the different categories.

Because Tennessee whiskey has only two distillers, each producing a limited line of offerings, choosing among them is easier.

What follows are my recommendations for a well-rounded selection.

 If you intend to mix the whiskey with water, try to find distilled water to make sure that you don't inadvertently add additional flavor, and use it in the form of ice cubes.

Kentucky straight Bourbon

The following Bourbons are all 80 proof (40 percent ABV) and four years old:

- Basil Hayden's
- Fighting Cock
- Four Roses
- Heaven Hill Old Style
- Henry McKenna
- Jim Beam
- Old Fitzgerald
- Old Forester
- Wild Turkey
- Woodford Reserve

Small batch Bourbons

If you're looking for the "best of the best," try one of these small batch Bourbons:

- Baker's Kentucky Straight Bourbon — 7 years old, 107 proof
- Booker's Unfiltered Cask Strength — 6 to 8 years old, 125.3 proof
- Elijah Craig — 12 years old, 94 proof
- Knob Creek — 9 years old, 100 proof

Single barrel Bourbons

These bourbons are of excellent quality and can be found in better taverns as well as a well-stocked liquor store:

- Basil Hayden's — 8 years old, 80 proof

- Blanton's — 12 to 14 years old, 96 proof

- Booker's — unfiltered, undiluted, 121 to 127 proof

- Elijah Craig — 12 years old, 94 proof

- Hancock's Reserve — 8 to 10 years old, 89 proof

- Knob Creek — 9 years old, 100 proof

- Maker's Mark — no age given, 90 proof

- Wild Turkey Rare Breed — 6 to 12 years old, 108.9 proof

Note that Maker's Mark is spelled "whisky," honoring its Scotch whisky tradition.

Tennessee whiskeys

As of this writing, Jack Daniel's (Brown-Forman Beverages) is the only fully operating distillery in Tennessee. The availability of George Dickel is limited, although you may be able to find inventory remaining in retail outlets. The following list goes up the ladder in price:

- George Dickel #12 — 12 years old, 90 proof

- Gentleman Jack — 4 years old, 80 proof

- Jack Daniel's Old No. 7 Black Label — 4 years old, 80 proof

- George Dickel Special Barrel — 10 years old, 86 proof

- Jack Daniel's Single Barrel — 4 plus years old, 94 proof

What your senses sense when you taste Bourbon or Tennessee whiskey

The flavors and aromas of these whiskeys are similar, but Tennessee whiskey may feel and taste smoother and smokier than Bourbon. However, what you smell and taste when you sample whiskey (or cheese or chocolate or lettuce, for that matter) depends to a large degree on your own senses.

What you find smooth may not taste smooth to the person across the table from you. In the end, what you like is what you like — and that's as good a guide as anything else.

Table 6-1 is a list of flavors and aromas experts often experience when tasting these whiskeys.

Table 6-1	Flavors and Aromas in Bourbon and Tennessee Whiskey
Flavor Category	*Specific Flavor*
Sweet flavors and aromas	Burned sugar (toffee), butterscotch, caramel, honey, malt/maple syrup
Fruit flavors and aromas	Apple, apricot, banana, cherry, citrus (lemon/orange), peach
Herbs and spice flavors and aromas	Cinnamon cloves, licorice, mint, nutmeg, pepper
Floral flavors and aromas	Violets
Barrel flavors and aromas	Charcoal, oak, smoky, vanilla

Pairing Foods with Bourbon and Tennessee Whiskey

Bourbon and Tennessee whiskeys have a mild sweet flavor that goes well with usually salty before-dinner hors d'oeuvres and appetizers.

At the main meal, roasted meats and poultry do well with Bourbon, but so do fruit and veggie side dishes (see Chapter 16 for recipes of two terrific examples: Green Beans with Pine Nuts and Tennessee Whiskey Candied Apples).

After dinner, you can pleasantly sip these whiskeys with sweet desserts; Bourbon is particularly good with chocolate. In fact, Bourbon Balls — a sticky cookie made of crushed wafers, nuts, and syrup and formed into, yes, balls before they're rolled in cocoa — are an old Southern favorite. To make these little wonders, type Bourbon Balls into your favorite search engine and sit back as thousands — okay, maybe tens — of different recipes rise up in front of your eyes.

Pick one and it's off to the races. With a Mint Julep. The recipe for that is in Chapter 15. Yum.

Branching out

Old-timers won't drink Bourbon with anything other than "branch water." This isn't a special water from some weird cave — it's actually water from any swift flowing creek. In Kentucky and its environs, a creek is often called a "branch" because it runs into a larger stream and ultimately to the Ohio, Kentucky, or Mississippi Rivers.

There's a reason behind this kind of aquatic devotion. The shallow creeks in the whiskey-making regions are understandably close to the rock underneath them. The rock around the distilleries and a good part of the region is limestone. Limestone is a wonderful mineral for settling out aromas and flavors, and limestone water is used almost exclusively during the distillation of Kentucky/Tennessee whiskeys.

If you're not in the neighborhood of good limestone washed water, a reasonable substitute is distilled water.

Touring the Bourbon and Tennessee Whiskey Distilleries

You don't need a passport or a lot of time — even a long weekend will suffice. Several Bourbon and Tennessee whiskey distilleries offer tours of the premises with options to taste the product (but *never* on Sunday) and buy really good stuff, such as drinking glasses and the ubiquitous and essential T-shirt of your choice. Here's a list of the distilleries:

Buffalo Trace
1001 Wilkinson Boulevard
Franklin County, KY 40601
Web site www.buffalotrace.com
Phone 800-654-8471

Four Roses
1224 Bonds Mill Road
Lawrenceburg, KY 40342
Web site www.fourroses.us
Phone 502-839-3436

Heaven Hill Distilleries
Bourbon Heritage Center
1311 Gilkey Run Road
Bardstown, KY 40004
Web site www.bourbonheritagecenter.com
Phone 502-337-1000

Jack Daniel's
Highway 55
Lynchburg, TN 37352
Web site www.jackdaniels.com
Phone 931-759-6180

Jim Beam
149 Happy Hollow Road
Clermont, KY 40110
Web site www.jimbeam.com
Phone 502-543-9877

Maker's Mark Distillery
3350 Burks Spring Road
Loretto, KY 40037
Web site www.makersmark.com
Phone 270-865-2099

Wild Turkey
U.S. Highway 62 East
Lawrenceburg, KY 40342
Web site www.wildturkeybourbon.com
Phone 502-839-4544

For the most pleasant trip, be sure to call ahead to check tour hours. Some distilleries are open only at certain times of the year. Or check with local travel agents or the tourism folks at

- **Kentucky Department of Tourism:**
  www.kentuckytourism.com
- **Tennessee Tourism Department:** www.tnvacation.com

And off you go.

Pining for home

It seems that everyone in the world, from Queens to commoners, wants to see the Kentucky Derby in Lexington's magnificent 19th-century Churchill Downs. Before every race, two songs are played and sung. One is the Star Spangled Banner. Guess what the other is.

Yup, Kentucky's national anthem, "My Old Kentucky Home," by Stephen Foster. Here's a snippet:

> Weep no more, my lady
> Oh, weep no more, today
> We will sing one song for the old Kentucky home
> For the old Kentucky home far away.

Stephen Foster had it right on. So, for that matter, did Redd Stewart and Pee Wee King when they penned "Tennessee Waltz," the endearing country number Patti Page and every bar in Tennessee made their theme song. Here's a sampling:

> I was waltzing with my darlin' to the Tennessee waltz
> When an old friend I happened to see.
> I introduced him to my loved one,
> And while they were waltzing,
> My friend stole my sweetheart from me.

Those good ole' boys and gals sure missed their homes. So sit down, hoist a glass of the native juice, drink a toast to them, and think how lucky you are.

Chapter 7

More Whiskeys from America and Other Parts of the World

In This Chapter

▶ Noting the special characteristics of American blended whiskey

▶ Naming the best-known blended whiskey and rye whiskey brands

▶ Traveling the American whiskey trail

▶ Examining whiskeys from Japan, India, New Zealand, and Wales

*A*merican blended whiskey is the youngest type of all-American distilled spirit, created after the Repeal of Prohibition in 1933. This chapter tracks its quick rise to a place as the world's best-selling whiskey and its consequent fall from grace as Americans developed a taste for global rather than homegrown spirits.

By the way, Chapter 6 is a companion to this chapter. It deals with the two other made-in-America distilled spirits stars: Bourbon and Tennessee whiskey. Ideally, you should have two copies of this book, one open to Chapter 6 and one open to this chapter so that you can read them side by side. On the other hand, you could just read one chapter at a time. Your choice.

I end this chapter with a few tidbits about some interesting whiskeys that are produced in other parts of the world.

The Character of American Blended Whiskey

Six distinctive types of whiskey are made in North America:

- ✔ Bourbon
- ✔ Tennessee whiskey
- ✔ Rye whiskey
- ✔ Corn whiskey
- ✔ Wheat whiskey
- ✔ American blended whiskey

Each of these distilled spirits is made in America using methods brought to the New World by Irish and Scottish farmer-distillers. Because there were more of the former than the latter, Americans spell the spirit they created *whiskey* (with an *e*) as the Irish do, rather than *whisky* (without the *e*) like the Scots.

I tell that story in Chapter 6. Repeating the whole shebang here would simply waste your time when you're raring to get on with the blended chapter. So if you need a refresher, take a minute, go back one chapter, and read about how Americans first distilled whiskeys. Then come back here to move ahead with the birth of the blends, a phrase so felicitous that it's the heading for the very next section.

The birth of the blends

Through the advent of blended whiskeys, everything in the history of distilled spirits seems to have happened by accident. Consider the following:

- ✔ **Accident #1:** The discovery of distillation while Arab alchemists were really looking for a way to turn base metals into gold (check out Chapter 1)

- ✔ **Accident #2:** The creation of whiskey as a way to turn a profit from surplus grain — shipping the grain to market in its original form was more costly than using it as the base for a distilled spirit and then shipping the spirit

- ✔ **Accident #3:** The creation of blended whiskey to make use of limited amounts of distilled spirits remaining in American distiller warehouses after national Prohibition began in 1919

In the last half of the 19th century and the first decade of the 20th, distilling was a booming and highly profitable business. If American distillers wanted to (and they did), they could walk through enormous warehouses — some as long as a half-mile — where hundreds, and sometimes thousands of barrels of Bourbon sat quietly, maturing on the racks, stacked often two stories high.

After Prohibition became the law of the land in 1919, some distillers were permitted to sell some of their products for medicinal purposes only. Others, faced with a product they couldn't distribute legally, simply sold off the inventory to whoever wanted it and left the business they had worked so laboriously to build.

That changed in 1933 when Prohibition was repealed. Faced with mostly empty warehouses, the wiser heads among the distillers recognized that they wouldn't be able to meet the expected new demand for American whiskeys. But then — Eureka! They realized they could *blend* the mature spirits they had left with *grain neutral spirits* (the first, un-aged distillate off the still — Chapter 2 tells you more).

Although Bourbon and Tennessee whiskey can be either straight (made from a single grain whiskey) or blended (a whiskey from a combination of several grains), rye, corn, and wheat whiskey are straight. What makes American blended whiskey special is that it was created specifically to deal with a business situation: the lack of aged whiskeys after Prohibition ended.

A man with a plan

Actually, blended whiskeys had always been popular in North America. From the first, Canadian distillers made blended as well as straight whiskies. After Repeal, some canny Canadian distillers had supplies of whiskies to sell to the United States to be used with their young straight whiskeys. The canniest among them, with a large inventory of aged Bourbon and rye whiskies, was a company called Seagram.

In the words of that company's founder, Samuel Bronfman,

> "Quality Canadian and Scotch whiskies generally were blended. I appreciated that by blending we could produce a better-tasting product, the quality of which would be uniform year after year and decided that we would produce blended whisky."

The names of Bronfman's blends were Seagram's 5 Crown and Seagram's 7 Crown. (Some people thought the numbers reflected years of aging. In fact, the "5" and "7" on the labels had been assigned to those particular blends in a series of tastings involving a large number different blends. These two were the winners.)

The brands were designed to enable the Seagram Company to offer two whiskies of the "same character with slight variations." One (7 Crown) was priced slightly higher and thus was slightly more profitable than the other (5 Crown).

To facilitate its move into the United States, Seagram purchased an existing unused distillery in Lawrenceburg, Indiana. There, they modernized the distilling equipment and renovated all the facilities for storing, aging, and bottling the whiskeys. Within a six-month period, they had also designed new bottles and labels for the American market.

Then Seagram introduced its brands nationally through a new network of distributors in every state. Or, as Bronfman (familiarly known as "Mr. Sam") reported to his Board, "In just sixty days, we were able to tell the public that the Seagram whiskeys were outselling all others throughout the country."

The sales success was buttressed with the first national spirits advertising campaign, designed to introduce consumers to the new whiskeys and assure them that Seagram — with more than 11 million bottles in inventory — was not about to run out of product.

And they didn't, in peace or in war, despite the World War II ban on making alcohol for anything other than the war effort (such as gunpowder). That ban did force Seagram to drop 5 Crown, but the company made certain that its limited production of 7 Crown was allocated evenly to its retail accounts, thus ensuring retailer loyalty while maintaining the brand's loyal customer base.

Regulating a new product

A new category of whiskey was born, and the Treasury Department, which is responsible for taxation and trade regulations to protect consumers against bad quality or mislabeled products, set the standards for that new whiskey.

Today, by law, American blended whiskeys are a combination of straight whiskeys made from various grains (primarily corn, wheat, and rye) plus a minimum of 20 percent grain neutral spirits — the flavorless, odorless, first distillate. Most commonly, the whiskey is 86 proof (43 percent ABV).

When the war ended, Seagram's 7 Crown came back with a roar, eventually selling a total of 9 million cases a year, outpacing worldwide sales of all Scotch whisky at the time.

Building a Blended Whiskey

Blended whiskeys don't just happen — they're built on the expertise of experienced still masters. Those masters choose from a variety of straight whiskeys and balance them perfectly so that what you taste is a unified flavor in which no one whiskey overwhelms another.

Most blended American whiskeys contain fewer than ten different spirits. But the most costly and sophisticated may have as many as 75 different straight whiskeys, plus neutral spirits, in a combination carefully balanced to produce the same unique light, mellow, smooth whiskey — year after year, bottle after bottle.

When first introduced, blended American whiskeys quickly came to account for about half of all domestic whiskey sold in the United States. Today, that's no longer true. Over a 25-year period, starting in the 1980s, the total market for blends was in continuous decline.

Still, their appeal and value as a mixing whiskey is so great that today Seagram's 7 Crown remains the leader of the category. It still sells about 2 million cases of 7 Crown a year, and the second place brand, Kessler, sells about 800,000 cases. And blended whiskeys can be found "in the well" behind most North American bars where, because of their lightness and inherent smoothness, they're still an integral part of almost every drink made with a whiskey.

Producing a unique American flavor

Americans didn't invent the notion of blending whiskeys to create a unique style of distilled spirits. The Irish and the Scots had already done that. Quite successfully, too.

The American differences arose when Irish and Scottish immigrants to North America began to experiment with grains native to America and to process the grains in different ways. For example, Americans started drying the grains in closed, smoke-free containers rather than over hot smoking peat or other burning material.

These simple changes made a big difference. The American grains and the smoke-free environment produced a robust but pleasant, sweeter, and less smoky flavor that was pleasing to the American palate. In addition, the new whiskey was great for mixing, and thus a boon to the American preference for cocktails.

Choosing whiskeys for the blend

The spirits used in making American blended whiskeys are, to put it simply, American whiskeys. In alphabetical order, these are

- ✔ **Bourbon:** Bourbon and Tennessee whiskeys (see Chapter 6), both made from a mash containing at least 51 percent corn, are the quintessential American spirits. By law, the only whiskeys allowed to use these names are those made in the United States.

- ✔ **Corn whiskey:** Straight corn whiskey, the predecessor to Bourbon, was made exclusively from corn, an early marketing ploy to use up surplus corn at a profit rather than letting it rot in the field or storage barn.

  Modern corn whiskey doesn't have to be aged in wood, but if it is, the barrels must be either uncharred wood (usually oak) or used Bourbon barrels.

  Straight corn whiskey, which has a strong corn taste and a nearly clear color, is still available in limited markets in the United States, made by local distillers. A few companies market it by calling to mind the "moonshine" of an earlier time. One company puts its corn whiskey into a wire-closed jar under the name Moonshine; others use jugs similar to those that delivered their product in old Ford flivvers straight from the backwoods stills in the hills of various southern American states. Most often, however, corn whiskey today is used in blending.

- ✔ **Rye:** Aficionados often said that anyone who liked rye bread would love rye whiskey, but the whiskey itself has a slight bitterness not found in corn whiskey. As a result, rye whiskey is less likely to be sold straight than to be used in blending Canadian and American whiskeys. Even when it's used in blending, it's used sparingly because of its higher alcohol content and more intrusive flavor.

  In Colonial days, rye was the most common grain, which is why early American distillers, predominantly in Pennsylvania, used it to make their whiskeys. As a result, even today Easterners are likely to call any blended whiskey a "rye." Modern rye whiskey is commonly distilled at 160 proof (80 percent ABV) or less and aged in new charred barrels for a minimum of two years.

- ✔ **Wheat:** Wheat whiskeys, distilled from, well, wheat, were never very popular with American drinkers. Today, finding a straight wheat whiskey is a near impossibility, but relatively small amounts of wheat whiskeys are used in some American blended whiskeys as well as in a number of Canadian whisky blends. Sometimes distillers use wheat to give a Bourbon a flavor differentiation — Maker's Mark is one such example.

Tasting American Blended Whiskeys

You can find the basic rules for tasting distilled spirits in Chapter 3. When you're ready for an American blended whiskey tasting, you can use the tasting sheet from that chapter as well.

Tasting Americans whiskeys is a three-part deal. To get the full range of American flavors, you should taste American blended whiskeys as well as rye whiskeys and, of course, Bourbon and Tennessee whiskeys. The latter are covered in Chapter 6.

To fully appreciate the flavor of American blends, try them straight (served cool but not cold), with water, and in a mixed drink.

- **Straight:** Pour about an ounce of whiskey into a wide-mouthed old-fashioned glass. Let the whiskey sit (breathe) for a few minutes, and then swirl and sip.

- **With water:** Mix the whiskey leftover from your first sip with an equal amount of water (distilled water or branch water is the classy version, but any plain water will do). Add ice cubes made from pure water if you prefer. Let the whiskey and water sit for a few minutes, and then sip.

- **Mixed:** The simplest American whiskey mixed drink is the classic 7&7 (an ounce of Seagram's 7 Crown in a tall glass plus 7-Up and ice). The classic American blended whiskey cocktail is the Manhattan (see the original recipe in Chapter 15). In tasting, the aim is to identify the whiskey underneath the other fine ingredients. A fine blended whiskey should stand up against the accoutrements.

Naturally, each of the steps listed for American blended whiskeys works as well for rye whiskeys. The one difference: No matter which rye whiskey you choose, the flavor will definitely carry a bigger punch.

Choosing the whiskeys

Selecting a few from the many is part of the fun in exploring the various types of distilled spirits, including the commonplace blended whiskey. Your local liquor store will have a number of blended whiskeys, some flavorful enough to taste neat or with a couple of ice cubes, and others that may be best used in mixed drinks.

Some brands are strictly regional or even local to a specific county. Check with your knowledgeable liquor dealer to find out what's popular, or ask a friendly bartender what brand he finds most useful for making cocktails (and why).

After all, tasting the whiskey made in the next town or county or state can be just as exotic an experience as tasting one made halfway around the world.

The list of the better-known American blended whiskeys includes the following, all at 80 proof unless stated:

- ✔ Kessler American Blended Whiskey
- ✔ Barton 80 and 90 proof
- ✔ Calvert
- ✔ Carstairs
- ✔ Corby's
- ✔ Guckenheimer
- ✔ Imperial
- ✔ Jim Beam 8 Star
- ✔ McCormick
- ✔ Schenley
- ✔ Seagram's 7 Crown

The list of time-honored names in rye whiskeys — 80 proof (43 percent ABV) unless indicated — are

- ✔ Jim Beam
- ✔ Michters Rye Whiskey
- ✔ Old Overholt 86 proof
- ✔ Rittenhouse Rye Whiskey 100 proof
- ✔ Sazerac Rye Whiskey 18 Years Old 90 proof
- ✔ Van Winkle Family Reserve Rye 13 Year Old
- ✔ Wild Turkey Straight Rye Whiskey

Just in case you want to try a wheat whiskey, here's one that's available in some markets:

✔ Bernheim 90 proof

Why no corn whiskey? Regional distillers make straight corn whiskey, but it's too costly and valuable to be put into a mass market straight whiskey, so it's primarily used for blending with the other whiskeys.

Blends and rye whiskeys, even the best of them, usually aren't as costly as other whiskeys. For example, if you're looking at a really good Scotch single malt whisky versus a value-priced blend, don't let the higher prices change your desires either way. Price isn't an indication of quality but of differences in the cost of production and tariffs and such.

What you see, taste, and smell when sampling American blended whiskey

As with all spirits, the distinctive characteristics of American blends are their color, texture (also known as *viscosity* or *mouthfeel*), flavor, and aroma. This list tells you more:

- ✔ **Color:** American blended whiskeys are traditionally a clear amber, sometimes with an orange overtone. The darker the color, the longer the whiskey has been aged, and — chances are — the smoother it will taste.

- ✔ **Texture (first impression):** Swirl the whiskey in the glass so that the whiskey rides up the side to the top — but not over, please — and then runs down again. The finger-like runnels coming down are called *legs*. The time it takes for the legs to run down the side of the glass is an indication of the whiskey's viscosity, which is an indication of its age. The older the whiskey, the slower the fall.

- ✔ **Aroma:** The aroma of American blended whiskey is slightly sweet with an alcohol overtone. Some say it smells like caramelized sugar (think caramels and toffee), tobacco, or coffee.

- ✔ **Texture (second impression):** In your mouth, American blends should be neither heavy nor oily, but should have a definite *mouthfeel* (translation: presence in your mouth and on your tongue).

- ✔ **Flavor:** American whiskeys have a pleasant, slightly sweet flavor — no smokiness, remember — that makes them perfect for sipping straight or mixing.

Planning an American Blended Meal

American whiskey is American-born, so it marries well with traditional, familiar, American foodstuffs. Here are just a few ideas:

- Bar-B-Q with a spoonful of American blended whiskey mixed into the sauce
- Franks and beans with a spoonful of American blended whiskey stirred into the beans before cooking
- Burgers with a spoonful of American blended whiskey mashed into the meat before grilling
- Apple pie with a spoonful of American blended whiskey stirred into the apples before baking

I'm sure you get the idea. Your spoon's gonna be busy.

President George: Distiller-in-Chief

Yes, George Washington was the father of our country, "First in Peace and First in War." But he was also the first major American distiller.

Running a distillery requires a managerial spirit, and in the history of the United States, few have been better managers than George Washington, the nation's leading distiller in the later 1700s.

At its peak, his distillery at Mount Vernon turned out 11,000 gallons of whiskey a year. The product was so popular that Washington made $7,500 in a single year (a lot of money back then) in sales. In 1709, the year before he died, Washington ordered three additional copper stills and enlarged the distillery at Mount Vernon to grow the business.

Unfortunately, after his death, his estate pulled down the distillery and put itself out of business. But then, in 2001, using funds raised under the auspices of the Distilled Spirits Council of the United States, the distillery was rebuilt and put back into operation using authentic 18th-century methods to make and sell souvenir bottles to visitors. (For the record, the retailer is the state of Virginia, which controls all sales and distribution of all alcohol beverages within the state.)

As the gateway of the American Whiskey Trail, General Washington's Mount Vernon Distillery also features a History Channel video story of the rebuilding effort, "George Washington's Liquid Gold," and a museum exhibit, "Spirits of Independence: George Washington and the Beginnings of the American Whiskey Industry."

For full information, e-mail edibelle@mountvernon.org.

Traveling the American Whiskey Trail

The American Whiskey Trail, a list of whiskey-related sites collected by the Distilled Spirits Council of the United States, is a visible history of America's romance with distilled spirits.

Some of the sites primarily associated with Bourbon and Tennessee whiskeys are listed in Chapter 6. The following list shows the locations associated primarily with American blended whiskey. Put the two together and you have one wonderful trip.

Gadsby's Tavern Museum
138 North Royal Street
Alexandria, VA 22314
Web site
dc.about.com/od/museumsinnorthernva/a/Gadsbys.htm
Tour information 703-548-1288

George Washington's Distillery
Mount Vernon, VA 22121
E-mail edibelle@mountvernon.org

Oliver Miller Homestead (the original home to one of the leaders of the Whiskey Rebellion; see Chapter 6)
South Park, PA 15129
Web site www.15122.com/OliverMiller
Tour information 412-835-1554

Oscar Getz Museum of Whiskey (one of the early Bourbon distillery families)
114 North Fifth Street
Bardstown, KY 40004
Web site www.whiskeymuseum.com

West Overton Museums
West Overton Village, home of the Overholt (rye whiskey) homestead
Scottdale, PA 15683
E-mail admin@westoverton.org
Phone 724-887-7910

Woodville Plantation
1375 Washington Pike
Bridgeville, PA 15017
Web site www.woodvilleplantation.org

For those who like their spirits mixed, an interesting spot not yet on the Trail is the Museum of the American Cocktail. The original is at 514 Chartres Street in New Orleans. Interestingly enough, it shares the building with the Museum of Pharmacy, where the creator of Peychaud's bitters lived and worked in the 18th century. Another branch operates at 3663 South Las Vegas Boulevard in Las Vegas. For information about both, click on www.museumoftheamerican cocktail.org.

Off the Beaten Whiskey Trails

Because of the global popularity of whiskeys, many other countries in the world have been producing their own versions of blended, single malt, and other types of grain spirits.

Some are good and some are not so good, but they're worthy of mention because four of these areas are getting high marks and selling a lot of whisky in their particular regions.

Japan is the oldest producer among non-European countries where whiskey is popular and made domestically.

India now ranks among the leading whiskey producers, and recently an Indian conglomerate magnate bought a Scottish distillery to meet that demand. Latest to join the party is New Zealand. The countries "down under" have long been noted for their wines, and soon the world will be talking about their spirits as well. And even Wales has joined the party. Why should the Scots and Irish have all the fun?

Although many of the products made in these countries aren't available in the U.S. or even in Europe, travelers to these lands should try their offerings. Flying on one of the countries' airlines should give you at least a taste of what they have to offer.

Book the ticket. Try the whisky. It's the only way to fly.

Japan

Initially, Japanese distillers called their whisky *Scotch*. But in 1988, at the request of the U.K., the World Trade Organization ruled that Scotch is a product of a specific geographical location and that no other country can call its whiskey a Scotch or Scotch-type. By 1990, this ruling was accepted throughout the world and enforced diligently by U.K. authorities.

However, starting as early as the 19th century, Japanese distillers — no slouches at their trade — had learned the secrets to making Scotch whisky. The small distilleries scattered throughout the Japanese islands began to use pot stills to double distill their malt whiskies using lightly peated barley. So, even though whiskies made in Japan can't call themselves Scotch, they do have a definite Scottish character — smoky, rich, and aromatic.

In 1920, commercial whisky-making started when Masataka Taketsuru returned to Japan after two years of studying chemistry and distillation in Scotland. His time abroad gained him not only a Scottish bride but also a burning determination to make Japan a factor in the world whisky trade. His goal was to convince local distillers to make real Scotch whisky rather than sweet-potato-based shochu or tinted grain neutral spirits.

Eventually he convinced the company that was to become Suntory that his idea was the way to go. When its new Scotch whisky became popular with consumers, others soon followed. Among those profiting from this burst of enthusiasm was Taketsuru himself who formed his own company, Nikka Distillery, in 1934.

Following World War II, the sales of spirits soared and have continued to grow. Whether the whisky is called Scotch or not, the business has grown to the extent that Japanese corporations bought into the Scottish distillery business. Today, they import their own Scotch whisky brands to sell domestically.

Some leading malted grain brands now made in Japan include the following:

- ✔ **Blended whiskies:** Karuizawa Master's Blend, 10 Years Old; Evermore 2004 Blend, 21 Years Old

- ✔ **Blended malt whisky:** Takesuru, 21 Years Old, Pure Malt

- ✔ **Single cask whiskies:** Yamazaki 119.2 proof, Japanese oak cask; Hakushu 1982, sherry cask

- ✔ **Single malt whiskies:** Fuijigotenba 15 Years Old, Single Grain; Golden Horse Chichibu 10 years old; Yamazaki 18 Years Old, Single Malt

India

Despite the general impression, many Indian people enjoy their whisky. Only Muslims prohibit alcohol; Hindus welcome it. The Muslim population is only a few percentage points of the huge Indian population. It's not surprising then that Vijay Mallya, who owns a $2 billion conglomerate, added to the holdings of his UB group (for United Brewing) by purchasing one of Scotland's top five whisky makers, Whyte & Mackay, for $1.18 billion. In addition to importing brands, including Dalmore and Isle of Jura brands, UB can also import bulk whisky for sale in China to be used for blending.

Above all, he hopes to meet the demands of the Indian marketplace, the biggest consumers of whisky in the world. In 2005, Indians drank more than 70 million cases, and sales are growing at the rate of about 9 percent a year.

That's big business even for a billionaire.

The only thorn in Mallya's side is India's high tariffs that are presently applied to imported whiskeys (and now under adjudication by the World Trade Organization). It's difficult to resolve this problem because most of the whisky made in India is made from molasses. (Chapter 12 tells you that sugar cane was first distilled in India.) Because of that, all Indian-made whiskies must be labeled *Indian spirit* or *rum*, according to WTO regulations. But Mallya is so optimistic about the tariff war outcome that he's expanding the Whyte and Mackay distillery in Invergordon to make it the largest in the world.

Brands to look for include McDowell's No. 1 Brandy (said to be the world's best-selling brandy) and Bagpiper Whisky, India's best-selling (more than 10 million cases a year), making it the largest selling non-Scotch whisky in the world.

New Zealand

After many years of trying, New Zealand vintners finally started producing some of the world's finest white wines a few years back. Demand now often outstrips supply. Now the self-nicknamed "kiwis" have discovered that their low-pollution climate, soils made for grain production, and the purest water in the world allow distillers to make fine single malt and blended whiskies.

The distilling business is said to have been started in 1850 by one Owen McShane who made a product called Chained Lightning. McShane went on to produce a gin, a brandy, and a rum — all using the root of the indigenous cabbage tree. Despite that, McShane's products must have been tasty because his non-tax-paying products (moonshine) became extremely popular, bringing his activities to the eyes of the government. In turn, the government passed the New Zealand Distillation Act of 1865, banning all distillers making fewer than 5,000 gallons of spirits a year — in other words, McShane and his buddies.

Over the years, New Zealand has permitted home distillation, changed that to no home distillation, totally banned all distillation, and finally relaxed most restrictions including those on home distillation. This naturally impeded the development of commercial enterprises. However, today, with the assistance of investors from Britain, the U.S., and France, the industry is slowly growing in popularity with its own people, and the word about the quality and purity of their alcohol beverages is piquing lots of interest in the global marketplace.

As for whiskies, Hokonui — which started life as moonshine — sent its first shipment of single malt blends and liqueurs to France. Other shipments followed to the U.K., Germany, and Norway. The whiskies are distilled by the Southern Distilling Company.

It's a definite sign of things to come. Drop in if you're visiting New Zealand's South Island. It's another reason to go to the paradise where the population of sheep is greater than that of people and the waters always sparkle.

Wales

Way back in the fourth century, a man named Reault Hir came to an island off the coast of Wales and started distilling whisky. He was the first to bring the art of making *aqua vitae* (or *gwirod* in the local language) to Wales, probably from Ireland. The soil was perfect for his needs. Wales is divided geologically; the coal in the north is separated from limestone by a range of hills. The first whisky was made from barley, yeast, and honey distilled into a basic raw spirit.

In 1705, a commercial distillery was started, owned by Evan Williams' family. That name became very familiar to Kentuckians when the family later emigrated to the U.S. Around the same time, another Welshman named Jack Daniel also moved across the Atlantic, winding up in Tennessee.

In the 19th century, another distillery opened in Wales, but it was forced to close in 1880 as a result of pressure from temperance advocates. That was it for Welsh spirits until the current millennium began with the first distillation in the new Welsh Whisky Company's Pendryn plant in Brecon Beacons National Park. Welsh Whisky was the successor to a previous company, which, although mandated to make pure and totally Welsh spirits, had cheated by using Scotch whiskies bought in bulk for use in a blended product.

Pendryn produced a purely Welsh single malt — Welsh Gold (*aur cymru* in Welsh) and, after aging, released it on Saint David's Day 2004 to honor Wales' patron saint. Welsh Gold is made from mountain spring water that flows over peat and through porous red sandstone and limestone caverns before coming directly into the distillery. There it's mixed with distilled malted barley spirits, matured in Bourbon casks, and finished in Madeira barrels. It's so well regarded that Pendryn is now busily exporting it to other nations.

Now you have yet another reason to visit this bastion of the United Kingdom where it's posited that once upon a time Arthur and his court held sway at Camelot.

Chapter 8

Channeling the Canadians

. . . .

In This Chapter

▶ Discovering what makes Canadian whisky different

▶ Following the effect Canadian whisky had on U.S. whiskeys

▶ Pursuing Canada's Prohibition-era salesmen

▶ Choosing Canadian whiskies to suit your needs

. . . .

This chapter takes North American whiskeys to extremes — the extreme North, that is — by detailing the origins of Canadian whisky, outlining the country's influence on worldwide whisky-making, recommending products for tasting, and naming the foods with which Canadians enjoy their spirits.

Starting at the Top (of the World)

The emergence of a special whisky from Canada is due almost entirely to the accident of a young British orphan's emigration across the Atlantic in 1782 and the subsequent arrival of a family of four Russian brothers in 1889.

Britain + Russia = Canadian whisky? In a word, yes.

Molson's multitudinous accomplishments

John Molson (1763–1836), the British orphan I mention earlier in this chapter, is best known to North Americans for the beer that bears his name (today: Coors Molson), first brewed at a Montreal brewery beside the St. Lawrence River. Molson bought the brewery in 1785 by using a small inheritance left to him by his parents.

Molson realized that the flat, mid-Canadian plains produced a bountiful grain harvest — so bountiful, in fact, that the farmers were being crushed by surplus crops year after year. Rye, in particular, was so plentiful that the prices kept dropping.

To get rid of the surplus, or at least find a way to profit from it, Molson took a logical next step — the one that matters in this book. In 1799, he opened the first grain-based distillery in Canada, thus becoming the first commercial Canadian spirits producer and the leading exporter of Canadian whisky.

For reasons that remain unknown, the spirits business didn't prosper, so no record remains of how Molson's whiskies may compare with modern Canadian products.

But, this much is certain: Molson's way of making Canadian whisky set the pattern for an entire industry because he

- ✔ Hired a staff of (what else?) Scottish distillers
- ✔ Distilled the whisky from corn and rye
- ✔ Spelled its name the Scottish way, without an "e": whisky

Entering the modern era with a bang

By the early 1900s, the distillation of Canadian style whisky was standardized, but the distribution and marketing (moving the whisky from the bottling line to the salesmen and on to the consumer) wasn't.

As in the United States, temperance groups waged a continuing battle against "the demon rum" (or wine or whisky), so fierce that eventually the Canadian Government decided to pass the matter over to the various provincial (in America, "state") legislatures for their consideration.

Molson's many talents

John Molson was a man of many talents. Not only did he create a Canadian style whisky, but he also went on to build the first steamship made entirely in North America, develop a fleet of 22 steam driven vessels (including the first of its kind to be used in war), finance the first Canadian railroad, serve as President of the Bank of Montreal, and sit as a member (at different times) in both the Lower and Upper Houses of the Canadian Parliament. Now that's a busy life!

A quick note on the birth of Prohibition in North America: As you'll see with other spirit types, governments were always willing to either impose huge taxes on alcohol beverages or ban their sale entirely (gin in England is one example). Much of that thinking came to North America with the first European settlers.

Modern sociologists know that abstinence isn't the same as temperance. Alcohol was recognized and accepted as a medication long before it was barred and long, long before it was recognized as a mood-altering substance. Even though it couldn't cure the plague or other diseases, it worked well with pain — remember the doctors in the Western movies who had no anesthetic?

However, the more mankind learned about this remarkable "gift from the gods," the better they learned how to deal with overuse when a joyous mood turned sour. Dr. Benjamin Rush, the Philadelphia doctor who was the first Surgeon General of the United States and an early proponent of ways to prevent Yellow Fever, had great respect for alcohol as a medicine, but strongly recommended temperance in its use (or as you'd say today, moderate drinking).

When some stern moralists came to the New World, they brought with them the belief that abstinence was the answer. Naturally they also brought ways to bring about abstinence, the easiest of which was a total prohibition against manufacture or distribution of the alcohol carrying beverages.

Robert Benchley, who was a well-known fan of the Martini, once said: "A Puritan is one who sits around all day worrying that someone else is having a good time."

The problem of prohibition

Having duly considered the matter of Prohibition, several provincial legislatures chose to enact forms of enforcing abstinence. These acts ranged from slight limitations, such as raising prices by higher taxation and putting the state itself in charge of distribution through ill-lit unappealing stores, all the way up to a total ban on the sale of beer and spirits.

Then, in 1916, the Canadian Federal government — explaining that all the alcohol produced in Canada was urgently needed for fighting the "Great War" (World War I) — enacted nationwide Prohibition, stopping the manufacture and sale of spirits and beer except for religious and/or medical use. Not surprisingly, the number of prescriptions issued for a glass of whisky every day rose astronomically.

Within three years, the majority of Canadian Provincial Legislatures declared Prohibition a failure. Every legislator didn't agree right away: Prince Edward Island, for example, didn't toss out Prohibition until 1940. Ah, well.

Governmental control of the industry

After they decided to end Prohibition, the Canadians got cracking on a system and moved to set up rules for controlling the sale of spirits and beer.

Each province was to control the distribution and sale of alcohol beverages within its jurisdiction. The provinces would

- Act as a purchaser to buy the products from the makers
- Distribute products to state-owned retail stores
- Set prices at the wholesale and retail levels
- Create laws to ensure the quality of the spirits and the equally important ethical performances of the distillers' trade practices

The American bonus

As the Canadians were beginning to wind down their experience with The Noble Experiment (also known as Prohibition), the Americans were just winding up starting theirs.

The 18th Amendment to the U.S. Constitution went into effect in 1919, thus opening an incredible opportunity for enterprising Canadians to open a huge market to the south, scooting in and out of the coastline with real whisky, courtesy of a network of illegal distributors called *booties,* short for, yes indeed, *bootleggers.*

The traffic was terrific until 1933 when the North Carolina became the last of the two-thirds of the State Legislatures needed to ratify the 21st (Repeal) Amendment of the Constitution. Once again, the U.S. was permitting the legal manufacture and sale of alcohol beverages.

After World War II, the Canadians, whose farmers were once more growing more grain than they could profitably sell, once again turned to converting the surplus corn and rye to whisky that they could ship across the border. It went to an American population with a great thirst for legal spirits and an appreciation for the fine Canadian whiskies they had enjoyed illegally.

Moving into the modern markets

Could the United States have had a successful distilling industry without Canadian whisky? That may sound foolish given the fact that, as Chapter 6 explains, Americans were making whiskey (with an "e") for almost a century before the Canadians entered the business.

In fact, the American whiskeys — eventually called Bourbon and Tennessee whiskey — were rough, not very tasty, and certainly not as pleasantly "mixable" as those made today are.

And that was America's second gift to the Canadian distillers.

Enter the king of the Canadian whisky entrepreneurs

In 1889, four Russian immigrant brothers named Bronfman — Sam, Allan, Abe, and Harry — opened a small inn located in what were then the wilds of Saskatchewan.

Like so many young immigrants, the Bronfmans were ambitious. Sam even set his sights on eventually being knighted by the King of England, which is pretty hot stuff for a young Russian immigrant in far-off Saskatchewan.

While operating a small hotel, Sam obtained a provincial license to distribute liquor. When Canada's Prohibition dried up the local whisky market, Sam turned his eyes to Joseph E. Seagram & Sons, a small distillery located in Waterloo, Ontario. Banking on the eventual end of Prohibition both north and south of the Canadian border, Sam purchased the company and went into the distilling business with his brother Allan. They aimed to position themselves to fill orders for whiskies made at the Seagram distillery, as well as imported Scotch whiskies, first in Canada and then in the United States.

Creating a signature brand (or two)

The Bronfmans' first big brand was Seagram's 5 Crown, a blended whiskey (with an "e" for the Americans who were used to seeing their previously highly favored Irish whiskey spelled that way). It was distilled from native American corn and bottled with a label carrying a Seagram crest prominently featuring the words *Integrity, Craftsmanship,* and *Tradition.*

"Mr. Sam," as he came to be known in the trade, shied away from personal publicity, but he believed strongly in promoting his brands in an ethical and effective manner. For example, one widely praised company advertisement during the Great Depression was headlined: "We Don't Want Your Bread Money." The copy underneath explained that spirits were a luxury and that basic needs came first.

Seagram's 5 Crown was so successful that the company introduced a second signature brand, Seagram's 7 Crown. It soon became the most popular spirit in America, making Joseph E. Seagram & Sons the world's leading distiller with four of the best-selling products of its type on the market (Calvert, Four Roses, Crown Royal, and Seagram's VO).

Having made their mark with American whiskeys, the Bronfmans also scored with Canadian spirits. Seagram's VO — the classic, smooth, slightly sweet Canadian whisky — is still a mid-price best-seller, while the even smoother Seagram's Crown Royal is the leading premium-price Canadian.

Not bad for four guys from Russia.

What Makes a Whisky Canadian?

All Canadian distillers must follow four specific legal guidelines. As with any whisky, it all starts with the grain:

- Canadian whisky must be distilled from a fermented mash of wheat, corn, rye, and/or barley.
- Canadian whisky must be made entirely in Canada, but it doesn't necessarily have to be a single grain whisky. Canadian whisky may be a blend of many different whiskies.
- Canadian whisky must be aged in oak casks for a minimum of three years.
- Canadian whisky must use water that's fresh and pure.

Traveling to Canada

Visiting Canada can be a wonderful tonic for the experienced traveler and an outstanding adventure for the first time visitor. You can find much to see and do, from Toronto's high-spot international lifestyle and Montreal's French culture, language, and cuisine, all the way west to the Asian-flavored sophistication of British Columbia and the rugged wilderness journeys into the Yukon Territory. Whether you want skiing in the Laurentians in the winter, boating in the Great Lakes, or hunting for gold up north, you'll find something for everyone, and at reasonable prices too.

Within these simple guidelines, distillers are permitted to apply individual skills to the making of their whisky. One example: A single Canadian whisky is often blended with others.

The guidelines not only led to the new type of whisky, but also helped create a new culture for the blank slate that was Canada in the early days. Its huge land mass was lightly settled but highly regarded for farming. The climate and topography dictate that Canadian agriculture is most profitable when it concentrates on growing grains such as corn, rye, and wheat. These were the grains to be used — with a little barley thrown in from time to time for variety. The new settler-farmers quickly learned that making whisky was a wonderful way to turn surplus grains into profits rather than burning them as rubbish.

Those farmers could often be found working in the fields with a pottery jug filled with the glowing whisky they or a neighbor distilled. When they rode into a nearby town for supplies, a cask filled with local whisky was standing at the front door of the general store for customers to dip into to clear the dust from their throats.

How Canadian Whisky Is Made

All Canadian whisky makers climb the same ladder to successful whisky, making and arriving at the high quality alcohol beverage that's regarded by almost every objective expert as the smoothest whisky made anywhere.

The distillation process that I describe here applies to the making of all spirits, including Canadian. For a quick refresher, turn to Chapter 2.

To create Canadian whisky, distillers follow these steps:

1. **Select the grain.**

   The most abundant grain grown in Canada is corn, so that's the grain that forms the base for most individual whisky recipes. However, each distiller uses a variety of different types of corn, and each adds small amounts of barley, malt, and rye so that each whisky has a different and distinctive flavor.

   Although rye is a very small part of the usual ingredient menu, it's the grain that adds the most flavor. When you can smell more rye in a glass of Canadian whisky, the distiller has used more rye in the blend.

2. Grind and malt the grain.

The grains that distillers use to make Canadian whisky may first be malted (heated), much as those used in making Scotch (see Chapter 5 for this and other similarities). Malted or not, all grains for the mash are ground to a predetermined, controlled level of fineness to permit the starches to reveal all the sugars they hold.

3. Select the water.

For every gallon of spirit produced, a distillery uses as much as 100 gallons of water. Outside of purity, the only requirement is that the water should contain a specific amount of lime, which is an essential element to making a quality whisky.

4. Cook the mash.

Under carefully controlled temperatures in sterile conditions, the distiller mixes the milled grain and water into a mash and cooks it to convert the starches into sugars as rapidly and evenly as possible.

5. Add yeast.

Under carefully controlled temperatures and sterile conditions, the distiller adds yeast (or several kinds of yeast) to the cooked mash to start fermentation. Each distiller obtains a number of yeasts and then uses them alone or in combination to gain the desired flavors. Those strains are then cultivated from isolated yeasts and used for years to give continuity of that flavor.

6. Allow for fermentation.

After about three or four days, the yeasts consume the sugars of the cooked mash and convert them into a liquid called *distiller's beer.*

7. Distill the whisky.

The fermented mash is passed into a still and heated to boiling. The alcohol vapors rising from the liquid are collected, condensed, and cooled in a collecting vat. To reduce the spirit to a required 86 proof (43 percent alcohol by volume or ABV) strength alcohol, distillers add pure water.

8. Barrel the whisky.

The distiller pumps the diluted alcohol into carefully selected wooden barrels — most often oak. (The unused mash is drained, compressed, and generally used for domestic animal feed.)

9. **Age the whisky.**

The filled barrels are stacked in a temperature-controlled warehouse for a minimum of three years. Many are aged longer than that, some as long as 25 years. The wood of the barrel imparts changes to the flavors of the whisky inside for the length of time needed to provide the desired taste.

10. **Blend.**

Distillers blend whiskies from various barrels to create the final taste that matches the permanent recipe of the distiller. Canadian whisky may also be flavored with up to 9.09 percent of imported whisky or spirit, or a domestic spirit other than whisky or wine. Caramel is often used for flavoring or coloring.

11. **Marry the blend.**

No preacher needed here. The distiller puts the blended whisky into a single barrel and lays it aside to mature for a short period of time, permitting the whiskies to *marry,* or, in other words, to blend.

12. **Package the whisky.**

Just pour the whisky into bottles, seal them, and slap on the labels.

The distiller removes the final blend and sends it to the bottling room where it's packaged for shipment to retail outlets all over the world.

Bottled Canadian whisky may legally be labeled "Canadian Whisky," "Canadian Rye Whisky," or "Rye Whisky." The last two give a distinct indication of the prime flavoring grain.

Tasting the Best of Canada

You can find the complete rules that turn tasting into an unforgettable experience in Chapter 3. Remember the importance of Rule Number One — always have a good, moderate time — and keep the results of the tasting where you can reference them easily to refresh your memory or help you discover something different. You can use the tasting sheet in Chapter 3 when you taste Canadian whiskies.

Selecting the whiskies for your tasting

Unlike some other types of spirits, such as cordials, Canadian whiskies are a relatively small group. As of this writing, Canada has 200 licensed distillers; some are *craft distillers* — small distilleries producing a limited amount of whisky a year, generally on less costly, small pot stills, and often without enough funding to buy grains and other items needed for production in the quantity that would put them up there with the big boys.

Licensed craft distillers are continuously overseen by government authorities to assure purity and quality according to the regulations. So, if you find a distiller in the woods of a small town in Saskatchewan, he may turn out some sensational whisky that's worth buying a bottle or two. But, his whisky may turn out to be a dud the second time around.

The majority of distillers are large enough to be members of the Association of Canadian Distillers, in operation since 1947. The output from its current members can be found all around the world, and their quality is unquestioned by a huge number of steady customers. Table 8-1 lists the members and their Web sites where available.

Finding a whisky with any of these names on the label assures you that the whisky was made by the producer under all laws and inspections.

Table 8-1	Canadian Whisky Brands
Producer	*Web Site*
Bacardi Canada Inc.	www.bacardi.com
Barton Brands	www.bartonbrands.com
Canadian Mist Distillers Ltd.	www.canadianmist.com
Corby Distillers Ltd.	www.corby.ca
Diageo Canada Inc.	www.diageo.com
Schenley Distilleries Inc.	www.bartonbrands.com
PMA - Peter Mielzynski Agencies Ltd.	www.pmacanada.com

For more information about the distillers and their brands, look for individual Web sites, or contact the Association at www.canadian distillers.com.

Although it's true that Canadian whiskies are the third-most-loved whiskies globally, it's also true that the number of brands available worldwide is limited. In looking for bottles to sample, decide in advance how you'll usually serve Canadian whiskies.

This is a whisky designed to be light in order to give it greater versatility in mixing. So, in this case at least, price does matter: The top priced brands have the cleanest and truest flavor.

To help you decide which brands to taste, the following sections list the leading brands arranged by price. I don't give exact prices because taxation varies from state to state, province to province, and retail outlet to retail outlet. However, I do give you three general price ranges, which I refer to as premium, popular, and value.

Premium priced brands

For the purest flavor, take the premium brands — often called *top shelf brands* because they're never put below eye level on store shelves ("eye level is buy level") or on back bars where they can't be seen ("a full value brand never goes in the well"). These whiskies are the brands that you'll want to sip slowly in front of a roaring fire, dreaming of days seeking gold in the Yukon.

I list them in approximate price order based on a 750-ml bottle, starting with the most expensive.

The following whiskies are priced between $25 (U.S. dollars) and $50. Newer brands may be even higher.

- ✔ **Crown Royal Special Reserve:** As in any other whisky category, a reserve is made of the finest whiskies put aside for just this brand. Crown Royal was named, blended, and given its unusual crown-shaped bottle in 1939 to honor the first-ever visit of a king and queen to Canada.

- ✔ **Tangle Ridge 10 Year Old:** This is called a *double-casked whisky,* because the whisky is first aged in casks for ten years and then blended with other whiskies for additional aging before bottling.

- ✔ **Crown Royal** (age unknown): The original premium Canadian whisky that comes in the purple sack (very useful for storing golf tees or golf balls). It's made from a blend of whiskies including some that are 21 years old and older.

- ✔ **Canadian Club Reserve 6 Year Old:** The second most popular premium Canadian whisky. The added age above the minimum three years certainly makes it worth a taste or two.

Popular priced brands

Are you having a party and want to have a couple of bottles of a good Canadian on hand for mixing those fancy new cocktails? This is the price range for multiple purchases. All have that wonderful Canadian flavor, but they're a little heavier so that the taste can cut through the clear soda or dark cola with which you mix them.

The following whiskies are priced from about $15 to $45:

- **Canadian Club 6 Year Old:** Made from "ordinary" 6 year old whiskies, and it's a little less robust than the reserve.

- **Seagram's VO Gold 8 Year Old:** For many years in the 1960s and 1970s the original VO was the best-selling Canadian whisky in the United States. This more recent version adds more aging, so it has a heartier flavor.

- **Seagram's VO 3 Year Old minimum:** Light, pleasant, and smooth. What more could anyone want for making a magnificent Manhattan?

- **Black Velvet Reserve 8 Year Old:** Probably the best value among all the whiskies in this category. In fact, it's probably too good to use for mixing and should be enjoyed as an aperitif with a little water and ice cubes.

- **Canadian Mist 3 Year Old minimum:** This blend of Canadian whiskies is extremely popular in some parts of the United States because of its mild unobtrusive flavor in cocktails.

- **Rich and Rare 3 Year Old minimum:** Another outstanding mixing whisky that lives up to its name — it's not rare, but the flavor is.

- **McNaughton 3 Year Old minimum:** Another regional neighborhood favorite.

- **Black Velvet 3 Year Old minimum:** If your favorite bar has this "in the well," you know the drinks are going to be better than average.

Value priced brands

Some people who drop in aren't your best friends, but you do have to show hospitality, so you whip out a bottle of what the trade calls "value priced" Canadian whisky and offer to mix them a drink. These are the brands almost always found in bar wells directly underneath the bar and are used primarily for mixing. They're good, pleasant tasting brands — but they're not quite the best.

The following whiskies are priced from less than $10 to $12:

- ✔ Windsor
- ✔ Campbell & Cooper
- ✔ Lord Calvert
- ✔ Canadian LTD
- ✔ Northern Light
- ✔ Seagram's Canadian Hunter

Savoring the flavor of Canadian whisky

No matter which brands you select for your tasting experience, all Canadian whiskies share a general taste profile. Your first sip tells you that these whiskies are

- ✔ **Smooth:** Unlike some whiskies, these have little alcohol "bite."
- ✔ **Even-flavored:** Because of the blending of various grains, the flavor is consistent and easy to recognize as Canadian.
- ✔ **Slightly spicy:** The aftertaste may be slightly spicy, depending on the amount of rye used.
- ✔ **Rye-flavored:** The flavor of rye bread may come through if enough rye is used in the distillation.
- ✔ **Full of other flavors:** These whiskies can be light or wintery, and they're often compared to Scotch due to the use of oats and barley.

The other Canadians

Never underestimate the inventiveness of Canadian distillers. In addition to offering the world rums and vodkas, they have also created a world-famed cordial, Yukon Jack. This drink is made on a flavored 100-proof Canadian whisky base. You can find it either in the Canadian whisky section or with other liqueurs.

Although this book deals primarily with spirits, it's difficult to mention Canada's contribution to the world's alcohol beverage pantry without calling attention to Canadian Ice Wines. These marvelous dessert wines have just recently been made available throughout Europe, thanks to a change in European Union import regulations. Ice wines are made mostly in West Coast wineries, primarily in Vancouver, but also in newer wineries on the Niagara plateau bordering the U.S. along the St. Lawrence River.

Overall, Canadian whisky has no single overwhelming flavor, so it mixes well and evenly with almost any kind of mixer, including with a judicious use of tropical fruit juices. The sweetness of the rye in Canadian whisky remains even when the whisky is mixed with sweet diet colas. Canadian whisky isn't even upstaged when mixed with dry vermouth and angostura bitters in a Manhattan.

Pairing Foods with Canadian Whisky

Canada is a really BIG country with a land mass of 3,851,800 square miles (9,012,112 square kilometers), making it the second largest country in the world. The population was estimated in January 2007 at about 33 million people, ranking the country 37th among the world's populous nations.

But in talking about the number of people living in this giant of a country, one is reminded of the famous line Spencer Tracy said about Katherine Hepburn in one of their early films together, "Not much meat on her, but what's there is cherce."

Canada is a multicultural country with a young population. Many Canadians brought with them to their new homeland the culture and cuisine of their original homelands. And they all seem to love Canadian whisky — that fact almost alone proves how well the whisky blends with virtually any style cuisine.

As you can see in Table 8-2, the foods Canadians serve with this universal whisky vary by province from the colder Atlantic side to the warm Pacific Coast and into the far north of the Arctic Circle.

Table 8-2	Canadian Provinces and Main Cuisine	
Province (Abbreviation)	*Location*	*Main Cuisine*
Alberta (AL)	Middle Canada	German-style food, such as pork and sauerkraut
British Columbia (BC)	West Coast	English, Asian, California; this is the most international cuisine you'll find west of Ontario
Manitoba (MN)	Middle	English, lots of grains

Province (Abbreviation)	Location	Main Cuisine
New Brunswick (NB)	East	Seafood and lobster; great New England influence
Newfoundland/Labrador (NL)	East	Fish and chowders
Northwest Territories (NT)	North	Picture Alaska — hearty meats and starchy vegetables; think moose, not mousse
Nova Scotia (NS)	Northeast	Scottish; prepared by early settlers
Nunavut (No abbreviation)	Far North	Inuit homeland cuisine
Ontario (ON)	Mideast	International foods for an international community
Prince Edward Island (PE)	Atlantic	Seafood, including the world's best mussels
Quebec (QC)	Mideast	Vive la France — A true touch of Paris in Montreal
Saskatchewan (SK)	Midwest	Polish/Russian influences; Kielbasa anyone?
Yukon Territories (YT)	Northwest	Lots of game and very hearty eating

Pin the label on the Canadian

Being one of the two neighbors to the United States has always been a bone of discontent with Canadians. After all, the northernmost parts of the continent were visited and settled by Europeans long before the rest of the continent. That alone would make Canadians happy — but it was not to last.

They had one stroke of good fortune: They beat the French, who were trying to take the vast land for their king, and they forced them into an enclave in Quebec and onto two islands off the Canadian coast that France still controls — Pierre and Miquelon.

Then they took on the upstart English colony to the south that had declared itself free. They even burned that nation's capitol, but they couldn't beat its navy and they had to settle on the 49th Parallel as the boundary line between them.

(continued)

(continued)

Ever since then, Canadians have suffered from an inferiority complex. However, the following quiz gives you some idea of how they've gotten even. It gives the names of a (baker's) dozen people in the limelight around the world in a number of fields. The trick is, are they real Canadians, or just wannabes? You decide and score yourself (no Googling allowed, please).

Person	*Career*	*Canadian?*
1. Ben Heppner	Opera Star	o
2. Joni Mitchell	Folk Singer	o
3. James Naismith	Inventor of Basketball	o
4. Mary Pickford	Silent Movie Star	o
5. Jim Carrey	Noisy Movie Star	o
6. Oscar Peterson	Jazz Musician	o
7. Kurt Vonnegut	Author	o
8. Saul Bellow	Nobel Prize Winner	o
9. Peter Jennings	TV Newscaster	o
10. Tom Brokaw	TV Newscaster	o
11. Leslie Nielsen	Movie Actor	o
12. Joe Schuster	Comic Book Artist (Superman)	o
13. Howie Mandel	TV Show Host	o

Canadians: 1, 3, 4, 5, 6, 8, 9, 11, 12, and 13

Wannabes: 2, 7, and 10

If you got three out of the thirteen, go back to the current events book. If you scored correctly on seven, you're halfway there. If you got all thirteen, you probably pronounce "house" as "hoose," end every sentence with "eh," and can sing all of "O Canada." Get your passport. You're a Canadian.

Part III

Surfing the White Waters: A Guide to "Clear" Spirits

The 5th Wave   By Rich Tennant

"I figured you for a vodka drinker. It too is completely tasteless."

In this part . . .

This part focuses on clear spirits, entrepreneurial products that are rewarding on their own, but entering profitably into mergers. The spirits listed here include the classic naturally flavored clear spirit (gin), an unflavored (or flavored) smooth competitor (vodka), two robust Mexican spirits (Tequila and mescal), plus the New World favorite (rum).

Chapter 9

Getting the Goods on Gin

· ·

In This Chapter

▶ Examining the origins of gin in Europe

▶ Noting the differences between Holland gins and London dry gins

▶ Figuring out why gin works so well in cocktails

▶ Deciding the best way to serve your gin

· ·

*W*hat could be simpler than gin? The plain distillate comes off the still, and presto! The distiller adds his own secret recipe of *botanicals* — that is, substances derived from plants — primarily juniper berries, plus other herbs and spices to make a mild and pleasant spirit.

What's amazing is how many complex and delicious drinks have evolved from this simple spirit. This chapter explains who, what, when, where, and how.

The Origins of Gin

In the beginning — or beGINning — alcohol beverages, especially distilled spirits, were regarded more highly as medicines than as beverages.

As Chapter 1 explains, the Christian missionaries who introduced distillation to Europe early in the 12th century were also medicine men who used their distillates to relieve an entire catalogue of ailments and illnesses. In doing so, the missionaries and monks may not have cured their patients, but they certainly left them happier.

But the imbibers weren't necessarily happy because the stuff tasted good. Most of the missionary meds were based on local plants ground up and boiled in a tea or soup, which left them tasting pretty much like, well, plants ground up and boiled in tea or soup.

Eventually, someone got the idea of making the medicines taste good by adding fruits and sweeteners and distilling them, leading to the introduction of liqueurs (cordials). One such liqueur was Benedictine, introduced around the turn of the 16th century by Dom Bernardo Vincelli at the Benedictine Abbey of Fécamp in Normandy. (For more on liqueurs, check out Chapter 14.)

A second result of this flavor revolution: Gin.

Hello, Holland; welcome, jenevre

By the end of the 14th century, the lowly juniper bush had already become famous as a flavoring. At that time, farmers in "The Lowlands" (modern Holland and Belgium) were practicing the new art of distilling grains, such as barley and oats, to produce alcohol beverages.

Farmers in Italy in the 11th century started using berries of the juniper to "soften" the harsh flavor of plain alcohol. In Germany, the problem of harshness was addressed by adding whole berries, crushed berries, or oil pressed from the berries to wine to make what they called *brentwine*. Today we recognize *brentwine* as the German word for what we now know as brandy (see Chapter 13).

Equally important, juniper was said to prevent or cure stomach problems and, for some unknown reasons, to even cure bubonic plague. That, probably more than its flavor, ensured its popularity.

Fast forward now to the mid-1600s. Franciscus de la Boie, also known as Dr. Sylvius, of Leiden University in the Netherlands, had already discovered that juniper berries were diuretics (chemicals that increase urination). Then he found that adding the berries to alcohol made the harsh grain alcohol taste better and the medicine easier to take. He called his new beverage *jenevre*, the Dutch word for juniper. So unlike most other spirit products, gin has a real, live, well-known historical originator: Dr. Sylvius. He's gin's father.

Dutch merchants, knowing a good thing when they tasted it, aggressively promoted their new spirit, even renaming it *genievre* (French for juniper) to make it more attractive on the Continent.

Holland's balm for British soldiers

The real impetus to spreading the fame of gin was a really long war.

In 1568, the House of Orange — Holland's ruling family — went to war to seek independence from Spain. The war expanded into a series of battles between Holland, France, and Sweden on one side and Spain and the Hapsburg Empire on the other. The conflict, lasting from 1618 to 1648 (later known as the 30 Years War), eventually drew Britain into the fray when England sent troops to join the Netherlands' side of the fight.

To offset the damp, cold climate of The Lowlands, the British troops drank a glass or two a day of Dr. Sylvius' wonderful juniper potion, which gave them "Dutch Courage." The result was so effective that not only did the Boys in the Red Coats feel fine about fighting alongside the Hollanders; but they also carried bottles of jenevre home with them, leading directly to yet another episode in the spread of gin's popularity.

The Brits Take Charge

Almost immediately on arrival in Britain, jenevre became terrifically popular both as beverage and medicine. But that created problems for British brewers and Scotch distillers who had a hard time keeping up with the new product from the other side of the Channel.

Protecting the home teams

King William III of Britain wanted to protect the home teams from the Dutch invasion. So, in 1689, he banned all imported spirits, thus making it much easier for local British distillers to produce jenevre — now known as *gin*. Coincidentally, this ban offered British farmers the opportunity to profitably dispose of surplus grains.

However, the new law failed to impose good quality control on the new distillers and their products. The law merely required the gin distillers to post a notice and wait ten days before doing business. As a result, the first British gins were very inferior — and very cheap. Not surprisingly, the inexpensive gin soon outsold other beverages, including beer. By 1730 more than 7,000 shops in London were selling only spirits; one in four of these shops primarily sold gin.

Records of the period suggest that Londoners bought 5,000 gallons of gin in 1690. That amount ballooned to 5 million gallons by 1720 when per capita (male) consumption of gin reached 14 gallons annually.

The increased gin consumption led to unpleasant civic behavior and street scenes, such as the one pictured in William Hogarth's famous etching, "Gin Lane." The etching shows a gin shop sign reading, "Drunk for a Penny/Dead Drunk for Twopence/Clean Straw for Nothing."

To bring the public drunkenness and proletarian debauchery to a halt, Parliament passed the infamous Gin Act of 1736. The legislation, which quintupled the price of gin and limited sale to two gallons at a time, led almost immediately to "gin riots" that grew so violent that the authorities conceded that the law couldn't be enforced. It was repealed in 1742.

Ultimately, this huge loss of market made British brewers very unhappy and led directly to the Beerhouse Act of 1830. This act was a Parliamentary attempt to stem the tide of gin sales and also to protect the beer business. The act allowed people to sell beer without a specific license, thus lowering costs so that brewers could better compete with distillers.

Spreading the gin gospel

The invention of the continuous still in 1831 (see Chapter 2 for details) made it possible to produce large amounts of spirits for a growing market. As a result, the modern gin business started making products used for a number of medicinal purposes (Gin and Tonic to help beat malaria in Britain's tropical commonwealth countries) as well as for simple taste pleasure (the Martini, for example, among other mixed drinks).

Much like the end of Prohibition in the United States, the repeal of the Gin Act brought about changes in perception. The spirit was no longer associated with degradation and abusive behavior by the poor working class when it was being consumed as medicine and for pleasure all over the world.

The gin makers and retailers responded to these changes by transforming their often shabby taverns into more inviting cabarets that offered music and entertainment. These cabarets were nicknamed "Gin Palaces." One such edifice was described by Charles Dickens as "[T]he gay building with a fantastically ornamental parapet, the illuminated clock, the plast glass window surrounded by stucco rosettes, and its profusion of gas lights in the richly gilt burners, is perfectly dazzling when contrasted with the darkness and dirt [of the street] where we had just left." These places attracted an entirely new class of drinker and turned gin into a fully acceptable drink in all walks of society.

Alexander the Great (gin guy)

London gin distiller Alexander Gordon took a major step forward in 1763 when he decided to remove sugar from the mixture used to flavor the raw spirit. He then added flavorings such as orange rind and coriander to create an entirely unique and less potent form of jenevre. The result was an unsweet gin, which, in the same sense as Champagne, was called *dry*.

Gordon's innovation, formally labeled *London dry gin,* eventually found its way across the Atlantic to the United States, where it was welcomed with open cocktail glasses, sorry, open arms. The dry formulation is by far the most popular type of gin all over the world. The gin can still be called London dry gin even if it isn't made in London. And, yes, Gordon also named the gin after himself, and Gordon's Gin is still among the world's leading gin entries up to the present day.

Riding out the rougher years

In the United States, similarly extravagant evening dining and drinking places flourished — until 1919 when the 18th Amendment to the Constitution made the production and sale of alcohol beverages for anything other than medicinal or religious purposes illegal in America. Canada had announced Federal prohibition a few years earlier. That left alcohol beverage sales in the hands of illegal distillers, smugglers, and retailers.

Many Americans did their drinking in illicit establishments called gin mills or speakeasies where the price of entry was a password ("Joe sent me") whispered to the guy eyeballing prospective patrons through a spy-hole in the door.

Others relied on an inexpensive spirit, hand-crafted, so to speak, in North America. "Bathtub gin" isn't an idle phrase; it perfectly describes the potion whipped up in washing tubs and, yes, bathtubs all across North America. People poured plain alcohol, distilled water, and suitable botanicals — or "flavor bricks" (compressed flavoring agents designed to "make medicine more palatable") — into a container, stirred the pot, and poured out a clear liquid to use as a mixer in cocktail making, more often than not for Martinis.

The 21st Amendment to the Constitution (passed in 1933) made liquor legal, but between 1919 and 1933, gin and its various mixers drew a large audience of men and flappers. This generation had discovered the soothing effects of the Martini. Even then, it took a while for gin to recover from its nasty Prohibition reputation. But, recover it did. Soon the clear spirit became a symbol of wealth and sophistication and an icon of upper-class American living. This reputation was perpetuated in movies, such as *The Thin Man;* in popular fiction by writers F. Scott Fitzgerald and Ernest Hemingway; and even in gag lines, such as Robert Benchley's classic on entering a room after walking through a rainstorm: "I must slip out of these wet clothes and into a Dry Martini." (Check out the Martini recipe in Chapter 15.)

Making Modern Gin

London dry gin and its sweeter Dutch cousin jenevre are clear spirits distilled from grains and flavored with juniper berries plus a variety of botanicals (herbs, spices, and other plant products) from all over the world.

- ✔ **London dry gins** are distilled from a mixture of 75 percent corn and 25 percent barley and other grains.

- ✔ **Holland gins (jenevre)** are made from fermented malt (malt wine) redistilled with juniper berries; the jenevre gins are aged in oak barrels for three months, so they're sometimes classified as "Old Gin."

- ✔ **German gins (steinhäger),** by law, must be made with a triple-distilled, 45 percent alcohol by volume (ABV) spirit and must contain juniper berries.

Protecting the secret

Gin distillers may use as many as 15 different botanicals to produce the distinctive flavor of a specific gin. The exact recipe for any one gin is the major difference between that product and its competitors, so the formula is always a well-kept secret, passed down from one generation to another and generally shared with no more than five or six people in distillery management.

Although modern distillers may create new recipes for new gin products, many modern gins are still proudly made with recipes dating back at least 300 years.

In America, by law, no matter what other flavorings are in the mix, to call itself *gin,* a spirit must include juniper, and be bottled at 45 percent ABV. It doesn't have to be aged.

Creating the flavor

Regardless of the particular mix of botanicals they select, gin distillers use one of four methods to arrive at the flavor and aroma demanded by the original recipe.

The first three methods in the upcoming list are used for gins made on continuous column stills. Method #4 is used by makers of the original jenevre with some modification for what was, in the United States, called "Old Tom."

Stop! Are the words "continuous column still" new to your vocabulary? Then stick a pencil between this page and the next page, and turn back to Chapter 2, which explains distillation — and the difference in stills.

✔ **Method #1** is the simplest way to match the recipe's desired taste profile for *compounding* the gin. (Compounding, in this use, is distiller talk for putting the two elements together.) The distiller crushes the botanicals fine enough to release their aroma and flavor, and then tosses the crushed botanicals into a vat filled with the amount of neutral spirit recommended to create the brand's desired flavor/aroma profile. He allows the mixture to "marry" by letting it sit together for at least a week before removing it to go directly to the bottling line. This method has no need for added filtration or alcohol proof dilution.

✔ **Method #2** involves crushing the botanicals, putting them in a mesh bag, and immersing the bag in the alcohol. This immersion allows the botanicals to steep the alcohol as if it were a tea, transfusing flavors directly into the liquid. The gin is filtered and diluted before bottling.

✔ **Method #3** is used for more expensive brands. The distiller crushes the botanicals and adds them to the fermented grain mash before distillation. He then heats and stills the entire package — flavorings and all.

✔ **Method #4** was first used by original gin distillers. It's an expensive process used only by those making the very top-level gins. First, the neutral spirits are diluted with distilled water in a pot still that's fired up. As the liquid heats and the vapors rise, they pass through a special "Gin Head," invented in the late 1800s by distiller James Burrough (who gave the world Beefeater Gin). The vapors pass through a basketlike device filled with crushed botanicals, where the botanical flavors and aromas are collected, condensed, diluted with distilled water to 60 percent ABV, filtered, and then sent directly to the bottling line with no further processing or filtering needed.

Touring the World of Gin

Unlike spirits named for their countries or locale — think Scotch, Irish whiskey, and Bourbon from Bourbon County, Kentucky — gins are truly universal.

Gins from Britain are generally more potent than those from the United States, while gins from Holland and Germany are heavier-bodied and even slightly malty.

What they all have in common is quality and versatility. The following is an abbreviated tour of the world of gins.

British gins

The Brits didn't invent the cocktail, but they developed some of the most popular uses for gin. Likewise, they didn't make the very first gin, but they did refine the process so well that today they make most of the best and best-selling gins around the world.

London dry gin

The world's most popular gin type is rarely made in London (only one distiller remains in the city) and is dry only in the sense that it lacks sugar to make it sweet. London dry gins, produced on column stills, tend to be high in alcohol — 90 proof (45 percent ABV) — with a characteristic citrus flavor and aroma due to the widespread addition of dried lemon and/or orange peels to the botanical recipe.

Some fine examples of London dry gins are detailed in the following sections.

Bombay distilled London dry gin and Bombay Sapphire distilled London dry gin

Despite having Queen Victoria's picture and funky lettering, the label was designed to give Bombay a feeling of age and great respectability — necessary because it's a recent product that was created by an American in the 1960s. None of this should detract from the fact that Bombay is a very smooth gin that can only be described as *non-juniperish* — possibly because the botanical flavorings are steamed as they're redistilled with the grain neutral spirits.

To its credit, even though it isn't required to do so, Bombay has always listed its main ingredients on the label. But don't read the label until you taste the gin — that way, you get to test your palate as well as the spirit.

Bombay Sapphire, introduced in 1988 in its distinctive blue bottle, is a bit spicier than the original, but both Bombays have good body. (Not sure what body is? Bookmark this page and turn to Chapter 3 where I define tasting terms.) Bombay Sapphire is the best-selling premium gin globally.

Beefeater London distilled dry gin

Beefeater is, as of this writing, the only distiller left in London. Founded in 1820 on the banks of the Thames by James Burrough, the distillery has since moved to larger quarters in Kensington. It was one of the earliest British gins to be imported to the United States (starting in 1918).

In making Beefeater, the botanicals are diffused in the spirit for a full 24 hours before redistilling the gin. The result is a highly perfumed product with a touch of citrus and a desirably long finish.

Tourist note: Although the label was recently modernized, the picture of the actual Beefeater guardsman from the Tower of London is still prominent; in fact, Beefeater uses it in its ads as well. He's still carrying that monstrous long lance, too.

Tanqueray Special Dry English Gin and Tanqueray No. TEN

Both Tanqueray types are made in pot stills that exactly replicate the original Tanqueray gin still. The still, which has a unique shape, was developed in 1830 by Tanqueray when it first created the recipe. Botanicals are added to the spirit just before distillation, which means no steeping time; the result is a fresh but complex herbal flavor that has made Tanqueray a worldwide brand and the number-two leading imported gin in the United States.

The latest member of the Tanqueray family, Tanqueray No. TEN, has been breaking records for introductory sales. It's more expensive, presumably because its botanicals cost more, and the bottle is a modernized version of the original — but it's still green. By the way, the Tanqueray bottle is known in the trade as "the fire hydrant." On the other hand, the company says the original bottle is meant to be a replica of a cocktail shaker.

Old Tom gin

Old Tom Gin dates back to the 18th century. It's heavy-bodied, about 80 proof (40 percent ABV), and sweetened with simple syrup. It was introduced to the United States only in the early 1950s. It's said to have been the spirit used to make the very first Martini (see Chapter 15 for the recipe). Today, only a few British distillers produce Old Tom, and although they import it to the United States, it's not easy to find.

Some new arrivals

Quintessential Gin, just recently introduced, is already generally available throughout the U.S. It's creating a stir, possibly because among its botanicals are lotus and lavender, which give it a distinctive flavor and aroma.

Hendricks, introduced to the world in 2004, is a super-premium brand of gin made in Scotland. It includes cucumbers and rose leaves among its list of more than ten botanicals.

Whitely and Neill is made by the heirs to a centuries-old British distilling family. What makes their gin different is an unusual bottle and the addition of botanicals from Africa, including baobab tree fruit and cape gooseberries. This gin is 42 proof (21 percent ABV).

Plymouth gin

Unlike London dry gins, which don't have to be made in London, Plymouth gin *must* be made in Plymouth, a city in southwest England that was once Britain's leading seaport and the point of departure for the Puritans headed to the New World.

The gin, first distilled there in 1793, is a highly aromatic, slightly fruit-flavored, very dry, wheat-based spirit. It's made with water from Dartmouth's granite hills and the addition of seven botanicals. It's also 94 proof (47 percent ABV). A great favorite with Royal Navy seamen, Plymouth gin became the worldwide favorite for Gin and Tonics because its fruit flavors nicely balance the bitter taste of the quinine-flavored tonic water.

Today, Plymouth gin is still made at the original distillery from the original 18th-century recipe. It's the seventh most popular gin in the United States.

Hayman's 1820 gin liqueur

Here's something very different: a gin liqueur, made to appeal to consumers who enjoy highly flavored gin. Hayman's 1820 gin liqueur is the first of its kind. The 80 proof (40 percent ABV) sweetened grain gin is made in London by the family-owned Hayman Distillers, who also make the century-old British favorite Pimm's Cup Liqueur. The "1820" refers to the year in which the family introduced Beefeater. Some experts have compared its flavor with Old Tom.

A drink for a penny

In his 1755 autobiography, British sea captain Bradley Bradstreet tells of his invention to circumvent requirements that drinkers purchase only two gallons of gin at a time. (This requirement made gin so expensive that few working class people could afford it.) In order to keep his customers from drinking too much gin, the good captain figured out a way to offer them gin for one penny per ounce.

He drilled two holes in the wall of his pub, leading to the street outside. On the outside of his establishment (the Black Cat), he painted an illustration of a black cat. Over the topmost hole, he painted an illustration of the cat putting a tube in a hole between its paws that led to the tavern inside. The customer would speak through the top hole and then insert his one, two, or three pennies. The bartender inside would pour the proper amount of gin into the customers' container and place it in front of the bottom hole.

Then, Captain Bradstreet tells of how he shopped for the best distiller in London. He bought gin from that distiller, and when the gin was in place, Bradstreet says, "I got a person to inform the mob that gin would be served by the cat at my window next day, provided they put money in his mouth, from whence there was a hole that conveyed it to me. At last I heard the chink of money and a comfortable voice say, 'Puss, give me two pennyworth of gin.'" At that moment, the Captain knew he had a success.

In fact, he reported that he made "upwards of two and twenty pounds" in one month. He didn't know it, but in addition to naming the gin "Old Tom" after his cat, he also invented the world's first beverage vending machine.

American gins

The United States, the world's largest gin market, prefers dry gins, most of it in cocktails. All American-made gins are London dry style and all, including Gilbey's and Gordon's (which are made in the U.S. under license from the British owners), are lower in alcohol than British-made London dry gins. As a result, American London drys are sometimes called "soft gins."

Some good examples of American-produced gins are included in the next section. All are the 80 proof (40 percent ABV) unless otherwise noted.

Barton gin

This traditional made-in-the-U.S.A. brand is a "value" spirit of good quality. This good mixer is primarily available in the Midwest where people whose parents — grandparents? great-grandparents? — have known the Barton name since it appeared right after the Repeal of Prohibition.

Burnett's London dry

It may be hard to believe, but this gin in a square green bottle is made in Kentucky by Heaven Hill, one of the world's leading Bourbon distillers. The Americans make it using the same English recipe developed by Sir Robert Burnett in 1769. It's distilled by a system of vacuums that evaporate the alcohol at a lower temperature. The full-bodied gin has a fairly long finish with an overlay of anise. This flavor makes it perfect for drinking with a lemon twist or tonic water.

If the term "finish" is new to you, bookmark this page and flip to Chapter 3. Then come right back for more on American gins.

Gilbey's London dry

Gilbey's (a well-known British brand) is made for the American market in the U.S. under license to Beam Global Wine & Spirits. Its outstanding characteristic is balanced flavor in a medium body with a mineral finish.

Gordon's London dry

Gordon's, like Gilbey's, is a British brand also made in the U.S. by Beam for the American market. The gin, produced from a recipe dating back to the 17th century, has more of an "imported" style. Translation: It has a well-balanced flavor but is somewhat harsher than most domestic brands. As a result, Gordon's is often found in the "well" (where you find the perfectly acceptable brands bartenders use to make a drink when the customer doesn't specify a brand).

Seagram's distilled dry gin

Seagram's is the leading American-made gin, slightly more expensive than other domestic gins but considered a great value for the price by its fans. The slightly golden color that differentiates Seagram's from other gins is the result of about three months of aging in oak casks. This aging is said to make the gin "softer," but it also reduces some of the juniper tang.

Holland gins

The original gin (jenevre) is still made primarily in Holland and Belgium. It's made mostly in pot stills from malted grains — barley, rye, or corn in equal proportions — at a lower proof than English and American gins. Holland gins are usually fuller bodied than other types. "Oude" (old) jenevres are aged for at least a year in oak barrels; "jong" (young) jenevres aren't aged.

Zuidam Dry Gin and Damrak Genever Gin, two higher-priced gins from Holland, made their first appearance in the U.S. in 2004. Zuidam is more aromatic and herbal, made with nine botanicals. Damrak, made in the traditional Dutch style, is slightly sweeter with a malt (grain-like) undertone.

Gins from other countries

A handful of other countries are in the gin business. The following sections outline those countries.

French gins

Citadelle is a super-premium gin that's making quite a stir among gin aficionados all over Europe and now in the U.S. Aside from a very handsome package, its main claim to fame is that it's a wheat-based spirit.

Another new French entry is the sibling of the hugely successful Grey Goose Vodka, called (what else?) Blue Goose. Naturally, it comes in a blue bottle.

A Dutch treat trick

Jenevre is a really "full" (viscous) liquid. Pour it slowly into a glass and it will rise over the top without spilling. Having astonished watchers, true Holland gin fans bet on their ability to do it, and then pick up the glass and drink it without breaking the protective "bubble" or spilling a drop of the precious liquid.

Warning: As it says on those car commercials where professional drivers zip their autos up and down walls without turning a hair, do not try this one at home.

Unless you're really, really practiced. And have a napkin handy.

German gins (steinhäger)

German gin is a jenevre-style spirit, lighter in body and more delicate in flavor than Holland and London dry gins. The best-known (and oldest) brand is Schlichte Steinhager Dry Gin — 80 proof (40 percent ABV) — a grain-based, slightly sweet gin with no flavoring other than juniper berries. Unfortunately, Schilchte — which is bottled in a brown clay crock — is rarely available in the U.S. On the other hand, Doornkaat, often called "schnapps" in Germany, is available on the Internet. A reasonably priced way to impress visitors from Germany.

Spanish gins

Spanish gin is dry and has a style similar to London dry. The best-selling gin in Spain, Larios Dry Gin, is also the best selling gin in Continental Europe. In Spain, it's consumed mostly with cola.

Sloe gin is no gin

Somewhere back in a time when gin was young, an unknown distiller ran out of juniper, couldn't find it in the first place, or determined it too expensive. So he decided instead to use sloe berries, the fruit of blackthorne shrubs, which were commonly used as hedges in parts of England. He took the berries, cured them, and infused them in his gin — virtually cost free. The distillate was between 15 and 39 percent alcohol by volume, so he felt justified in calling it sloe gin. That was a mistake.

To start with, sloes aren't berries at all; they're related to plums. They lack that *je ne sais quoi* taste of juniper, and, when crushed, their juice is red. It probably wasn't very long before his customers started to complain that his gin just didn't taste very ginny anymore and asked, "Whoever heard of a red gin anyway?"

Trying to make a purse out of a plum's ear, he added some cherry juice as flavoring and also to give the drink more color. That worked for a while, but soon the British government stepped in. They pronounced that henceforth all gin would be made with juniper berries — the real ones.

That should have been the end of that, but in the time between introducing it and being told to stop, the unknown distiller had built a following for sloe gin. So, he was permitted to call it just that.

It entered the lexicon — and bartender mixing guides — and can still be found in some establishments where it's a liqueur used primarily as a flavoring for mixed drinks that may or may not be made with gin.

So, go slow when you ask for sloe gin — you might get it.

Speak Spanish? Read more about Larios and the distinguished family that made it famous at `larios.com`. Finding the gin itself is more difficult. Although Larios is sold in 40 countries around the world, and imported to the U.S. by Pernod Ricard, it isn't widely available on this side of the Atlantic.

Tasting the World's Gin

Tables 9-1, 9-2, and 9-3 list popular gin brands by price categories.

If you're a traveler, take a look at prices in the international airport duty-free shops. They often have some startling bargains. Just be sure to check customs regulations to see how many bottles an individual can bring into the arrival destination.

Table 9-1	Value Gin Brands ($9–$15)	
Brand	**Country**	**Alcohol Content**
Barton London Extra Dry	United States	80 proof/40% ABV
Taaka Dry	United States	80 proof/40% ABV
Booth's London Dry	England	90 proof/45% ABV
Glenmore London Dry	United States	Varies
McCormick Dry	United States	80 proof/40% ABV
Fleischmann Extra Dry	United States	80 proof/40% ABV
Gordon's London Dry	United States	80 proof/40% ABV
Seagram's Extra Dry (Aged)	United States	80 proof/40% ABV
Burnett's London Dry	United States	80 proof/40% ABV

Table 9-2	Premium Gin Brands ($20–$30)	
Brand	**Country**	**Alcohol Content**
Broker's London Dry	England	94 proof/47% ABV
Boodles London Dry	England	90.4 proof/45% ABV
Beefeater	England	94 proof/47% ABV
Bombay Dry	England	80 proof/40% ABV

Table 9-2 *(continued)*

Brand	Country	Alcohol Content
Tanqueray London Dry	England	94.6 proof/47.3% ABV
Beefeater Wet	England	70 proof/35% ABV
Bombay Sapphire	England	94 proof/47% ABV
Hendrick's	Scotland	88 proof/44% ABV
Damrak	Holland	83.6 proof/11.8% ABV

Table 9-3   Super-Premium Gin Brands (More than $30)

Brand	Country	Alcohol Content
Bafferts	England	80 proof/40% ABV
Blue Goose	France	80 proof/40% ABV
Quintessential	England	90 proof/45% ABV
Tanqueray No. TEN	England	94.6 proof/47.3% ABV
Whitley Neill	England	42 proof/21% ABV
Van Gogh	Holland	94 proof/47% ABV
Zuidam	Holland	Genievre: 80 proof/40% ABV London Dry: 89 proof/44.5% ABV
Magellan	France	80 proof/40% ABV
Old Raj	England	110 proof/55% ABV

What to look for when tasting gin

When you're ready to taste gin, pour about an ounce of it into your tasting glass. Then look at the gin. With rare exceptions, the liquid should be crystal clear. (Those exceptions include Seagram's, which is slightly golden because it's slightly aged, and any gin with an added botanical that may affect the clarity.) The body, or viscosity, is fairly uniform. An exception is the heavily viscous Holland jenevre. Other than that, as the man says, when you've seen one, you've pretty much seen 'em all.

What to sniff and sip

The pleasure of gin is, in no small measure, derived from its intriguing aroma. Juniper is the primary botanical in gin, so when you're sampling gins, juniper should be the first thing you smell. And, of course, the first thing you taste.

Which brings up an interesting question: How many people know exactly what juniper smells like or tastes like? Not many. So the first step in tasting gin may be to put down this book; go down to the supermarket or health food store; pick up a packet, jar, or whatever of juniper; bring it home; and smell and taste it. It can always be brewed as a tea. Who knew?

But juniper's just the tip of the flavor and aroma iceberg. Table 9-4 lists some of the important flavoring agents used in making gin. In addition, some distillers may include *aloe, fennel, hyssop, oregano, rosemary, star anise, turmeric,* and any one of more than a thousand different botanicals. Exactly which botanicals go into which gin and in exactly what proportions is a secret.

Most, but not all, of the ingredients listed in Table 9-4 are familiar. You probably know what orange peels smell and taste like. If you see something on this list that you haven't experienced, taste or smell it before you start.

Table 9-4	Flavoring Agents Found in Gins
Botanical	**Description**
Juniper (*Juniperus communis*)	These are the berries of an evergreen shrub. They're the primary flavoring agent in gin and, by law, must be included in any product labeled "gin." Also used to flavor pork, sauerkraut, and root beer, and as a marinade. Medical effect: A mild diuretic. The oil of the juniper may relieve some types of gastric upset stomach.
Angelica root (*Angelica archangelica*)	This is the root of a plant belonging to the carrot family. It's also known as archangel, European angelica, or dong quai. Its licorice flavored seeds and stalks are also used in cordials. Stems may be candied and used as garnish. Native to North America.

Table 9-4 *(continued)*

Botanical	Description
Anise (*Pimpinella anisum*)	This annual plant is a member of the carrot family. The seeds have a slight licorice flavor and aroma; used to flavor anisette and ouzo as well as gin. Native to India, the Middle East, and Southern Europe; cultivated in the United States. Medical effects: Used to flavor cough syrups and dentifrices; may relive some gastric upset and respiratory congestion.
Cardamom (*Elettaria cardamom*)	Whole and powdered seeds and seed pods. Cardamom has a flavor ranging from mild to intense, and it's used in curries.
Cinnamon (*Cinnamomum verum*)	These are the powdered or rolled sticks of the dried inner bark of a tropical evergreen tree. It's called "true cinnamon" to distinguish it from cassia, a similar spice with which true cinnamon may be blended. Native to Sri Lanka, Sumatra, and Borneo.
Coriander (*Coriandrum sativum*)	The leaves (cilantro) and seeds (coriander) of this plant are both used to flavor gin, as well as sausages and chewing gum. Native to Morocco, Rumania, and the Czech Republic. Medical effects: Oil is a possible allergic sensitizer (a substance that increases sensitivity to other substances).
Orange peel (*Citrus sinensis*)	This is the grated fresh rind of the sweet orange, also known as orange zest. Native to China and Northern India. Cultivated in the United States, West Indies, and Israel.

Natural or artificial?

Artificially flavored gins, such as the newer fruit flavored versions, were designed to keep up with vodka in the mixed drink derby. Tasting them can be, well, tasty, but what you're really tasting isn't gin. It's the essential oils or essences of the featured flavor, such as strawberry. Nothing wrong with that, of course. In fact, flavored gins can be a real timesaver at a party. However, when it comes to true tasting, stick to the main event. The gin, the whole gin, and nothing but the gin. Cheers!

Serving Gin

Obviously, to get the true flavor of a gin, you must taste it *neat* —
that is, unadorned. But gin is so rarely served straight that it may
make more sense to serve it in a cocktail.

Right. And wrong.

In fact, some gins are tasty on their own. Others work better as
mixers. As a general, but definitely not a definitive guide, Table 9-5
suggests which gin to serve which way. If you decide to go with
cocktails, check out *Bartending For Dummies,* 3rd Edition, by Ray
Foley (Wiley).

Table 9-5	How to Serve Your Gin
Gin Type	*Serving Tip*
American London Dry	Serve it in cocktails. What cocktails? Martinis.
German	Serve it chilled and straight.
Holland	Serve it chilled and neat with a Dutch favorite fast food snack — green herring.
English London Dry	Serve it with tonic water, as in a Gin and Tonic, or with Italian Vermouth, as in a Gin and It, which could be considered an English Martini.
Old Tom	Serve it neat, as a rarity, just to experience the flavor of gins past.
Plymouth	Serve it chilled, in fruit flavored cocktails.
Spanish	Serve it in cocktails with cola.

A Martini made with vodka rather than gin is correctly a
"Vodkatini." (See Chapter 10 for the scoop on vodka.)

However you serve it, "To your health!"

Chapter 10

Vodka: Toasting the Russians

In This Chapter

▶ Identifying vodka's origins

▶ Describing vodka's unique characteristics

▶ Considering vodka's flavors

▶ Comparing vodka with its siblings from different countries

*T*his chapter describes the super-fast rise of vodka and its European cousins (including Scandinavia's aquavit) from their humble origins as the oldest European distilled spirit to blockbuster status as the (current) most popular spirit in the world.

And, of course, I explain how to enjoy the drink. In moderation.

What Is Vodka, Anyway?

Early on in vodka's history (as with all spirits), no local government or global administration set standards defining alcohol beverages. You call it *vodka,* I call it *wodka* — who's to say who's right?

Today, however, every country that produces a vodka agrees: Vodka is diluted ethyl alcohol, the clear liquid produced when any plant food (grains, fruits, potatoes) is distilled. And of course, ethyl alcohol is the only alcohol used in alcohol beverages.

Do you need a refresher or a first run-through the distillation process? Stick a pencil in this page, turn to Chapter 2, and then come back when you're done reading about the process in detail.

In Continental Europe, distillers and their governments are happy with the definition of vodka. But in Eastern Europe, not so much. Over there, the folks want to define vodka as a spirit distilled only from grains or potatoes — not sugar cane, grapes, or other non-traditional agricultural products.

Sooner or later, they'll all agree. Meanwhile, you can consider a brief history of the clear spirit.

The Birth of a "Breathless" Spirit

Who gets credit for vodka? Was it the Russians who first drank the "breathless" spirit? Or did the "dear little water" first speak Polish? Don't forget the Scandinavians, specifically the Danes, and yes, the Germans.

Each claims to have been first out of the gate with vodka, and lest you think this is a passing quarrel, you should know that the argument has been raging since the 15th century.

Actually, no one knows for sure where vodka first saw the light of day, but everyone knows the story of its name.

The name *vodka* comes from the Russian phrase *zhizennia voda,* most commonly translated as "water of life," or (in the shortened form) *voda,* meaning "dear little water." Either way, the Slavs clearly recognized that they had something special with vodka (*wodka* to the Poles). But they're not absolutely certain about when it was first produced.

Local histories suggest the first vodka was consumed during the 12th century or maybe the 14th century or — an outside guess — the 16th century. One reason why nobody can pin down the date is that nobody is actually sure what the original vodka was.

The monks move north

As you can read in Chapter 1, the original Johnny Appleseeds of the spirits crowd came from the monasteries of Spain and Portugal. There, Moorish alchemists — having failed to convert base metals, such as lead, into gold — invented distilling, thus settling for converting grains, fruits, herbs, and seeds into medicinal (and highly potable) alcohol beverages.

The monks called their clear spirit *aqua vitae,* water of life. The Scandinavians translated that to *akavit.* The Western Europeans called it *eau de vie.* And the Eastern Europeans translated it as *vodka* (or, in Poland, *wodka*). Whatever you call it, historians suggest that an Ecumenical Council in Rome in 1430 decided that using alcohol (rather than the often rancid local waters) to make medicines palatable was a really good idea.

The Russians stake a claim

The Russians say vodka was first distilled at an abbey and/or fort named Viatka in the 12th century. Unfortunately, many documents dealing with the initial distillation of vodka were destroyed when the Russian Orthodox Church labeled it a "tool of Satan" and destroyed all documents detailing how to make the demon spirit.

That was the first time — but certainly not the last — that vodka became part of a serious political debate. Peter the Great (1672–1725) saw how popular vodka had become, so sometime in the 1700s, he decided to give all rights for making, selling, and keeping the profits for that work to the royal family. That took it all away from the traditional owners, the Russian Orthodox Church.

Naturally, now that Satan was now out of the picture, the Church administration objected and asked Peter to return some control over the distillation and distribution of this marvelous medicine. Peter had seen the possibility of getting great revenues from controlling the manufacture and sale of vodka, so he turned down their requests. The control rested with the czars until the state took over after the 1917 revolution.

In 1936, while distillation remained a state-controlled product, the ban against higher proof beverages meant the return of legal vodka. After the overthrow of Communism, the state maintains an interest in some of the distilleries. Almost all are located in Moscow, but most of them are privately owned either by Russian national companies or by French- and English-based global companies such as Pernod Ricard and Diageo.

Huzzah for Ivan IV, the not-so-terrible czar

The next time you sit at a table in a swank restaurant, sipping Cosmopolitan, lift your glass to the man who came up with the idea of having a social drink with friends in a friendly place away from home: Ivan the Terrible (1530–1584), the first czar of the Rus, which was made up of all the Russian tribes.

Nasty though Ivan may have been, he knew how to keep the *oprichniny,* his palace guards and secret police, happy.

Ivan IV's predecessor, Ivan III, didn't appreciate the fact that alcohol consumption among the peasants was interfering with their work, which was to keep the economy moving and his coffers full. So he banned all drinking except during religious holidays.

Ivan IV, who didn't care much about the peasants but had a better grasp of labor relations at home, rewarded his guards with a drink when they were stressed — possibly from knocking those pesky peasants about — and even established a place for them to go on Christmas and Easter to drink all they wanted.

The places, called *kabaks* (translation: taverns) sold nothing but vodka. Not surprisingly, soon there were kabaks everywhere throughout the land. The guards were happy, the people were happy, the distillers and tavern owners were happy. And best of all, Ivan was happy because the taverns soon became a steady source of income as well as a place to socialize and relieve the tensions of living in difficult surroundings.

Regulations, regulations, and more

If Ivan codified public drinking, Peter the Great (all 6 foot 8 inches of him — constituting probably one of the world's champion drinkers) was the one who established a system of licensing production and sales of spirits. He established this system near the start of his reign, which lasted from 1682–1725.

Peter's grand idea was to permit spirits to be produced by state-owned distilleries for the benefit of the general populace (and Peter) and by individual land owners for their personal use.

That system held until 1765. Catherine the Great, whose appetite was for things of the flesh rather than the vodka bottle, made distilling vodka illegal for anyone other than members of the aristocracy.

That situation continued for a while, but was eventually relaxed. By the early 19th century, regulations had been put into place, setting the standards for making vodka. Now the illegality was making a spirit in a manner that wasn't established by the state and calling it *vodka*.

Vodka Takes a Long Voyage

In the United States, until just after World War II, vodka was rarely served outside of neighborhoods with a large Russo/Polish population.

But the War had taken millions of young Americans overseas, introducing them to new foods and drinks. Now, with the growth of commercial air travel, ordinary folks could hop a plane to Europe, visit the Old Country, and taste new pleasures, including vodka.

Aquavit: The Scandinavian alternative

Aquavit (or *akavit* or *akevit,* depending on where in Scandinavia you're drinking it) is a clear spirit like vodka, but its character is different.

The Swedes, who were the first to produce the new spirit, didn't like a flavorless drink, so they tossed in some herbs and spices. The most popular turned out to be caraway — yes, the same ingredient you find in rye bread.

And while other Europeans were distilling their clear spirits from grapes, the Swedes — who lived too far north to grow the fruit — learned to make theirs from hardier and less expensive grains.

That was sometimes problematic. From time to time, Scandinavian winters were so cold that even the grain crops failed, and production of aquavit was banned. Luckily, in 1763, after the potato had been introduced to Europe from the New World, a smart Norwegian distiller promoted potatoes as a substitute for grains in making the spirit.

Perfection! The potato thrived in the northern climate. It was less expensive than grain to grow and distill. So, since then, all aquavit has been made from a potato base. Flavored with caraway, of course.

And then somebody mentioned the name *Smirnoff.*

"Why would people pay money for this stuff?"

Historians of distilled spirits are a tad wobbly on the exact date, but one fine day sometime in the 1860s, a Russian distiller named Piotr Smirnov set out to create the world's finest vodka. His secret? He was the first person in the whole wide world to filter his vodka through charcoal, thus producing a spirit so well regarded that the Smirnov distillery was soon named the official purveyor to the Russian court.

Fast forward to 1917. Revolution. Confiscation. Vladmir Smirnov (grandson of Piotr) was imprisoned and sentenced to death. But Our Hero, ever resourceful, escaped to Constantinople, moved to Poland, changed his name to Smirnoff, and — with success at hand — opened a second distillery in Paris.

Then came The Great Depression. Facing economic disaster, Smirnoff sold his company to Rudolph Kunett, another Russian émigré. Kunett, even more resourceful than the Smirnovs, saw an untapped market in the United States. So, posthaste, he moved across the ocean to begin the search for an American distiller to make and distribute his vodka.

Kunett's first call was to Samuel Bronfman, founder and head of Seagram's Ltd., then the world's best-selling distiller. But "Mr. Sam," as he was known to friend and foe alike, had a quick answer: "Why should anyone pay good money for this liquor with no color, aroma, and taste?"

Bronfman suggested that Kunet go up the East Coast to Connecticut and call on Heublein, Inc., a major importer of foods and beverages. Heublein executive John Martin made a recommendation to the company: buy the Smirnoff vodka recipe, trademarks, and rights to sell everywhere in the world.

And thus was history made, one fortune won, and another lost.

With a kick like a Moscow mule

World War II halted most production of alcohol for beverage use, but John Martin over at Heublein insisted that this Russian spirit could find a place on America's store shelves and back bars.

In due course, Martin visited his friend Jack Morgan, owner of Los Angeles' Cock 'n' Bull restaurant. In the course of a lunch, Martin said that he didn't know what to do with this new vodka. Morgan said that he understood because his restaurant was overflowing with a surplus of ginger beer.

Just as in a cartoon, a light bulb lit up over their heads: They decided to make a mixed drink from the two beverages, adding a dash of lime for an extra touch of tartness.

The pair invited Heublein's Los Angeles distributor to suggest a name and serving style. At the time, the famous Young's Market in Los Angeles had a surplus of copper mugs. Vernon Young's suggestion was to create a drink to be served in the copper mugs that could then be presented as souvenirs. So the mugs were engraved with an illustration of a kicking mule and the drink name: the Moscow Mule. The gifts were a big hit with Hollywood celebrities who visited the Cock 'n' Bull often and allowed the eatery to inscribe their names on mugs and hang the endorsed mugs on a wall.

Once again, it was light bulb time. The success of the Moscow Mule encouraged Heublein to promote its vodka and Smirnoff. Heublein hired an advertising agency that came up with a simple explanation of why Smirnoff should be on every drinking person's menu (especially drinking persons expected to return to the office after lunch): "It leaves you breathless."

Spasibo, Piotr.

Yesterday, the Cold War; today, the world

Every so often, while East and West were staring at each other over the walls of the Cold War, Stolichnaya — the first Russian vodka to be imported to Western Europe and the United States — became the object of noisy, messy boycotts.

But it's an ill wind that blows nobody any good, and newspaper and television pictures of bartenders pouring Stoli down a sewer opened the U.S. markets to vodkas from other countries, especially those in Western Europe.

First the Swedes arrived with Absolut. Then the Finns delivered Finlandia. And after that? A flood of vodka filled the nation's drinking glasses. Here's some evidence:

- ✔ In 1935, when the first *Old Mr. Boston,* a classic drink recipe book, was published, it contained not a single recipe made with vodka. When the "Platinum Edition" came out in 2006, there were 123.

- ✔ In 2005, 25 percent of all spirits sold in the United States were vodka; more than 2.5 million cases of ultra-premium vodkas were sold that year.

- ✔ In January 2007, New York state retail stores and bars had a choice among 132 imported vodkas (from countries as far apart as Iceland and Lithuania), and 163 domestic brands to offer for sale.

And, boy, did those brands bring in the big bucks. In 2004, Bacardi paid an enormous sum estimated to be around $2 billion to buy Grey Goose, made in France, then the world's best-selling vodka. Just a single brand, not the entire company behind it.

Today, the world is awash in vodka. *Spasibo,* once again, Piotr.

The Japanese "vodka"

Shochu is a Japanese clear spirit distilled from a number of plant products, including sweet potatoes (*imo-jochu*), rice, buckwheat (*soba*), barley, and other similar so-called "small grains" such as oats, and even brown sugar and chestnuts.

Each plant food lends a specific flavor to the finished product, so shochu from one area doesn't taste entirely like that of another. The flavor depends on the climate and type of agricultural product used.

The Japanese use two methods of distillation for this spirit. The oldest, in use since the 14th century, most likely came to Japan from China. In this process, the mash is distilled only one time and uses only one ingredient. This is called *Otsu-rui* or *Honkaku* — "the real thing."

The second type of distillation, legal only since 1949, is called *Kou-rui*. This process requires multiple distillations of several ingredients, including the choice of different types of sugars used to speed fermentation.

Shochu is also made in Korea (*Soju*), Okinawa (*Awamori*), and Southeast Asia. Interestingly, despite the global popularity of vodka as vodka, more shochu than vodka is sold throughout Asia, which earns it the title "world's best-selling spirit."

Distilling Vodka

Here's today's standard global definition of vodka: A neutral spirit distilled from any material at or above 190 proof (95 percent alcohol by volume, or ABV), if bottled at no less than 80 proof (40 percent ABV). Filtered after distillation with charcoal or other material so as to be without distinctive character, aroma, taste, or color.

The distinctive characteristic of vodka is that it not have any distinctive character. Go figure.

The basic steps for producing distilled spirits are spelled out in detail in Chapter 2. What you read here is how to make vodka — and how to make one vodka different from another while still adhering to the definition of a product "without distinctive character, aroma, taste, or color."

The drawback of that tasteless, aromaless, and colorless attribute is the importance of brand differentiation. Making a new vodka brand different from the thousands of other flavorless, aromaless, and colorless vodkas available from all over the world brings with it a new set of challenges for the vodka distiller.

This challenge also flings wide the doors to a sacred temple. Gaining entrepreneurial admittance to that temple is supposedly reserved for those with the huge amounts of investment money that are necessary for equipment. That challenge has brought about new and often better variations of an old theme without sacrificing the traditions of the old.

First comes the mash

The almost indiscernible differences between vodkas become more obvious as you taste and evaluate them more carefully. Those differences begin with the choice of a recipe for the mash to be fermented.

Despite popular belief, not all vodkas are made from potatoes. Even the ones that are made from that tuber may vary the type of potatoes used. The flavor and texture of an Idaho-grown baking potato is vastly different from a Southern France-grown russet, just as organically grown grain is different from ordinary grain.

Grains are used more than any other material in vodka distillation, and this is where differentiation is first revealed. Distillers of vodka use grains of all kind, primarily corn, wheat, and rye. They also use touches of "small grains" — such as barley, oats, and rice — along with other agricultural products, such as sweet potatoes, white potatoes, sugar cane, molasses, and even fruits.

Next comes fermentation

Ingredients for vodka, just as those for any other spirit, must be heated with water to speed up the fermentation to come. For that purpose, distillers need either or both cultures and "wild" yeasts. To speed the process even further and add another element of flavor to the mash, distillers can use brick-shaped bars of white or brown sugar or a combination of both.

Don't forget the water

Although going far away to find pure water to use in fermentation isn't necessary, some distillers have done just that to give their particular vodka greater differentiation from others.

One brags that icebergs are towed to his distillery and melted there for water that has been untouched for centuries. Another uses melted water from a 12,000-year-old glacier. The ultimate is

Icelandic vodka distilled in Scotland, and then shipped over water to Iceland where glacial water is added to the clear vodka spirit in order to lower the alcohol level before bottling.

Into the still

Vodka is usually made on column (continuous) stills. But the more premium-priced the brand is, the more likely it is to have at least one pot still involved, if for no other reason than for the sake of tradition.

No matter which method is used, in order to remove all the *congeners* (flavoring agents), the fermented mash must be heated. The heat boils the liquid out of the mash and then turns the vapors back into liquid.

In most cases, three distillations will do the desired work. Some producers may make a "cleaner" product by using as many as six distillations. But because no spirit is ever 100 percent free of flavor (maybe 99 percent can be achieved), the number of distillations is a choice that depends on which congeners the distiller wants to leave in, and how often the alcohol must be distilled to remove all the others.

Although it isn't necessary, it sounds sexy to tell consumers that this vodka has been distilled six times (unlike most of the competition). Or that it uses the purest water in the world to make certain it has no unwanted flavors. Alternatively, you may hear that the additive used, such as glycerin or sweeteners, gives it enough taste to make your cocktails brighter, newer, and more colorful (or tasteful).

And then into the bottle

Another way to create differentiation among vodkas is in packaging. When Absolut was first introduced, competitors derisively called it the "medicine bottle." When it became the leading imported vodka, they all rushed around finding designers to create new bottles (even architect Frank Gehry designed the latest bottle for Wyborowa).

In 1992, Maurice Kanber, who had no experience in distilling but had written a book titled *Secrets From an Inventors Notebook,* said that he wanted to create a domestic U.S.-made vodka. And so he did. He called attention to it by distilling it four times and filtering it three times. Then he put it into a cobalt blue bottle. Skyy Vodka got noticed, took off immediately, and is still going.

How do consumers choose a vodka?

The goal of distilling vodka, as I say throughout this chapter, is to make it as flavorless as possible. With every brand trying to achieve this same goal, you have to wonder how consumers latch onto one particular brand or another. What is the perceived value of one vodka over another? The answer is clearly that value is in the eye of every single beholder. Vodka enthusiasts seem to enjoy being experimental. The distillers understand this enjoyment and are always trying to come up with new and exciting vodkas to try, which contributes to the "Flavor Revolution" (discussed in an upcoming section) that began in the U.S. and is now global.

Add to this mix packaging, advertising, and promotion. Because premium and ultra-premium vodkas are highly profitable, a lot of money is available for all those externals. Believe it or not, developing all those beautiful bottles and the extra packaging to protect them costs into the thousands of dollars. (Frank Gehry's great talent doesn't come cheap.) Then the bottles have to be put on display in the most magnificent way so that potential buyers can look on them with great favor. Marketing folks call this *perceived value,* the extra value consumers get from the satisfaction of having a beautiful or unusual bottle to call attention to their taste in the products they own.

The Second Vodka Revolution: The Flavor Factor

As early as the 15th century, the vodka-drinking population of Northern Europe recognized the need for some flavor in their drinks — if for no other reason than to be able to tell a wodka from an akavit. Therefore, they were the first to add flavor at the distillery.

To their clear, tasteless Zubrowka, the Poles added eight blades of "Bison grass," so named because the wild Bison of the time once grazed on it in open fields. Russian distillers regularly added sweet syrup to vodka for women to drink because, so the story goes, women didn't like their spirits unless they were sweet.

Fast forward to the 20th century when food technologists found ways to make artificial flavors that sometimes tasted even better than natural flavors. Borrowing the 400-year-old system of flavoring their beloved vodka to hide some of the inconsistencies of taste, they added lemon flavoring to Stolichnaya Límon. From then on, it was off to the races as far as the Western world was concerned.

Not only did distillers use some of the traditional Russian flavorings, but they also added many new ones. Traditional examples include *Pertsovka,* black pepper and chili flavor; *Limonaya,* lemon with some sugar added; and *Kubanskaya,* dried lemon and orange peels. The new flavors also include all kinds of berries and mixes of berry flavors, citrus fruits, spices, and even chocolate. All thanks to the wonders of science or nature. Whenever and however flavored, the bottle label must say so and tell you how they were captured for use in the spirit.

Seeing the success of flavored vodkas, now a major element in that spirit's highly successful growth, distillers of other spirits began to brighten up their traditional unflavored products with flavors. Thus, you can find Bacardi Límon, which began a revolution in rum, a spirit type that would appear not to need additional flavoring. In addition, distillers added berry flavorings to Alizè Cognac, where tradition said that the brandy alone — not berries — was the taste that people liked.

Although the purists may blanch at seeing something as bizarre as a green appletini made with vodka, the younger generation loves it — the more highly flavored, the better. And, as the revolution that began in the U.S. caught fire, the rest of the world followed, adding not only flavor, but also aroma (it doesn't leave you breathless anymore) and color (a white melon vodka would look odd to anyone, young or old). The revolutionaries won in a walk.

Do-it-yourself flavored vodka

In the 1960s, Finlandia came up with an idea to help bolster its slipping sales: Give bartenders a way to create flavored vodka right there on their bar. The Finlandians provided an appropriately labeled five-gallon jug with a spigot and instructions on how to create flavored vodkas.

It was a moderate success and once again brought Finlandia to the attention of those bored with Absolut, which came out with its own flavored versions shortly afterward.

Today, some people want to create their own flavored vodka to make certain that the flavors are real and come from organically grown sources and also to control the amount of flavoring their vodka drinks have. Here's a safe and sane way to do it yourself. First check with local regulations on how much you can make without paying taxes.

STRAWBERRY VODKA INFUSION

Purchase two one-liter glass Mason jars with airtight covers. It helps if one has a spigot. Then follow these steps:

1. Get a 750 ml bottle of your favorite unflavored vodka and four pints of fresh strawberries. Best types: California and Alpine.

(continued)

(continued)

2. Wash everything you're using — from the berries to the Mason jar — so that it's all clean and free of any disinfectant.

3. Remove the green leafy hull and cut the berries in half using a sharp paring knife.

4. Add the berries and the vodka to one of the glass jars and allow them to infuse for a few days in a cool, dark place.

5. To get the most out of the strawberries, line a strainer with layers of cheesecloth and decant the initial mixture from one Mason jar into the second. Use a plastic spoon to press every bit of juice from the berries through the cheesecloth into the second jar. Make sure you add the entire mixture from the first bottle.

6. Let the mixture rest in its new home for a few hours. Sample it. If needed, sweeten with simple syrup — 1 cup of refined sugar plus ½ cup of water; boil them together until syrupy. Add to the jar when finished.

For information about the stuff you need to infuse vodka at home plus recipes, materials, and how-to information, click on www.infused-vodka.com.

Tasting Vodkas

Chapter 3 provides basic information on how to set up a spirits tasting. This section applies the rules to vodka.

Creating the tasting sheet

First, make a tasting sheet on which to note your personal evaluation of every vodka you sample. Table 10-1 gives you a sample tasting sheet that you can copy or adapt to your preferences.

Table 10-1	Vodka Tasting Sheet	
Vodka	**Special Characteristics**	**Aroma/Flavor**
#1		
#2		
#3		
#4		
#5		

Aquavits: A simple choice

There are dozens of vodkas but very few aquavits, which makes choosing the ones to sample as easy as, well, one, two, three. The leading brands available practically everywhere are the Danes' Aalborg Akavit, the Swedes' obvious Absolut and O.P. Anderson, the Norwegians' Linie, and the Finns Finlandia. If only all life's choices were that simple.

Classifying vodkas

One practical way to simplify the long, long, *really long* list of vodkas available is to group them into easy-to-handle categories. For example, as an adventurous and discriminating drinker, you can classify vodka by

- Price levels
- Country of origin
- Food from which the vodka was distilled
- Flavorings

You may choose to sample several vodkas from one category or one vodka from each of several categories. But real experts testify that the differences between vodkas are generally so subtle that it makes tasting sense to compare like products — that is, all unflavored vodkas or all flavored vodkas from, say, Sweden or among those costing more than $20 a bottle.

Choosing vodkas by price

Is price the best guide to vodka quality? Yes. No. And, maybe. Some expensive vodkas are excellent, but so are some lower-priced brands. For example, in January 2005, a team of experts assembled by *The New York Times* sampled ten different 80 proof (40 percent ABV) vodkas, from various countries, made from various foods (in other words, grains versus potatoes). And the winner was — drumroll, please! — Smirnoff, made in the U.S., and the least expensive of the lot.

You can set up your own price-based tasting to see whether you agree with the *Times'* panel of men and women. Choose from a range that includes the following:

✔ **Ultra-premium vodkas:** These brands are priced higher than $40 per 750 ml bottle. Examples of ultra-premium vodka brands are:

- Belvedere
- Danaka
- Grey Goose
- Ketel One
- Tanqueray Sterling

✔ **Premium vodkas:** These brands are priced between $25 and $40 per bottle. Examples of premium vodka brands are:

- Absolut
- Boru
- Fris
- Hangar One
- Level
- Three Olives
- Wyborowa Estate

✔ **Popular priced vodka:** These brands are priced between $15 and $25 per bottle. Examples of popular priced vodkas are:

- Effen
- Finlandia
- Seagram's Extra Smooth
- Skyy
- Stolichnaya
- Teton
- Vincent Van Gogh

✔ **Value brand vodkas:** These brands are priced up to $15 per bottle. Examples of value brand vodkas are:

- Fris
- Georgi
- Nikolai
- Smirnoff
- Svedka
- Tito's Handmade

Choosing vodkas by country of origin

What countries make vodka? Chances are good that if you spin a globe and stick a pin anywhere it stops, you've found a vodka source. Table 10-2 is a representative list of products from a representative list of countries. *Note:* No prices are shown because of the differences in taxation between one state in the U.S. and another and the differences of import excise taxes on goods from one country to another.

Table 10-2	Choosing Vodkas by Country of Origin
Country	*Vodka Brands*
Canada	Pearl
Denmark	Danska, Fris
England	Blavod Black, Three Olives, Tanqueray Sterling
Estonia	Turi
Finland	Finlandia
France	Ciroc, Grey Goose, Vertical
Holland	Effen, Ketel One, Vox, Vincent Van Gogh
Iceland	Iceberg
Israel	Mishka
Ireland	Boru
Italy	Mezzaluna
Norway	Viking Fjord
Poland	Belvedere, Chopin, Luksusowa, Wyborowa
Russia	Cristall, Kremlyovskaya, Stolichnaya (Stoli)
Scotland	Armadale
Sweden	Absolut, Svedka, Level
Switzerland	Xellent
United States	Charbay, Gilbey's, Teton Glacier Potato, Tito's Handmade, Gordon's, Rain, Seagram's Extra Smooth, Skyy, Smirnoff, Square One

Choosing vodkas by the base

Basically, the choice of the foods from which popular vodkas are distilled boils down (that's a joke, folks) to two: Grains and potatoes.

Examples of grain-based vodkas are:

✔ Absolut (Winter Wheat)

✔ Belvedere (Polish Rye)

✔ Skyy (Corn)

Examples of potato-based vodkas are:

✔ Chopin

✔ Spudka

✔ Teton

✔ Blue Ice

Pure foodies may be interested to know that the American-made Square One boasts of being made from organic rye. The latest organic to join the list is Rain, which is made from organic corn. Hey, whatever floats your vodka Martini.

Choosing vodkas by flavor

Many regular vodkas also have fruit flavored versions. For example, Smirnoff produces lemon and other flavored versions. Table 10-3 lists vodkas available in flavored versions.

Table 10-3	Flavored Vodkas
Flavor	*Brand (Country of Origin)*
Banana	Hamptons Banana (U.S.)
Berries	Citadelle Raspberry (France), Olifant Raspberry (Holland)
Citrus	Zone Lemon/Tangerine/Banana/Melon/Peach (Italy), Olifant Orange (Holland), Orange V (U.S.)
Peach	Zygo Peach (U.S.)
Herbs/spices	Shakers Rose (U.S.), Zhitomirska Herb (Russia), Zubrowka Bison Brand (Poland)

Follow the leader

Are your eyes glazed? Does the incredible number of choices leave you, well, breathless? For consumers looking for the easy way, here's a list of the ten best-selling domestic vodka brands and the ten best-selling imported vodka brands for 2005. These lists were compiled by *The Adams Liquor Handbook,* a seriously respected liquor industry publication.

✔ **Domestic best-sellers:** Smirnoff, Skyy, McCormick (regional), Popov, Gordon's, Barton, Skol, Kamchatka, Fleischmann's Royal, Seagram's

✔ **Imported best-sellers:** Absolut, Grey Goose, Stolichnaya, Ketel One, Svedka, Three Olives, Finlandia, Belvedere, Fris, Tanqueray Sterling

By the way, lest you think that Europeans have a lock on the market, Adams wants you to know that domestic vodkas accounted for 70 percent of all vodka sales in 2005. Take that, you furriners.

Tasting vodka neat

To freeze or not to freeze, that is the question.

Nobody argues that warm vodka is good. In fact, warm vodka is decidedly unpleasant to the nose and the palate. But how cold is the right cold?

The Russians traditionally stick their vodka in the freezer. Some wags suggest that this practice comes from the fact that the inside of the freezer is warmer than the room temperature during a Russian winter.

In fact, the vodka won't freeze in your freezer because ethyl alcohol doesn't freeze until the temperature hits –117 degrees Celsius. That's a tad lower than the freezer in your kitchen.

In other words, putting the vodka into the freezer is a pleasant but meaningless affectation. Want it colder than room temperature? Chill the bottle in the fridge, chill the glasses in the freezer, or add ice cubes.

Sampling vodkas: What to see, sniff, and taste

If pressed, most people say that vodka is a truly neutral distilled spirit — that is: no flavor, no aroma, no color.

"Most people," as usual, aren't absolutely right.

Vodka tasting experts — such as the people who make vodka — can almost always tell one brand from another. They've been tasting vodkas for a long time and have perfected the ability to detect virtually undetectable flavor notes and degrees of *smoothness* (lack of a harsh alcohol bite).

Can an ordinary everyday vodka drinker do that? Maybe. But it takes practice. Lots of practice with one sip (no swallowing, please) at a time. Some of the terms the experts use most often are "smooth," "creamy" and a "long finish," which means that the taste stays in the mouth for a while. The flavor most often identified is vanilla. Occasionally a vodka may be "spicy," particularly those vodkas with a little more rye or wheat in the mash blend. Keep in mind that while five distillations may remove all the flavor, some is put back in through additives, such as glycerin, to help smooth the spirit.

Serving vodka after the tasting

After you taste vodkas neat and choose the one(s) you prefer, you may wish to move on to vodka mixed drinks.

That may be as simple as adding an olive or a twist of lemon; if you have a sweeter palate, a pitted sweet cherry should do it. Vodka purists, however, frown on salting (as with tequila) or putting something with a hot flavor (such as a chili pepper) into the glass. The pepper used in flavored vodkas is much milder than those usually used in cooking. Whatever you add to the drink, remember that vodka's flavor is very subtle — learn how to find it, not smother it.

Ice, the common vodka companion, is best made with distilled water — unless your town's tap water is absolutely tasteless (believe it or not, some are).

Mixers are a mixed bag. Fruit juices do well. The less acidic the flavor (think peaches), the clearer the subtleties of the vodka. But lemony vodka drinks are very popular. Go figure!

Colas are a no-no, even the diet versions, because they're so strongly flavored. But tonic — whose flavor is anything but shy — is A-okay. That's another "go figure." Some bartenders frown on loading the spices into a Bloody Mary, while others go for broke. (Speaking of the Bloody Mary, see Chapter 15 for the recipe.)

Toasting with vodka

So what are you supposed to say when you toast with vodka? It depends on the language:

✔ Denmark: Skaal (pronounced skohl)

✔ Finland: Kappis (pronounced kip-piss)

✔ Germany: Prost (pronounced prohst)

✔ Netherlands: Proost (pronounced prohst)

✔ Norway: Skaal (pronounced skohl)

✔ Poland/Russia: Nahz'droh vee'ah (pronounced phonetically, naz-dro VEE-ah)

✔ Sweden: Skaal (pronounced skohl)

In any language, these toasts mean: To your health.

Do you get the picture? Vodka is so versatile that what you like in a vodka mixed drink is what you should get.

Let everyone else go figure!

The Foods That Match the Drinks

Surprise! Vodka drinks go well with typical Northern European cuisine, be it salty, savory, or just plain rich. Examples are listed in Table 10-4.

Table 10-4	Vodka-Friendly Foods
Flavor	*Food*
Salty	Caviar, smoked fish (herring, salmon), olives
Savory	Dumplings (pirogi), baked meat pies (piroshki)
Rich/creamy	Blini (rolled, thin pancakes) with crème fraiche or sour cream

The Russians are coming?
The Russians are here

Hollywood has had a long love affair with all things Russian. Grand balls, assassinations, musical extravaganzas, political intrigue — American movies about Russia and the Russians have it all. Sometimes, all in the same film.

What ties all these movies together is the fact that at some point in the movie, some character tosses back some vodka. Match the stars to the movie and you're a winner.

And you get extra points for knowing the Americanized names of the following film personalities of Russian ancestry: Natalya Gurdina, Mikhail Igorevich Peshkovskiy, Issur Demsky, and Vadim Plemiannikov.

Stumped? How about actress Natalie Wood, director Mike Nichols, actor Kirk Douglas, and director Roger Vadim. But you knew that!

Movie	*Stars*
1. Ninotchka (1939)	a. Merle Oberon, Robert Ryan
2. Berlin Express (1948)	b. Matt Damon, Angelina Jolie
3. War and Peace (1956)	c. Carl Reiner, Eva Marie Saint
4. Silk Stockings (1957)	d. Robin Williams, Maria Conchita Alonso
5. From Russia With Love (1963)	e. Fred Astaire, Cyd Charisse
6. Doctor Zhivago (1965)	f. Omar Sharif, Julie Christie
7. The Russians Are Coming, The Russians Are Coming (1966)	g. Sean Connery, Michelle Pfeiffer
8. Moscow On the The Hudson (1984)	h. Sean Connery, Daniela Bianchi
9. The Russia House (1990)	i. Greta Garbo, Melvyn Douglas
10. The Good Shepherd (2006)	j. Henry Fonda, Audrey Hepburn

Answers: 1. i; 2. a; 3. j; 4. e; 5. h; 6. f; 7. c; 8. d; 9. g; 10. b

Chapter 11

Tequila: Unearthing the Aztecs

In This Chapter

▶ Discovering Tequila's prehistoric history

▶ Exploring the agave

▶ Describing the difference between pulque, Tequila, and mezcal

▶ Mapping the Tequila regions

*T*his chapter shatters the Euro-centric myth that the Western hemisphere had no fermented beverages before the arrival of the Europeans. In fact, virtually every group of Amerinds, natives in the north and those in the south as well, had its own fermented beverage. Primary among them was the Aztecs' *pulque*.

The Europeans brought with them the art and science of distillation, which the Amerinds had never developed — much like the Incans failing to invent the wheel but building a marvel of a road system throughout their empire.

Because the northern natives were hunter/gatherers, they obviously had little time to further develop any type of beverage that couldn't be swallowed at the moment of thirst or distress. However, the Incans and Mayans were another story. Witnessing their ancient cities and seeing their pictograph language shows that these were a highly organized and forward-thinking group of people.

But credit for creating and developing the present worldwide thirst for Tequila, mezcal, and variants goes to the Spaniards. It was their idea to bring the agave to a higher level by making it more acceptable for Europeans and certainly ultimately for Norte Americanos.

The First North American Spirit

As North America's first distilled spirit and first commercially produced alcohol beverage this side of the Atlantic, Tequila's history is long and rich. Its roots reach back into pre-Hispanic times when the natives fermented sap from the local *maguey* plants (which the Spanish conquistadores called *agave*) into a low-alcohol fermented beverage they called *pulque*.

The history of Tequila's development from that traditional beverage to the modern spirit parallels the often turbulent, chaotic growth of Mexico herself, and is often equally obscure to outsiders.

The history of Tequila is really the history of one plant and three beverages. The plant, of course, is the maguey, which isn't a cactus but rather a succulent assigned to the *amaryllis* family and a cousin to the *century plant,* also known as the American aloe.

The three beverages are:

- ✔ **Pulque:** First naturally fermented in Mexico almost two millennia before the arrival of Europeans

- ✔ **Mezcal:** A strong wine made from the maguey plant by the invading Spanish

- ✔ **Tequila:** A distilled spirit so popular that it took on the name of the city in northwest Mexico where it was first made — and from there it was shipped to Europe and ultimately around the world

Tequila is customarily spelled with a capital "T" as an indication of its appellation status (a specific region of a specific country), similar to Burgundy wine produced in the Burgundy, France region or Bourbon for the Kentucky whiskey.

Ancient history

When you're dealing with the origins of Tequila, "ancient" doesn't mean before the founding of the Republic of Mexico (1921), or before guitarist Don Gaspar Vargas created the first modern Mariachi band in Tecalitlán (1897), or even before the Spaniards landed in Mexico to take the land from Montezuma (1519).

No, in Tequila talk, "ancient" means r-e-a-l-l-y long ago, as in 100,000 BCE when — historians suggest — a volcano erupting in the northwestern part of that land near modern Jalisco tossed tons of

Agave, the mother of all Tequila

The Spanish renamed the maguey plant *agave,* a name accepted by later botanists. Those botanists include Sweden's Carolus Linnaeus (1707–1778), also known as Carl von Linné, who first identified the maguey as a member of the amaryllis family, and Germany's Franz Weber, who recognized that the maguey from northern Mexico wasn't the same as the maguey in the south. In 1902 he put the stamp on his discovery by naming it *Agave Azul Tequiliana Weber* after — who else? — himself.

The species name *agave* honors the original Agave, who, in the ancient myth, was the mother of a Greek king, Pentheus of Thebes. Pentheus promoted himself as a moral sort of guy, the man who banned festivals celebrating Bacchus, the god of wine, because the parties were characterized by unseemly behavior. In a word or two, drunken orgies.

Pentheus' dictate was okay with Agave until she discovered her son having a high old time at one such event. Straight away, Agave rounded up all the women in her family and they dismembered Pentheus. That's certainly a dramatic way of showing that nobody loves a hypocrite.

Other than that rather tenuous connection with alcohol beverages, nothing ties Agave to the plant that produces Tequila.

But it's certainly a good story.

mineral-rich ash into the air. The ash fell back to earth, creating a rich soil on which the agave thrives.

And that pesky volcano did more. An Aztec legend has it that the heat of the lava set fire to some maguey plants and filled the air with a smoky sweet odor. When the residents went to learn what was what, they found burnt plants with sap seeping from their hearts. The Aztecs tasted the sap and yelled "Huzzah" or whatever their word was. They were drunk with, and because of, their discovery. Tasting it resulted in a feeling of euphoria that led them to say that the juice — which they called *pulque* — was a gift from the gods.

As time went by, pulque was commandeered by Aztec priests for their exclusive use; non-priestly folk caught with a bowl of pulque were sentenced to death. The survival of the plants was so important to their religious observances that the priests often offered human sacrifices to defeat droughts or plant diseases — at which point the designated donor was permitted a drink of pulque to help ease the pain of the execution.

That's the way it went, with the Aztecs planting and cultivating the remarkable plant they named *maguey* (origin unknown) and cutting the plants to drink the sap that the Nahluatl Indians called *mezcal* from *mexcalil,* which looks a lot like *Mexico.*

Then came the conquistadores, led by Hernando Cortez, who eventually conquered all of Mexico, including the region in the northwest that they named New Galicia after the Spanish state. And along the way, they discovered the maguey and its lovely powers.

Thus began the modern — or at least the middle — history of Tequila.

Tequila's middle ages

This era in Tequila history stretches roughly from the moment when Hernando Cortez marched into Tenochtitlan (Mexico City) to be greeted by Montezuma as the legendary white god who taught the Aztecs how to farm. Befitting his status, Cortez got a glass, or a bowl, of pulque and wanted more. With more kick to it. He immediately sent off to Spain for a still. When it arrived, he taught the locals how to use it and so kicked pulque up a notch to mezcal.

In the mid 1500s, another Spanish explorer, Don Pedro Sanchez Tagle, the Marquis de Altamira, established the first Mexican distillery on his maguey farm at the village of Tuiquila in the northwestern section known today as Jalisco. He started turning pulque into mezcal and offering it as *aguardiente* (literally "fire water") for sale locally. Eventually, business boomed; the name of the village was Spanish-ized to Tequila, and bingo! A center for exporting a Mexican spirit was born.

By the 18th century, mezcal was selling so well that the taxes collected on the mezcal trade within Mexico as well as to Spain were sufficient for the government to subsidize building much of Guadalajara, the country's second largest city. In fact, sales were so good that they were cutting into Spanish spirit sales at home, leading the then-king, Charles III, to prohibit importation of any Mexican spirituous beverages.

Fortunately, the ban lasted only a decade until the next king reversed it in 1795 and issued the first retail license to sell mezcal (or mezcal brandy and agave brandy as it was also known) to José Antonio Montaño y Cuervo. Immodestly, he named his place

La Taberna de Cuervo. Shortly thereafter, the king issued the first right to distill the spirit to José Jr. and so established a dynasty that lasts into the 21st century.

Like all those who distilled the country's favorite spirit, José Jr. was no slouch at promotion, even to his putative enemies. People from the United States got their first taste of mezcal in 1846 during the Mexican-American war (also known as "The Fight For Texas"). During the U.S. Civil War, enterprising Mexicans put the mezcal into discarded whiskey barrels and sold it by the ladleful to soldiers along the border. When the French invaded Mexico in 1862 by winning a battle now memorialized by the Cinco de Mayo holiday, the Mexican civilians were there to greet them with rifles — and mezcal.

Shortly thereafter, all spirits made in Jalsico were renamed Tequila, and a good old high time was had by all.

Jose Cuervo: Hero of the Tequila revolution

The commercial Tequila business can trace its origins to the first land grant by a Spanish king to a nobleman in the New World. The nobleman was José Antonio Montaño y Cuervo. His family name means *crow*. And a crow is part of the family heraldic shield that appears on every bottle of Cuervo, even to this day.

The grant was soon followed by the first license ever granted in Mexico to a planter to sell his Tequila at retail. Don Cuervo took his thousands of acres and converted them to a plantation for cultivated maguey. When the plants matured for cutting, his son José Guadalupe, who inherited the family business, opened La Taberna Cuervo in the former village of Tequila, then a city of more than 20,000.

But the family had many years of little wealth due to Spanish taxation and other unresolved political questions. These came to an end in 1821 when Mexico gained its independence from Spain. Cut loose from Spanish goods, the Mexicans started to govern their own industries.

By the mid-19th century, the Cuervo family fields were growing more than three million agave plants. When these plants matured, in 1880, Cuervo enjoyed annual sales of an estimated 10,000 barrels of its Tequila in nearby Guadalajara alone.

Despite the invasion and occupation of Mexico by France, the family persevered and stuck to its guns — or rather its plans for growth — so that in the 21st century, Cuervo is the world's leading Tequila producer, and the Cuervo descendants still operate the plantation and the distilleries.

Tequila's trek north

As it was for Canadians to the north of the United States (see Chapter 8), the U.S. experiment of Prohibition was a boon to Mexico and its Tequila on the southern border. Gringos traveled to Mexico by the thousand to pick up a bottle or two or three or more.

The end of Prohibition may have impeded the continued growth of the Mexican distilling business, but World War II — with its consequent U.S. government request for local distillers to switch from making alcohol for drinking to making it for gunpowder — was enough to keep the Mexican industry booming. One expert estimates that 21,000 liters of Tequila were produced in 1941, which leaped to more than 4 million liters by the end of the war — most for export to the U.S. After the war, several U.S. companies, such as Heublein (now a division of the Diageo company), swung into action by importing Jose Cuervo.

The rest, as they say, is history.

Defining Tequila: New Standards for a New Global Spirit

In an effort to make Tequila into a more widely accepted and recognized spirit type, in 1974 the Mexican government asked that Tequila be granted an *appellation of origin*. The request was granted in 1994. This term means that the product is named after a specific geographical region — one that throughout time has been devoted to the product's production. The region gives the spirit its special characteristics due to the climate, location, and cultural tradition of the area.

This appellation of origin puts Tequila in the same class as Champagne, Cognac, Roquefort cheese, Bourbon, Tennessee Whiskey, and other similar products. The appellation carries with it an assurance of compliance to a set standard as established by the individual government.

The U.S. Standards of Identity, as set down in the Federal Register by the former Bureau of Alcohol, Tobacco, and Firearms (now known as the Alcohol and Tobacco Trade Bureau) define Tequila as "a regional alcohol drink obtained by distillation and rectification from musts originally made from ground 'heads' of ripe Agave Tequiliana Weber Blue variety which were cooked or hydrolyzed subject to alcohol fermentations with cultured or non-cultured yeasts. These yeasts can be enriched with other sugars up to a ratio of not more than 49 percent. Subsequent mixing of subsequent mixing of the producer's finished products is not allowed."

Tequila is a colorless liquid that can turn a yellowish or caramel color when aged in white or yellow oak containers, or with the addition of permitted additives. The "Denomination of Origin" law of 1994 defined the area in which the blue agave is grown. It includes the state of Jalisco (see Figure 11-1) and some regions in other states that have similar reddish volcanic soil and climate.

✔ The original Tequila region located around the town of Tequila, which is in Jalisco

✔ Guadalajara, which is Mexico's second largest city and the capital of Jalisco state

✔ The other best-known Tequila-producing towns: El Arenal and Amatitán, which are a few miles west of Tequila

✔ The Los Altos highlands east of Guadalajara that include Atotonilco, Tepatitlán, and Arandas

✔ Lowland towns Tesistán and Capilla de Guadalupe in Jalisco, and Corralejo in Guanajuato

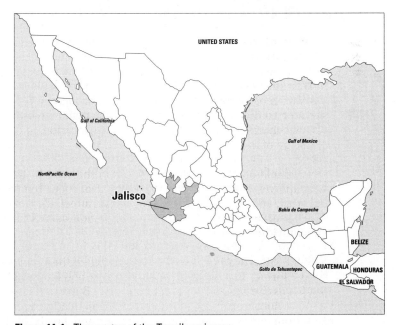

Figure 11-1: The center of the Tequila universe.

How Tequila Is Made

As with all distilled products, the process begins with choosing the base and then slowly and deliberately converting it to a satisfying beverage. Throughout the production of Tequila, representatives of the Tequila Regulatory Council oversee activities to ensure that standards of identification and quality regulated by Mexican law are followed.

During the distillation process, some producers add cane sugar or *piloncillo* (brown sugar cones) to speed up fermentation and save money by permitting the distiller to produce the Tequila using fewer mature agaves. Made this way, the Tequila is called *mixto* and can be sold in bulk for export or bottling outside Mexico, but it can't be labeled 100 percent agave.

For more information on Tequila standards, e-mail the Tequila Regulatory Council (CRI) at crt@crt.org.mx.

Choosing the base material

Tequila distillers have been trying for decades to dispel the idea that Tequila is made from cactus, but the myth is still around. Despite growing alongside cacti, agave isn't a cactus. Tequila is made of distilled sap from the root of a specific blue-green agave succulent plant that's called the Blue Weber agave.

Mexico has 136 species of agave, including 26 sub-species of which only *Tequiliana Azul Weber* is allowed for use in making Tequila. A mature agave has leaves that are 5 to 8 feet tall, is 7 to 12 feet in diameter, and has a life span of 8 to 15 years depending on the climate and soil.

Agaves are grown in cultivated orchards called *porteros* (pastures, also called *campos de agave* or *huertas*). These *porteros* often resemble vineyards, and you're likely to see corn or beans growing between the rows of the 1,000 to 2,000 plants in a typical acre. The agave plants are propagated from shoots (*mecuates* or *hijuelos*) taken from adult plants four to six years after planting. At that time, the shoots are at least a year old, and about the size of a leek or small onion. They're left to dry in the field for about a month and then removed to a nursery for another year. Only then are they planted in the field.

Forget Disneyland — Visit Tequila Land

Want to travel and visit Mexico? And why shouldn't you? If you have the chance, be certain to visit "Tequila Land," not only for its lovely scenery and hospitality, but also for the opportunity to visit several of the country's leading distilleries. Here's a listing of the ones that have special programs for visitors, along with contact information. Use this info to find out whether you need appointments and whether you'll be charged when you visit.

✔ **La Cofradia** produces Casa Noble Tequila. Visitors are welcome before 5 p.m. A nominal fee includes a complimentary tasting. Check out www.tequila cofradia.com for more information.

✔ **Casa Herradura** is located in Amatitán, 17 miles from Guadalajara. Tours of the Hacienda — amid outstanding scenery — last 90 minutes and conclude with a complimentary tasting. Check for times of the tour: Toll-free phone: +1-800-710-9868; Phone: 52-333-942-3900; Web site: www.herradura.com.

✔ **Mundo Cuervo** offers a journey through "La Rojeña." Tours are every hour on the hour. For a full schedule: Phone: 52-374-742-2170; E-mail: tours@ cuervo.com.mx; Web site: mundocuervo.com.

✔ **Museum of Tequila** is a well-designed display of visual materials showing the history of Tequila. It's open Tuesday through Sunday from 10 a.m. to 4 p.m. Phone: 374-742-0012 and 742-2170.

✔ **Sauza Family Museum** has a collection of memorabilia of one of the oldest families in Tequila and is located in what was once the family home. The fee is less than $3.

For more information on the Tequila Land region, check out www.iTequila. org/region.htm. For more information about the distilleries, go to www. Tequilasource.com/distillerytours.htm.

Pressing the agave

The part of the plant used for Tequila is the giant root called the *piña*, also known as the *head* or *cabeza*. As the word *piña* suggests, the root looks like a large pineapple. As it pushes its way upward through the earth, the piña puts on weight; when it's fully grown after 8 to 12 years, it may weigh between 77 and 308 pounds. Fortunately for the harvesters (or *jimadores*), most roots weigh fewer than 200 pounds. The piña is ripe when the leaves develop a maroon coloration with red spots. Only then is the piña cut from the stalk to start its way through the distillery.

Let's hear it for the jimadores

The skill of harvesting is passed down from father to son, and some fields have three generations of *jimadores* (harvesters) working in them. Methodical but efficient, a good jimador can harvest more than a ton of piñas in a day. Full truckloads are carried to the factory where the piñas are usually quartered or halved before baking. Harvesting is done year-round because the plants mature at different stages in the fields. Some large distillers pick young agaves, but others, like Herradura, use only plants that are 10 years old or older.

Before the piñas can be processed, jimadores cut the 200 or more spiky thorn-covered leaves (*pencas*) off them using a sharp, long-handled tool called a *coa.* They do this process almost entirely by hand because of the softness of the piña.

Each 15.4 pounds of piña yields about one liter of Tequila; the average piña yields 5 to 20 liters.

Preparing the mash

Traditionally, distillers let the piñas soften in steam rooms or slow-bake ovens for 50 to 72 hours. The traditional stone or brick oven is called a *horno,* which is where Sauza got the inspiration for its Hornitos brand name.

This softening process bakes the agaves at around 60 to 80 degrees Celsius. The slow baking softens the fibers and prevents the natural sugars from caramelizing, thus reducing the chances of bitter flavors in the juice.

Some Tequila distillers precook the piñas to remove external wax and solids to remove any possibility from adding bitterness to the final juice.

After the piñas are precooked and then slow baked or steamed, they're cooled and then beaten with mallets. Finally, distillers move them to a *tahona,* a giant grinding wheel or mechanical crusher or shredder that presses out the juice while removing and discarding waste. That waste may be used as animal foods or fertilizer, in a process similar to what occurs with the waste from grains used in making whiskeys (see Chapter 6).

The piñas are minced and strained to remove juices called *aquamiel* (honey water), and then mixed with water in large vats to produce a mash (wort) that's sprinkled with yeast — traditionally a strain that grows naturally on the plant leaves. Some distillers use cultivated yeasts or even a commercial brewer's yeast.

Fermenting the wort

The wort is left to ferment in wooden or stainless steel tanks for 7 to 12 days. At this point, some producers add piña residue for more flavor in the wort. When fermentation is complete — meaning that the conversion of sugars in the wort have an alcohol concentration of about 5 to 7 percent alcohol by volume — the wort may be left standing for another 12 hours to let the flavor richen and settle. Next, the distiller sends the fermented wort to the still, at which point he may set some of it aside to be used as a starter in the next mash very similar to the "sour mash" method used in Bourbon (see Chapter 6).

Distilling not once but twice

The liquid strained from the wort is distilled twice, once each in either a copper pot still or a stainless steel column still. Distillation takes 4 to 8 hours. The first distillation (*ordinario*) takes 1½ to 2 hours to produce a spirit that's about 40 proof (20 percent alcohol by volume, or ABV). The second distillation takes 3 to 4 hours to reach a spirit that's about 110 proof (55 percent ABV).

As in other spirit distillations, the process yields three distinct liquids:

- ✔ The *cabeza* (head) has more alcohol and more of the unpleasant flavoring agent called *aldehydes,* and it's discarded.
- ✔ The middle part of the distillation, called *"el corazon"* (the heart), is put aside as the final spirit.
- ✔ The end of the run, called *colos* (tails), is either discarded or re-distilled to add more flavor to triple distilled Tequila. Some distillers believe that the third distillation actually causes the spirit to lose flavor.

Aging the spirit

As with all spirits, Tequila is clear when it comes off the still. Aging adds color and helps classify the type of Tequila into one of the following:

- ✔ **Blanco** (silver) is basically un-aged Tequila, bottled right after distillation or after the distiller allows it to rest for no more than two months in stainless steel vats.

- ✔ **Joven** (gold) is also known as *suave* or *abocado.* These terms imply youth and freshness. Joven is un-aged Blanco with added coloring or flavoring agents — such as oak tree extracts, glycerin, or sugar — to soften the spirit. Joven may also be Blanco blended with aged or extra-aged Tequilas.

- ✔ **Reposado** (aged) is Tequila that has been stored in barrels made from charred American oak for a minimum of two months but no more than 12 months.

- ✔ **Añejo** (vintage aged) has been aged in barrels with a capacity of no more than 600 liters for at least one year and sometimes as long as three.

- ✔ **Extra Añejo** (ultra-aged), the newest type of Tequila, was first standardized in October 2005. It's a distillate aged for a minimum of four years in wooden barrels with a capacity of no more than 600 liters.

Distillers age their Tequilas in barrels that may have been used before to age other spirits — such as Bourbon, other whiskeys, sherry, or Cognac — in order to get different flavoring agents from the wood into their Tequila. Barrels may be used for 50 years or more.

Another way to create different flavors than the competition is to add actual fruit essences or even fruit juice. But those who love the earthy undertones of Tequila say that flavored versions should be used only for cocktail making.

Although aging does add color and certain flavor undertones to all spirits, including Tequila, the color of the spirit itself may not be a reliable guide to either its actual age or flavor. As more Tequila drinkers go after the richer flavor, some less-than-perfect distillers simply toss in a coloring agent, such as caramel. Honorable distillers, of course, lengthen the time spent in the barrel to deepen the flavor, or they may practice the art of blending as allowed under the regulations to produce a fuller flavor.

Blending and bottling

The contents of barrel-aged Tequila are usually blended with similar aged Tequilas from different barrels. This process enables a distiller to maintain a brand of consistent flavor, aroma, and color from year to year.

Mezcal: The "other" Tequila

Tequila is globally recognized as the king of Mexican spirits, but some confusion exists between Tequila and the "other" Tequila — mezcal. Tequila can be made only from the blue agave grown in specific appellation areas, but several different species of agave are permitted for use in mezcal, including *tobala,* a rare wild species.

Although similar, the agaves used in mezcal are harvested younger than the Tequila agave. This youth means a rawer, less complex flavor in the finished product, which feels very "hot" on the back of the throat. Because of this heat, mezcal is often considered a more masculine drink than Tequila.

To make mezcal, the sugar-rich piñas are baked slowly in a rock-lined pit oven over charcoal, and covered with layers of palm-fiber mats and earth. This process gives mezcal a strong, smoky, and leathery flavor. Larger distillers often cook piñas in a single day using steam pressure cookers. Distillers with a more limited production may simply buy agave syrup to save still more time and cost.

Tequila is distilled twice or occasionally three times; mezcal goes through only a single distillation. The result is that mezcal has more *congeners* (flavoring agents) while Tequila achieves a more balanced, yet still complex, flavor.

Despite the difference in flavors, Tequila and mezcal contain about the same level of alcohol — 38 to 40 percent ABV — partly because of Tequila's careful blending to keep the taste in balance.

Clearly the choice between mezcal and Tequila rests on a simple fact: More people like the balanced earthiness of Tequila than prefer the rough edges of mezcal. Currently you can find between 400 and 600 brands of Tequila and only about 100 brands of mezcal.

Before bottling, the blended Tequila is filtered through activated carbon or cellulose filters and diluted with distilled water to reduce the alcohol content, most commonly to 80 proof (40 percent ABV).

The Different Brands of Tequila

The standards permit two different kinds of Tequila. The first is the top level — Tequila 100 Percent Agave — that must be made from 100 percent Tequiliana Weber Blue Agave only. The second category is Tequila made from a minimum of 51 percent of blue agave sugars together with 49 percent other sugars, often called *mixto,* a word that doesn't appear on labels. However, both categories are clearly identified.

A number of outstanding Tequilas are available throughout the world in the following ranges (all prices are U.S. dollars for a 750ml bottle):

- ✔ **Ultra-premium** Tequilas run more than $40 a bottle.

- ✔ **Premium** Tequilas include a fine selection of $30 brands.

- ✔ **Value-priced** Tequilas cost $20 or less, and many of these mass market products are mixto.

Of course, price alone shouldn't be the final decision maker in selecting a Tequila or mezcal brand favorite. Taste should always be the ultimate factor. Some people prefer the rougher edge of the young Blanco Tequilas or mezcal with its more distinct agave flavor. Others like the sharper, almost peppery flavor of a mid-aged Reposado. And some may prefer the smooth, woody aroma in an even older Añejo. Like single-malt Scotches, or craft brews, Tequilas vary according to the company making them, the process, and the ingredient-growing environment. The temperature, soil, types of equipment, age of the plants, means by which the plants are pre-pared, and the blending and aging all affect the flavor and body.

Eeek! There's a worm in my drink!

You may have heard an interesting urban legend related to a worm in a bottle of Tequila. Some American-bottled brands of mezcal put a worm — usually made of plastic — in their bottles. The object seems to be to impress the *gringos* and boost sales with a legend that the worm was added to show that the beverage inside the bottle was actually alcohol, and to show that the proof indicated was accurate. In addition, the legend said that eating the worm was an aphrodisiac.

In actuality, the worm is far from being a Mexican tradition. It was a marketing ploy in the 1940s, started by an importer whose name has been lost to history.

So, the worm in the bottle isn't real — but you may find a bottle with a real moth caterpillar inside. Two types of caterpillars are used — the red, *gusano rojo,* con-sidered superior because it lives in the root of the maguey, and the less-prized white or gold *gusano de oro,* which lives on the leaves. Both larvae are commonly eaten as food and are still today sold in Zapotec markets.

Yes, the drinker is meant to eat the non-plastic worm. Don't worry, it's quite well pickled and free of pesticides — these worms are often raised just for use in mezcal and then pickled for a year. But, despite the fact that the word *mezcal* sounds like it's associated with the drug *mescaline,* it has no magical or psychotropic proper-ties, as either an aphrodisiac or the key to an unseen world.

It's merely protein and alcohol — but it's very rich in imagery.

Fancy packaging, wooden boxes, and elegant bottles are now common with ultra-premium Tequilas. They have become collector's items in their own right. Although they don't add to the basic quality of the drink in the bottle, they do add to its charm and certainly its visual appeal.

For more information on Tequila standards, contact the Tequila Regulatory Council (CRT) at crt@crt.org.mx.

Tasting Tequila and Mezcal

As usual, the tasting is the good part. So pull up a glass or two and get going. The basic rules for setting up a Tequila tasting are much the same as those for tasting any food or drink: Choose your samples, smell and taste them, and decide which you like best.

Chapter 3 lays out the details of a general tasting, along with an explanation of how your nose and palate transmit signals that your brain interprets as, "Oh, boy that's good," or "Eeeeew. Take that stuff away."

To apply these details to a Tequila tasting, try one of the following:

✔ Choose a minimum of three brands, each representing one type of Tequila.

✔ Select three samples from one distiller, such as Jose Cuervo, to experience the difference within a family of Tequila.

Making a tasting sheet

See Table 11-1 for a typical Tequila tasting sheet.

Table 11-1	Tequila Tasting Sheet	
Tequila	*Aroma/Legs*	*Flavor*
#1		
#2		

Tequila	Aroma/Legs	Flavor
#3		
#4		
#5		

Choosing the Tequilas to taste

Examples of outstanding Tequilas abound, ranging in price from less than $20 (value brands) to $30 (premium brands) to as high as $200 (ultra-premium brands). All price ranges are in U.S. dollars for a 750 ml bottle.

In other words, you can sample a really well-made premium Tequila for about the price of a mid-range single malt Scotch.

Which to choose? The following list is representative of Tequilas in the various styles:

- **Blanco:** Gran Centenario Blanco (Jose Cuervo), Chinaco Blanco, Two Fingers Blanco, Don Julio, Partita, Jose Cuervo Classico

- **Joven:** Two Fingers Gold, Montezuma, Pepe Lopez

- **Reposado:** Gran Centenario Reposado (Jose Cuervo), 1800 Reposada (Jose Cuervo), Sauza Commemorative (Sauza), El Tesoro de Don Felipe, Chinaco, Oro Azul Artesanal, Cabo Wabo

- **Añejo:** Gran Centenario Añejo, Oro Azul Artesanal, Corazon, Herradura Seleccion Suprema, Sauza Tres Generaciones (Sauza), El Tesoro de Don Felipe

- **Extra Añejo:** Assombrosso Del Porto, Reserva del Dueño Añejo, Rey Sol Añejo, Casa Noble, Chinaco, Milagro

Tasting the Tequilas

As you go through the following steps, note your reactions on your tasting sheet so that you can review them later.

First, look at the color. Pour about an ounce of Tequila into a tall, wide-mouthed glass. Next, hold the glass against a clean white sheet of paper with the light behind it. Depending on the type of Tequila, the color should range from clear (blanco) to a deep rich gold/amber (añejo).

As for body, swirl the glass so that the Tequila goes up the side. Aged Tequila will roll back very slowly — the greater the viscosity, the slower the legs give it up, and the older the Tequila.

Good Tequila smells and tastes good. If you notice an off aroma, such as oil or gasoline, don't even waste time tasting it. Check out Table 11-2 for a guide to the aromas and flavors expert tasters find in good Tequila. See how many you can actually identify.

Now add water to the Tequila in your next tasting glass (you want to add about two-thirds water compared to one-third Tequila). Repeat the aroma and flavor tests.

Finally, do as the Mexicans do, and have a bite or two of a taco or some unsalted nachos to cleanse your palate. And move on to brand or type #2.

Table 11-2   Flavors and Aromas Commonly in Tequila

Sweet Flavors/Aromas	*Spicy Flavors/Aromas*	*Hearty Flavors/Aromas*
Banana	Spices	Burnt oak
Caramel	Earthy	Light oak
Pears	Vanilla	Pine
		Smoke
		Leather

Pairing Food with Tequila

North Americans have been voting with their feet when trying cuisine while dining out or making something relatively simple at home. For many years, their first love was French, and then they discovered Italian. Years ago, North Americans relished spaghetti and red sauce (some people even used catsup) accompanied by that height of sophistication — a bottle of Chianti covered with a net that could, when empty, be used as a candle holder. The people of this great continent have come a long way since then.

The same will happen with the present number two menu choice — Mexican cuisine. Today, it's still widely considered tacos and a bottle of beer. But that's all changing as Americans become more familiar with the wonders and glories of the best meals that can come from south of the border. What better beverage to wash a Mexican meal down with than a fine Tequila or a cocktail made with a tasty Blanco?

After all, most alcohol beverages were created to augment and enhance the local style of cooking. So, although Tequila may go well with virtually any spicy, earthy type of food (even Italian), it does pair best with Mexican dishes.

Generally, Blancos are more food friendly than Añejos. The Blancos need food to take the edge off their "peasant" flavor, while the aged Tequilas can be sipped.

Of course, many Tequila fans say that you should never waste any Tequila in a cocktail, and certainly not in a slammer. Sipping a well-aged, balanced Extra Añejo is as pleasant as sipping a fine brandy — and for some people maybe more so.

There's a cultural reason for that too. Consider: The most popular alcohol beverage today in Mexico is not Tequila but brandy. Hmmm.

You've come to the end of this chapter on Tequila. As they say in Mexico when hoisting a glass:

> *Salud, amor y pesetas y el tiemppara gustarios!* (Health, love, and money, and the time to enjoy them!)

Chapter 12

Yo Ho Ho and a Bottle of Rum

In This Chapter

▶ Discovering the place where rum was born

▶ Tracking rum's travels around the globe

▶ Tasting the basic rum types

▶ Naming popular brands of rum

*T*his chapter explains how rum is made. It lists the various types of rum made in countries from Australia to Antigua, and serves up a splendid dish of rum history, including the fact that the Dutch in New Amsterdam opened the first rum distillery in America in 1664. This proves again, as New Yorkers like to say, "If you can make it here, you can make it anywhere."

And, if any spirit ever did make it anywhere, rum certainly did. It started as the juice from pressed sugar cane in New Guinea several centuries ago. It traveled through India to Persia, to the Mediterranean, and it went with Columbus to the New World. There, it turned the Caribbean into today's global center of rum production. Ever changing, today's rum keeps up with the demand for greater variety in spirits with more aged products, new flavorings, and new drinks — but it never loses sight of "Rum and Coca-Cola."

The History of Rum

The basic ingredient used in making rum is sugar cane, a tall reed grass first cultivated in New Guinea an estimated 10,000 years ago and much later in Indonesia, India, and the Philippines. How tall is this reed grass? It can reach as high as 30 feet.

Europeans got their first glimpse of sugar cane around 327 BCE when Nearchus, a general with Alexander the Great's army in Central Asia, reported finding "an Indian reed, which brings forth honey without the need of bees, from which an intoxicating drink is made."

No fools they, Nearchus and Alexander toted cuttings of this mira-
cle grass back home. They planted the sugar cane in the northern
Mediterranean where it quickly became known for its ability to
give sweetness without stinging. This episode laid the groundwork
for millions of rum drinks in the centuries to come.

From arak to rum

By the seventh century, people were converting sugar cane in
northern Africa and the entire Mediterranean basin, including the
islands. Ultimately, the Moors brought the sugar produced there to
the Iberian Peninsula. In every place it was grown, the folks

- ✔ Crushed the cane to release a sweet liquid
- ✔ Put the liquid out to sit, enabling yeasts floating naturally in
  the air to fall into and ferment the liquid
- ✔ Enjoyed the benefits in the form of *arak,* a fermented beverage
  still made and enjoyed throughout the Middle East, India, and
  Central and Southeast Asia

The Moors used crystallized cane juice to sweeten foods and make
medicines more palatable. Later on, Abu Musa Jabir ibn Hayyam
(for more on him, see Chapter 1) invented distillation. He (or one
of his assistants) poured the cane juice into a pot still, heated it,
collected the vapors and gave birth to — drumroll, please! — rum.

Hooray for Christopher Columbus

In 1493, on his second trip across the Ocean Sea (translation:
Atlantic Ocean), Admiral Christopher Columbus landed on an
island he named Hispaniola (now home to Haiti and the Dominican
Republic). On this island, he planted the first sugar to grow in the
Caribbean region.

The island was warm (not hot) and moist (not wet), the perfect
climate for sugar cane, which flourished like, well, the grass it is.

Soon the Spanish planted their flag (and sugar cane) on Cuba
(1511), Puerto Rico (1598), and Jamaica (1599). The Brits grabbed
Barbados; the French took Maritius and St. Kitts. The Portuguese
established their sugar cane production on plantations in Brazil,
where they had the dubious distinction of being the first to use
slave labor, keeping the workforce quiet by giving each a daily
glass of *garapa doida* (crazy sugar cane juice).

By 1625, Brazil had become Europe's leading sugar mill, and the entire Caribbean area became the world's leading source of sugar cane production, outstripping the Spanish Canary Islands and Madeira, the refueling and restocking islands that were formerly the sugar bowl for European ships traveling to the East.

The Caribbean was doing well, too. For example, by 1655, the sugar crop on the island of Barbados alone was valued at $5 million annually (in modern dollars).

And then came rum.

Rum rises

The invention of distillation and the creation of rum added tremendous wealth to the "sugar colonies" in the Caribbean and South America. And the American colonies, which carried the kegs back and forth across the waters, did well too. In fact, the rum trade was so profitable that some historians suggest that taxes on rum, not tea, were what triggered the American Revolution.

Rum was also a pretty good business for *privateers* (privately owned trading and raiding ships) and *corsairs* (outright pirates) who roamed the seas under any flag that would hire them. These "businessmen" were so powerful that one, Captain Henry Morgan, bought a sugar plantation on Jamaica and eventually became deputy governor of the island and a knight (as in Sir Henry Morgan) as well.

Legend has it that Captain Morgan is the one who came up with the single name — rum — for the distilled spirit made from cane sugar. Certainly, no British "sir" would accept the Spanish name *aguardiente* or the French *eau de vie,* and it's unlikely he even heard of the Portuguese designation *cachaca.* But the English *rum,* a transliteration of the Spanish *ron* and the French *rhum* was just fine.

Thank you, Captain Morgan. Hey, isn't that the name of a modern brand of rum? Right-e-o, mate. Check out the later section, "Hola! Rums from the Caribbean," for more information.

Sugar into rum: A trade bonus

After its discovery, sugar was a culinary delight and an economic boon to the Europeans. But it wasn't until the 1700s that the British realized that the real value of sugar was in distilling the cane into an alcohol beverage.

Bay rum

No, you don't drink this one. Bay rum is a simple distillate made in the Virgin Islands and on nearby Granada by adding crushed bay leaves to a rum spirit straight off the still. Originally used as a cure-all for skin and scalp conditions, bay rum evolved into a male cosmetic when men started using a splash or two to "close the pores" after a shave and a hot towel at the barber. The scent was grand and the shock of alcohol on a recently shaved face was exhilarating. With the advent of the electric razor, bay rum lost its almost universal popularity, but many men still use it as an aftershave.

In 1690, Sir Dalby Thomas, the governor of Jamaica who just happened to own a sugar cane plantation on the island, sent a memo to the British Colonial Office suggesting "the spirits arising from melasses (sic) which is sent from the 'Sugar Colonies' to other colonies and to England, if it were all turned into spirits would amount annually to above $800,000, at half the price the like quantity of brandy from France would cost."

In other words, Sir Thomas realized what farmers in Scotland and Ireland already knew and what Americans would soon learn: It's cheaper and more profitable to ship some foodstuffs, such as grains and sugar, as a highly desirable liquid. That is, as alcohol beverages.

Quick as a wink, farmers in many lands began turning their sugar cane into a commercially acceptable alcohol beverage and exporting the spirits under a variety of names, all of which ultimately translated to *moneymaker.*

And so it has been ever since.

How Rum Is Produced

As with other spirits, the process of making rum includes five basic steps:

- ✔ Choose the base from which to make the spirit
- ✔ Distill the spirit
- ✔ Age the spirit
- ✔ Blend the spirit
- ✔ Bottle and sell it

The "Triangle Trade"

While Britain ruled the North American colonies, the Americans were required to buy all their imported goods from either Merrie Olde England or other British colonies, such as those in the Caribbean. No surprise, then, that as the Brits expanded their cane growing and rum distillation in the Caribbean, rum became the alcohol drink of choice from Virginia to Maine. Distilleries opened frequently in New England where the merchant ships were built and docked. And casks of rum arrived regularly in Newport, Rhode Island; Boston; and New York to be poured into punches, toddies, flips, and other rum drinks. In addition, it was poured into medicinal concoctions, such as rum drinks (called cocktails for the first time), and in rum-and-mustard, which was used to "cure" respiratory problems ranging from a mild cold to tuberculosis.

To meet the demand, Caribbean plantation owners needed laborers willing or forced to work 17 hours a day under the most horrible conditions. The result was an importation of ever-increasing numbers of African slaves. Soon a regular trade route was established with the New Englanders sailing to Africa to bring slaves to the Caribbean and then loading the now-empty slave ships with casks of rum for the return trip to North America.

This route, soon dubbed the Triangle Trade, continued until the early 19th century when Haitian slaves revolted against the French and took control of their island, creating the first Caribbean republic. To avoid a similar revolt among the "workers," Britain abolished slavery in 1833, cutting the arms off the slave triangle.

What could be more straightforward? (Well, flavored rums are an additional wrinkle worth mentioning, and I discuss them later in this section.)

Stop! If you're reading this chapter before you've read Chapter 2, some technical terms — such as *fermentation, mash,* or *pot still* — may require definition. No problem: Just stick a bookmark here, go back to read quickly through Chapter 2, and come back when you're done.

The base

Rum is made from one of three "starters" — fresh cane juice, cane syrup, or molasses.

> ✔ **Cane juice** is the liquid extraction gained simply by crushing one type of sugar cane (several types are listed under the Latin genetic designation *saccharum officinarum*). After the

juice is extracted, it's strained; some distillers add a bit of lime juice to clarify the cane juice.

✔ **Cane syrup** is the thick liquid produced by reducing cane juice. As any cook knows, *reducing* means boiling the cane juice so that some water escapes as steam, leaving behind a more concentrated, thicker liquid.

✔ **Molasses** comes from the Latin word *mellaceus* and the Spanish word *melaza,* both of which mean *like honey.* It's the liquid left behind when all *sucrose* (simple sugar) has been crystallized and removed from the boiled sugar cane juice. To achieve a deeper flavor, some rum distillers use *blackstrap molasses,* a very dark liquid produced when the syrup is caramelized (heated and darkened) during three rounds, rather than one round of boiling-and-removing-the-sugar crystals. Fun fact: The word *blackstrap* comes from the Dutch word *stroop,* which means *syrup.*

 Occasionally, a distiller may use a base made of matter skimmed from the tops of the liquid in the pans that are used to process the sugar cane. This base, however, isn't as common as cane juice, cane syrup, or molasses.

Fermentation

The second step in making rum is to add water and yeasts to the base, creating the mush known technically as a *mash* (more about that in Chapter 2). As the mash sits in fermentation tanks for anywhere from one day for lighter rums to three weeks for the heavier types, the yeasts convert the sugars in the liquid to alcohol in a chemical reaction. This reaction also creates flavoring agents called *esters.* As a rule, the longer the fermentation time, the more complex the final flavor. As for the yeasts, some of the mass distillers use their own yeast cultures; others rely on the local yeast population to do the work.

Distillation

After the mash ferments, it moves on to the stills. Rum distillers use both pot stills and column stills to distill the mash once, twice, or even three times. As a general rule of thumb, darker, more flavorful rums are distilled in pot stills. Those rums come off the still at about 98 proof (45 percent alcohol by volume, or ABV), while the lighter rums — made on column stills — emerge from the still at higher alcohol rates (as high as 151 overproof or 75 percent ABV). These higher rates are due to greater removal of flavoring agents.

Aging

The benefits of aging rum were discovered by accident sometime in the 17th century. That's when a couple of barrels of rum bound from the Caribbean for England were somehow left to stand on a dock for a longer-than-usual period of time before being loaded onboard. When the barrels were opened and the rum poured, eureka! It tasted a whole lot better than the normal run-of-the-still, sorry, run-of-the-mill, product.

That was then. This is now, and various governments have set rules about what to call an aged rum:

- ✔ **Silver rum (white rum)** is rum as it comes off the still, usually after two or three runs through a continuous still.

- ✔ **Light rum (golden rum)** is rum aged a minimum of one year, either in oak barrels or stainless steel tanks.

- ✔ **Dark rum (reposado)** is rum aged three years or more in charred oak barrels.

Often the barrels used for aging rum were formerly used for aging whiskey, sherry, or brandy. Rums aged in these used barrels have more complex flavors than rums aged in new barrels.

Some distillers darken their light rums with *caramel* (a sugar syrup), but only aged rums can be legally labeled "dark rum."

The color of aged rums may vary depending on how long they age. For example, golden or amber-colored rums are usually aged at least three years; the darker rums are usually aged for five years or more.

Blending

Virtually every bottle of rum sold anywhere in the world is a blend of rums from different locations, stills, or ages. The art of blending rums, as with the art of blending whiskeys, rests with a person with the skill and experience to produce a palate-pleasing flavor. His (yes, this is a very male-dominated profession) intuition, tasting ability, and knowledge of what's expected of the product is the "make or break" of success for any brand. At any time, a distiller's warehouse can have thousands of barrels sitting and quietly aging. Sometimes this inventory can be valued in the hundreds of thousands of dollars, which is a very big investment resting on the blender's shoulders. Or, more accurately, his palate.

Now there's an image for you: A man with barrels balanced on his tongue. Never say a *For Dummies* book fails to titillate your imagination!

Flavoring a favorite

In 1983, a new element was added to the versatility of rum with the introduction of Captain Morgan Spiced Rum. This Puerto Rican-made blended rum ranks among the top five sold worldwide, and its success spurred the creation of many other flavored rums.

The Captain Morgan line now includes a lighter flavored version (Parrot Bay), plus Black Label Jamaican, Private Stock, and Tattoo (a very dark rum with a berry/citrus flavor). Each of these rums is distilled and blended in Puerto Rico, and then bottled in Baltimore, Maryland.

Bacardi's first flavored entry, Limon, sold so well that the company now also produces Ciclon (rum plus 10 percent blue agave Tequila and a touch of lime), Tropico (Bacardi Gold rum plus tropical fruit

---

Talking about rum

Wherever rum is made and whatever flavor it carries, the spirit has also added a rich list of words to the English language. *Rummy* was once a synonym for one who abused alcohol. *Rum* meant *bad.* Before Prohibition, America's temperance queen, Carrie Nation, cut straight to the chase, calling all beverage alcohol *demon rum.* And the guys who ferried alcohol into the United States illegally during Prohibition were called (what else?) *rum runners.*

But when it comes to inventing nicknames for rum itself, the all-out champs are the Brits. A partial list culled from a report by the British Broadcasting Corporation lists the following:

✔ Barbados water

✔ Demon water

✔ Kill-devil

✔ Navy neaters

✔ Pirate's drink

✔ Rum bastion

✔ Rumbullion

Whew!

juices), Bacardi O (rum plus orange essence), Razz (rum plus raspberries), Vanilla, Coco (coconut, of course), and Grand Melon (watermelon).

Cruzan, made in the U.S. Virgin Islands, has eight different flavored rums, including mango and banana. Presumably, by the time you read this, you'll be able to find even more.

Where That Rum Is From and Why It Matters

Just as Scotch whiskies from the Highlands taste different from Scotch whiskies from the Islands (see Chapter 5) and London dry gin is different from Dutch gins (see Chapter 9), a rum from, say, Puerto Rico has a character and flavor different from one born down under in Australia. In the following sections, I fill you in on the most important information about rums from around the world.

Hola! Rums from the Caribbean

The epicenter of the rum world is still the Caribbean, where the world's oldest rum distillery — Mount Gay — continues to produce rum good enough to rank in the top ten bestsellers in the United States.

The following is a handy-dandy synopsis of the kinds of rum made on the various Caribbean islands. For a quick look at some specific brands from specific islands, check out Table 12-1.

Table 12-1	Caribbean Rums
Country	*Representative Brands*
Antigua	Muscovado
Barbados	Cockspur, Doorley's, Mount Gay
Cuba	Havana Club
The Dominican Republic	Brugal, Matusalem, Ron Barcelo, Ron Bermudez
Haiti	Rhum Barbancourt
Jamaica	Appleton Estate, Myers's

Country	Representative Brands
Martinique	Duquesnes, Mauny, Trois Riviéres
Puerto Rico	Bacardi, Don Q, Ron Del Barrilito, Captain Morgan
Trinidad and Tobago	Angostura, Fernandes "19," Royal Oak, Ten Cane
Virgin Islands	Cruzan

According to U.S. government rules, rum made in one part of the Caribbean may not say that it's made somewhere else. For example, if your rum is made in Puerto Rico, you must say that right on the label.

Alas, many Caribbean island-made rums are hard, if not impossible, to find outside the countries in which they're produced. That's as good a reason as any to book a trip to the Caribbean. So what are you waiting for? Pick a destination from the map in Figure 12-1.

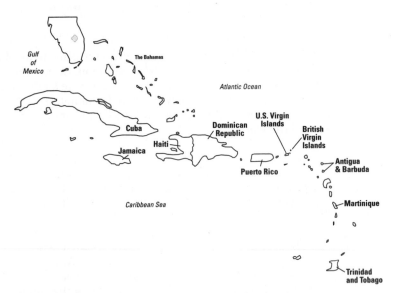

Figure 12-1: The world of rum.

Antigua

Originally a minor player with no distillery of its own, Antigua made do with simple, light-bodied rums that were homemade on local plantations. That changed early in the 1900s when a group of rum shop owners banded together to create Antigua Distillery.

In the 1950s, the Antiguans introduced Muscovado, a molasses-based rum. Ten years later, they switched to producing rums from fresh cane juice. Their most recent introduction is English Harbor 5 Year Old, a brand that's won awards in various countries. The line has expanded to include a 25 year old and a 1981 Vintage English Harbor.

Barbados

This island in the West Indies has a porous soil made of sandstone, coral, and volcanic ash deposits, so it's perfect for growing sugar cane. The only drawback is a lack of surface water; all water used for irrigation comes from an underground aquifer or from rain-water captured in cisterns.

Most Barbados rums, made on both pot stills and column stills, are molasses-based, fairly light in both color and body, with a soft smoky or "leathery" aroma and flavor. Some Barbados rums are aged, giving them a depth comparable to a good brandy (the spirit about which you can read more in Chapter 13).

Cuba

Rum exports from Cuba to the United States came to an abrupt halt with the advent of the Castro Revolution. At that time, the Cuban government appropriated the sugar cane lands, and the United States banned trade with Cuba. Nonetheless, Cuba — Bacardi's original home — continues to distill and export rum around the world.

Cuban rum is commonly made on column stills. The finished spirits are designated Carta Blanca (white label) or Carta Oro (gold label). The white label is, naturally, a light rum. The gold label often has caramel added to darken the color and add flavor to the run.

Modern Cuba's primary export rum is Havana Club. The globally popular brand is partially owned by the Cuban government, and to protect its investment, the Cubans have filed World Trade Organization action against any brands that describe themselves as being Cuban-made or of Cuban origin when they aren't.

The Dominican Republic

The Dominican Republic occupies two-thirds of the island of Hispaniola, the place where Columbus landed in 1493 to plant the first sugar cane cuttings in the Caribbean, effectively becoming the father of rum. (Flip to the earlier section "Hooray for Christopher Columbus" for more info.)

Dominican rum is made from molasses, on column stills, and aged for a minimum of eight months. Some brands are aged as long as seven years.

Brugal, Ron Bermudez, Matusalem Grand Reserve, and Red Flame (whose label says "spirit of Cuba," but whose rum is now made in the U.S.) date back to the 19th century. The Ron Barcelo brand-name first appeared in 1929.

Haiti

Haiti, the country that shares the island of Hispaniola with the Dominican Republic, was controlled by the French. The French were eventually tossed out by a slave revolution, and those former slaves started the first republic in the Caribbean in 1803.

However, the Haitians still speak French and they make their *rhum* (not *rum*) with a French accent, producing a spirit by means similar to those used to make Cognac. That's no surprise when you consider that the soil in the area where Haitian sugar cane grows is similar to the soil in the Cognac and Champagne regions of France.

Haitians press the cane, pasteurize the juice, and ferment it immediately with local yeasts. The first run off the pot still is redistilled and then aged in oak barrels for three years or more. The raw, un-aged rum called *clairin* is commonly sold not for export but by street vendors during local feast days, celebrations, or religious voodoo rituals.

Aficionados often describe one Haitian brand in particular, Rhum Barbancourt, as the world's finest rum. Unfortunately, Haiti's political instability sometimes interferes with rum production, raising export prices. This instability can make it difficult to find this treasure outside of Haiti or duty free shops in Caribbean airports.

Jamaica

Traditionally, Jamaican rums were made on pot stills and were darker and more aromatic than rums from many other Caribbean islands. Today, Jamaica has joined the mainstream, and its distilleries now make virtually every variety of rum.

Flavors range from light to dark. The best-known well-regarded light Jamaican rums are those from Appleton Estate. Myers's (originally known as Planter's Punch) is a standout among the dark rums.

Like other British-oriented islands, Jamaica sometimes ships its rum to England in casks for aging and bottling, thus saving various tariffs and creating a special category of rum appropriately called London Dock.

Martinique

Martinique is still part of Metropolitan France, which means that residents are French citizens with all appropriate rights and duties, including the ability to vote in French elections. This island has two claims to fame. First, it has the greatest number of distilleries in the Eastern Caribbean. Second, it's the place where the Empress Josephine (Napoleon's wife) was born.

Martinique produces two types of rum, *rhum agricole* and *rhum industriel.* Rhum agricole, which is made in Martinique and in nearby Guadaloupe, is distilled from just-pressed sugar cane juice. Rhum industriel is distilled from molasses. Both are produced on column stills and stored in steel vats or oak barrels. Both are aged for a minimum of three years. To be called *rhum vieux* (aged rum), the rum is aged for several years more.

All the island's agricultural rums were granted a French appellation designation in 1966, meaning that the cane fields and distilleries are regularly inspected to make sure they meet government standards.

Puerto Rico

This one island is the world's largest single rum distilling area, home of the magnificent Bacardi facility. Bacardi is the world's leading rum distiller with nearly 50 percent of the export market and is distributed in virtually every country in the world. Other fine Puerto Rican rum brands include Don Q, Ron Del Barrilito, and of course Captain Morgan Spiced Rums. In addition, Puerto Rico distills *overproof* rums, which are sold primarily for use in cooking and in flambé-ed cocktails — drinks the bartender lights with a match so that it flames for a moment as most of the alcohol burns off.

Puerto Rican distillers produce two styles of rum, White Label (very light) and Gold Label (slightly darker). The white label rums must be aged a minimum of one year. Gold label rums must be aged three years. The gold labels are the local favorites, as exemplified by brands such as Palo Viejo and Ron Llave. Some Puerto Rican distillers are aging their rums for even longer than three years; for example, Bacardi now offers an 8-year-old rum.

All Puerto Rican rums are made from molasses, and each of the island's distillers cultivates its own yeasts, which are considered the secret behind the light, dry, yet aromatic quality of the finished spirit. Remember that Puerto Rico is part of the United States, so its products must meet the same standards as those made on the mainland.

Trinidad and Tobago

The rums from the Republic of Trinidad and Tobago are made on column stills. They're primarily light, molasses-based spirits, similar to those from Puerto Rico. This similarity marks a move toward a standard Caribbean flavor, which is indicative of how island rum making is going.

Angostura, the same distiller that makes Angostura Bitters, offers an 8-year-old rum in French-made, hand-blown, individually numbered glass bottles. Other brands from this island are Fernandes

Rum's musical

During World War II, the United States Armed Forces established a base on Trinidad where more than 100,000 servicemen were posted at one time or another and where many got their first taste of, yes, rum.

The Caribbean spirit quickly became the beverage of choice among the itinerant servicemen, especially when mixed into a Cuba Libra (the local rum plus Coca-Cola and lime juice). The new cocktail was so famous that an island Calypso singer named Lord Invader sang a song about it. In 1943, radio comedian Morey Amsterdam (later to star as Buddy Sorrell on TV's *Dick Van Dyke Show*) heard the song while on a USO tour.

Amsterdam knew a winner when he heard one. He updated the lyrics, and brought the music back to the U.S. As luck would have it, he played the Calypso-style ditty for the popular Andrews Sisters the night before they were to record "One Meat Ball." The Sisters put "Rum and Coca-Cola" on the flip side of "One Meat Ball," and the rest is clearly history.

Eventually, the record sold nearly seven million copies, making it the third best-selling record of the 1940s, right behind Bing Crosby's "White Christmas" and Patti Page's "Tennessee Waltz."

Things didn't turn out so well for Morey. In 1947, Lord Invader invaded the U.S., having heard about the song's success and learning that Amsterdam was taking full credit for creating it. He brought with him the 70-year-old composer of the melody. They sued, they won, and, after several trials, the courts awarded them all future royalties, thus sending a very happy composer and lyricist back to Trinidad.

Happy drinkers around the world continued to enjoy "Rum and Coca-Cola" — the cocktail and the song.

"19", Royal Oak, and Ten Cane. The latter is rapidly growing in popularity in the U.S and is made from fresh pressed cane juice.

Virgin Islands

Even though the Virgin Islands are owned by Great Britain and the United States, rum is made only in the U.S. territory. The molasses-based spirits, made on column stills, are predominantly light rums.

The Islands' major distiller, Cruzan, also produces more flavorful darker rums designed for leisurely sipping. Maybe on a veranda overlooking the blue, blue waters.

The most famous saying about rum: "Yo ho ho"

Here's some more fun with rum. It's been said and heard many millions of times — children sing it, movie pirates chant it, people growl it out. Before you read any further, where did the saying "yo ho ho" come from? Think you know? No peeking.

The year was 1883, and British writer Robert Louis Stevenson (1850–1894) had just published his most successful (and most enduring) novel, *Treasure Island*. It's regarded by many as a children's book, but it deals with many adult situations and questions. What most people don't realize is that it's a story based on a true occurrence — the fate of the crew on a ship that wrecked on Dead Man's Chest, a reef close to Tortola.

A contemporary of Stevenson's, Young E. Allison, was so impressed with *Treasure Island* that he wrote an epic poem based on the book. The poem was called "Derelict," and it started with the lines:

"Yo ho ho and a bottle of rum.

Drink and the devil had done for the rest."

In 1901, the poem became a song in a Broadway musical, "Fifteen Men on a Dead Man's Chest."

Six film adaptations of *Treasure Island* have been released since 1911. Those films include the following:

✔ **The more recent:** *Muppet Treasure Island,* and an animated film from Japan.

✔ **The most famous:** The 1934 MGM blockbuster with Wallace Beery and Jackie Cooper, followed by the Disney version of 1950 starring Bobby Driscoll and Robert Newton.

✔ **The strangest:** A TV film in 1990 that was produced, directed, and written by Fraser Clark Heston and starred his father Charlton as Long John Silver.

Other places, other rums

Rum is made in virtually every area where the sugar cane flourishes, including the Philippines, India, South America, Mexico, Hawaii, and even the U.S. mainland. Yes, some American bottlers still package rum sent in from other countries and *rectifiers* (bottlers who buy in bulk right off the still and dilute the distillate to produce drinkable rum).

Asia

Asian distillers produce white and golden rums made on column stills for sale primarily in the Philippines and Thailand. India has begun making rums for its Hindu population (Hindus, unlike Moslems, drink alcohol beverages).

Australia

The Aussies make their white and golden rums via a double distillation on column and pot stills. The process must be effective: Rum is the second most popular alcohol beverage in Australia, right after beer.

Bermuda

Bermuda first made rum to satisfy the demands of sailors and ship owners who stopped at the island to resupply on their way to the U.S. Today, Bermuda's claim to rum fame rests with Gosling's Black

---

To your health, Aussie style

When Lachlan Macquarie arrived in Australia in 1819 as governor of New South Wales (the state in which Sydney is located), he found a town hospital that was nothing more than a collection of tents.

Macquarie immediately went about remedying the situation, putting aside land for a new hospital. When the British government refused to fund the building, Macquarie enlisted a group of local businessmen to build the hospital with convict labor in exchange for a monopoly on importing 45,000 gallons of rum. When the contractors complained about the price, Macquarie upped their compensation to the rights to import 60,000 gallons.

Even so, the hospital — completed in 1816 and nicknamed the Rum Hospital — turned out not to be profitable. Today, the building houses staff for the Sydney mint.

And that definitely makes money.

Label and Gosling's Gold Label. These pot-stilled spirits are shipped in bulk to the U.S. for bottling before being shipped back to (where else?) Bermuda.

Brazil

Brazil's sugar cane spirit isn't rum, it's *cachaça* (pronounced ca-cha-cha), a medium-bodied cane-juice product that's well-suited for aging. Cachaça is growing in popularity because it serves as a base for the *caipirinha,* a Brazilian cocktail made up of sugar, lime juice, and cachaça.

Canada

The North American northerners have been importing rum for more than 300 years, ever since sailing merchants first used it to barter with Atlantic Maritime fishermen for dried fish.

Canadians don't distill their own rums, but they do take bulk shipments of Caribbean rums (rums shipped in barrels rather than in bottles), and age the rum onshore for up to five years. This process produces a spirit known to Nova Scotians as (no kidding) Screech.

Europe

Europe's climate isn't friendly to the sugar cane, but its business-minded distillers are well aware of the profits to be made by aging and bottling spirits that are shipped to them in bulk.

The French and British ship their finished product primarily to their current and former colonies. The colony-bereft Germans bring in heavy Jamaica rum and mix it with neutral spirits (yes, you can read about neutral spirits in Chapter 2) to make *Rum Verchnitt.* The Austrians do pretty much the same.

Guyana

This former Dutch, English, and French colony is on the northern tip of South America. Its proper name is the Cooperative Republic of Guyana, and it's home to Demerara rum, a specific type (as well as brand) that's named for the river that runs through the region where the sugar cane is grown.

The molasses-based, high-alcohol rum is fermented with local yeasts and produced on pot stills as well as column stills. It starts out dark and becomes even darker with the addition of caramel. Despite its dark color, Demerara has a relatively mild flavor because the base is fermented very quickly (from 36 to 40 hours rather than over a period of days). This quick fermentation reduces the incidence of the chemical reactions that produce *esters* (flavor ingredients).

Even though the flavor is relatively mild, Demerara rums have a higher alcohol content than most other rums. The product line includes overproof rums and rums aged for as long as 25 years.

 Aged Demerara rum is often blended with lighter Caribbean rums. An example is Pusser's Rum, which was named for the *purser,* the man who measured out the tots of rum on British Navy ships. (For more on this topic, see the nearby sidebar "An ounce a day keeps the mutiny away.") This blend of Demerara plus rums from Jamaica and Trinidad was served exclusively on British Navy ships until 1970, when Pusser's was finally marketed to the public.

United States

No, the U.S. has no sugar cane fields used for making rum. But, as a relic of earlier times, the U.S. still has bottlers and rectifiers (people who add water or other ingredients to the distillate) who process rum shipped into New England in bulk — that is, in the original casks used for aging. Who knew?

An ounce a day keeps the mutiny away

What really made rum so popular? Forget flavor. Forget price. It was the British Royal Navy.

On long voyages, even the best of the Brits became disruptive from time to time. To keep order and prevent mutiny, the Brits came up with the *tot,* an ounce of rum diluted with several ounces of water, and allowed one per man per day.

Edward Vernon, a British admiral, ruled that the tot should be measured out in full view of the crew to prevent claims of one sailor's getting less than another. Vernon also decreed that the really good guys should get an extra dash of lime juice (the natural anti-scurvy medicine) plus sugar to make the rum even tastier. It worked. No more mutinous glares such as the ones Fletcher Christian handed Captain Bligh aboard the *Bounty.*

While on duty, Admiral Vernon always wore a coat made of a waterproof fabric called *grogram.* To honor his creating the drink-a-day practice, the navvies (Brit speak for sailors) named the rum/water/lime juice/sugar combo "grog."

Later, grog also became known as "Nelson's Blood" in honor of the great British naval hero — properly Vice-Admiral Horatio Nelson, First Viscount Nelson, Duke of Bronte, KB, RN (1758–1805) — whose body is said to have been preserved in a cask of rum on its trip back to England after Nelson was killed in the Battle of Trafalgar.

Tasting the World's Rums

Chapter 3 explains the rules of a spirits tasting. You can skip back there for the details, or simply follow the simplified procedure here.

Prepping your tasting sheet

Create a tasting sheet so that you can jot down your impressions as you sample each rum. Table 12-2 shows a typical tasting sheet.

Table 12-2	Rum Tasting Sheet		
Rum Name/Type	*Color*	*Aroma*	*Flavor*
#1			
#2			
#3			
#4			

Selecting the rums you want to sample

Which rums you choose depends on whether you want to try a simple beginner's tasting or a more advanced and adventurous one.

For the beginner's tasting, the logical plan is to compare a white or silver un-aged rum, a golden and slightly aged rum, and a reposado (rum aged for several years). You may also want to add a very old rum — that is, one aged for as long as 25 years or more.

For a slightly more sophisticated tasting, sample a variety of rum styles from different parts of the Caribbean. If you're working with an especially knowledgeable (or well-stocked) spirits merchant, you may also want to add rums from other countries, as available.

Finally, consider a flavored rum tasting. You can compare several brands with the same added flavor (say, vanilla) or a variety of brands with different flavors (say, vanilla versus spices). This is definitely a tasting that requires a cooperative storeowner, but the rewards of working together can be dee-li-cious.

Want more information about the rums in your taste competitions? Table 12-3 lists some of the most popular rum brands, the name of the company that distills them, and the Web site to get all the information you could ever want about that brand.

Table 12-3	Rum Brands	
Brand	**Producer/Importer**	**Web Site**
Appleton	Brown-Forman Beverages	`appletonrum.com`
Bacardi	Bacardi USA	`bacardi.com`
Brugal	Shaw Ross International	`rum.cz/galery/ cam/do/brugal`
Captain Morgan	Diageo	`captainmorgan.com`
Cruzan	Cruzan, Ltd.	`cruzanrum.com`
Mount Gay	Remy Cointreau	`mountgayrum.com`
Rhum Barbancourt	Crillon Importers	`crillonimporters.com`
10 Cane	Moet Hennessy USA	`10cane.com`

Gettin' to tastin'

Start your engines, sorry, taste your rums. Your first taste should be plain rum, no mixers. Here's what you do:

1. **Pour about an ounce of rum into your tasting glass.**

2. **Observe the color.**

   As with all spirits, the darker the color, the longer the liquor has been aged.

3. **Swirl the glass and watch how quickly the liquid flows back down the sides.**

   Slow sliding is another sign of aging.

4. **Inhale the aroma.**

5. Taste the rum.

For plain rums, the predominant flavors are brown sugar, caramel, leather, molasses, sugar, tobacco, and vanilla.

For flavored rums, the important point is that the flavor tastes just as the flavor should — vanilla flavored rum should taste like vanilla; a spiced rum should taste spicy. And in all cases, they should taste clear and pleasant rather than heavy or "off."

Trying the rum with mixers

To get a real feel for the versatility of rum as a spirit, try the same rums (minus the flavored ones) with mixers other than tap water. Cola is by far the favorite, but other possibilities include sparkling bottled water, club soda, lime juice, other citrus juices, and pine-apple juice or similar not-so-sweet tropical fruit juices.

Yo ho ho, Hollywood style

Now, it's time for a break to take a short quiz. If you score 100 percent, you earn yourself a cocktail made with some top grade rum. Fifty percent entitles you to a beer. No fair checking with Netflix or the Internet Movie Database. This test shows how good a memory you have of the movies you've seen (or at least heard about).

Match the actor with the role by answering the question "Who starred in this film?"

1. The Pirate (1948)	a. Steve Reeves
2. Pirate Warrior (1964)	b. Buster Crabbe
3. Pirates (1986)	c. Lex Barker
4. The Pirates of Penzance (1983)	d. Johnny Depp
5. Pirates of the Caribbean (2003)	e. Kevin Kline
6. Pirates of the Coast (1961)	f. Walter Matthau
7. Pirates of the High Seas (1950)	g. Ricardo Montalban
8. Pirates of the Seven Seas (1962)	h. Jon Hall
9. The Pirate Movie (1982)	i. Christopher Atkins
10. Pirate Ship (1949)	j. Gene Kelly

Answers: 1. j; 2. g; 3. f; 4. e; 5. d; 6. c; 7. b; 8. a; 9. i; 10. h

---

Part IV
Enjoying the "After Dinner" Specials

The 5th Wave   By Rich Tennant

"It says here the word 'brandy' comes from a Dutch word meaning burnt wine. At last, something appropriate to serve at one of your barbeques!"

In this part...

At the end of the meal at the end of the day, two special spirits treats await: Cordials/liqueurs and brandy. The former is the spirits' singular bow to sweetness; the latter is the *ne plus ultra* (translation: absolute tops) in sophisticated spirits.

Chapter 13

Cultivating Brandy

In This Chapter

▶ Discovering how brandy is made

▶ Appreciating brandy's worldwide fame

▶ Deciphering the initials on a Cognac label

▶ Deciding how to drink your brandy

*T*his chapter explores the wide world of brandy, the spirit many people mistakenly consider to be a wine. It explains why brandy is the most luxurious spirit and, some say, among the most complex in flavor as well as production. I also identify the different types of brandies and lay out standards for tasting and other matters that make drinking brandy one of the more satisfying rituals in fine dining (and fine living as well).

Brandy has always been one of the "luxury" spirits in terms of cost, taste, and general reaction. Brandy snobs may believe that all brandies are too expensive for a working class individual to purchase. Tell that to the young people in the hip-hop culture and the jazz buffs before them. Those snobs may consider the working class the least likely to drink brandy regularly because of the cost, but today they make up a good percentage of the total brandy market.

Obviously only a handful of individuals can afford to spend $1,200 for a bottle of Remy Martin Louis XIII — or even to purchase a single drink. But all social boundaries have been broken by the use of fine brandies in mixed drinks — one of the most popular for years in many poorer neighborhoods was called "Yak and Coke," referring to Cognac and the well known cola, and more recently Hennessy and orange juice has become popular.

Brandy snobs may mock this trend, but modern brandy makers don't. They've accommodated their markets by producing outstanding new brandies in packages that break the stereotypical brown bottle syndrome. Many outstanding brandies are made in other lands, and you can try them at moderate prices. And if you really want that bottle of Louis XIII, you can find it at a discount as low as $1,150.

The "Champagne" of Distilled Spirits

The word *brandy* comes to English from the Dutch word *brandewijn.*

The direct translation is *burnt wine,* which is how the straightforward Dutch traders described it to potential buyers when introducing their distinctive alcohol beverage to Northern Europe. They carried it through France and on to Germany sometime in the 16th century.

Italian vintners often take umbrage at the Dutch claiming credit for naming this spirit. In Italy, the name *brandy* is said to be descended from the Peidmontese word *branda.* But the Italians may be treading on thin etymological ice: The Italian-English dictionary at www.freedict.com defines *branda* as *a folding cot* or *hammock.*

In fact, even the Italians don't take the argument too seriously because they prefer their own version of brandy: *grappa,* a harsher distillation from the *pomace* (leftovers) of fruit fermented for brandy.

However, despite discussions about who invented the name, the following generalizations about brandy are true:

- ✔ All brandies are distilled from fruit wines, most commonly grape wines.

- ✔ All brandies are aged in wood, much like whiskeys (although brandy may be called by different names, such as *slivovitz* in Poland, *metaxa* in Greece, and *pisco* in Peru).

- ✔ All brandies, everywhere, are considered luxury products that conjure up the world of paneled libraries, fragrant cigars, and old-fashioned manners.

Where Do Brandies Come From?

Put a map of the world on the wall, toss a dart, and no matter where it lands, you've probably hit a country that makes brandy.

Yes, the Big Four — France, Spain, Italy, and the United States — dominate the market, but other places off the beaten brandy path make some interesting spirits.

France

Although France wasn't the first nation to make brandy, the French were the first to make their brandies a must-have in the salons of France and later the world. French brandy became the distilled spirit of royalty.

Today, French Cognac and Armagnac are the world's most regulated brandies, a situation that makes them the most expensive, long-lasting, and presumably best tasting. Figure 13-1 shows you where Cognac and Armagnac are located in France. Other French brandies include Calvados (apple brandy) and a variety of less serious fruit brandies.

Figure 13-1: The homes of Cognac and Armagnac.

Brandy, Cognac, and Champagne

Regardless of the type or where it's made, from time to time, aficionados describe brandy as the Champagne of the distilled spirits family.

Not because it has bubbles — it doesn't. Not because it's made from grapes — even though it is. Not because only the brandy made in Cognac, France, can be called Cognac, just as only the sparkling wine made in the Champagne region of France can be called Champagne. Brandy is the Champagne of distilled spirits simply because brandy — in particular Cognac — takes the most time to produce and requires the greatest skill to maintain consistency.

This brings up another brandy conundrum. Question: Is it brandy Cognac or is Cognac brandy? Answer: All Cognac is brandy, but not all brandies are Cognac. Only brandy made in the Cognac region of France is Cognac. Got it? Good.

Cognac

The vineyards of Cognac grow Ugni Blanc, Colombard, and Folle Blanche grapes planted by the Roman Emperor Probus (232–282 CE). The wines made from them were first shipped to Northern Europe in the 14th century.

By the 16th century the wines were distilled into *eaux-de-vie* (the clear spirit that's called by many other names, including vodka), and today's Cognac was born.

The Charentes region and six subdivisions were legally defined specifically for production of Cognac only. The six subdivisions are Grande Champagne and Petite Champagne (regarded as the two finest and mentioned on the label when their eaux-de-vie are used) as well as Bois Ordinaires, Borderies, Fins Bois, and Bons Bois (which are all considered lesser subdivisions).

In the 20th century, the Charentes region was recognized worldwide under agreements with the World Trade Organization. The agreements decree that if the label says Cognac, the brandy inside must have been made only in the Charentes region. Every Cognac brand is made from a blend of eaux-de-vie from various subdivisions during a specific year (read more about blending later in the chapter).

The designation "Champagne" in the two subdivision names is believed to arise from the fact that the place where Cognac is made and the place where the bubbly wine is made share similar *terroir* (translation: soil and climate) that produces low alcohol, highly acidic wines.

Armagnac

The second-ranking French brandy in the world is Armagnac, first documented and recognized as a brandy in the early 15th century.

It's made in the Armagnac region of Gascony in Southwestern France. As with the Charentes region where Cognac is made, Gascony is divided into several districts: Bas-Armagnac, Haut-Armagnac, and Tenareze.

Like Cognac, Armagnac is made from Ugni Blanc, Colombard, and Folle Blanche grape wines. And like Cognac, if the bottle says Armagnac, the brandy inside must have been made in that region.

So why is Armagnac usually ranked second to Cognac? One reason is that Armagnac was historically made by local farmers for home consumption. As a result, the brandy didn't always have the same consistency from batch to batch — Cognac did. And it was lacking a certain sophistication in the flavor.

However, since 1970, the use of portable stills brought by cart to the local vineyard by itinerant distillers (*bouillers de cru*) have been banned by French law, thus leading individual farmers to bring their goods to stills operated by more sophisticated cooperatives.

As a result, modern Armagnacs are more mellow than their predecessors. The reputation, however, has yet to catch up with the improved production.

Calvados

This well-loved brandy is made from Normandy's tart apples similar to American crab apples. Calvados comes from several regulated appellations. Contrôlée Pays d'Auge near Deauville is the top grade, followed by ten nearby districts called Appellation Reglementee.

All Calvados are aged a minimum of two years and have the same alcohol content. Although most brands carry an aging statement, unlike Cognacs, they're not legally bound to do so.

Eaux-de-vie (fruit brandies)

Fruit growing regions along the upper Rhine River produce what are generally considered the best brandy distillates (eaux-de-vie) in Europe.

In France, the Alsace region is well-known for berry brandies (particularly strawberry and raspberry), cherry brandies, and pear brandies (*poire*).

Talking Cognac and Armagnac

The most often asked questions about Cognac have nothing to do with the brandy itself. The questions, instead, are about the label. What in the world do all those designations mean?

The labels tell you how old the Cognac inside really is, as dictated by the very strict French laws governing such things. And you don't even have to know how to speak French. Just follow this handy guide:

- ✓ **A.C.:** Two years old. Aged in wood

- ✓ **V.O., Very Old:** Aged a minimum of four years

- ✓ **V.S., Very Special:** Three years of aging in wooden casks. Very often called Three Star

- ✓ **V.S.O.P., Very Superior Old Pale:** Minimum aging is eight years in wood for the youngest in the blend. Industry average is between 10 and 15 years old, which is why it's sometimes known as Five Star

- ✓ **X. O., Extra Old:** Also called Luxury. Has a minimum age of eight years. This class also can include Napoleon and Vielle ("Reserve")

- ✓ **Napoleon/Extra/Vielle Reserve:** Napoleon had nothing to do with it, except to order this type of Cognac. At least four years old, but generally much older than that

- ✓ **Varietal:** Made using only one type of varietal grape

- ✓ **Vintage:** Aged and was put into the bottle in the year of the vintage

- ✓ **Hors d'Age:** Too old to figure out the age. A true gem

Surprising consumer note: Armagnac is blended with older vintages than similarly labeled Cognacs. Hence, a V.S.O.P. Armagnac could be considered a better value than a similarly aged Cognac.

Many mass produced brandies simply labeled *French Brandy* are exported throughout the world. All are made on continuous stills, aged for an unregulated period of time in oak casks, and labeled with designations that have no meaning under French regulations. These brandies, sometimes blended with grape juice, wines, oak flavoring, and other brandies (including some Cognac), aren't unacceptable, but often the prices are obscenely high for what they are, so watch out for that.

Spain

Quick now, globally, where do the most popular brandies in the world come from? Chances are you said France. You'd be wrong. It's Spain, where the whole idea of differing spirits was born and where those spirits were sent to all the nations around the world conquered by the force of Spanish arms. Because of this, the world has a lot more Spanish-speaking people than French-speakers. And the Spanish-speakers in the many heavily populated parts of the world are culturally used to brandy.

The best known type of brandy is produced in a unique way. It uses the same system for aging, called *solera,* as port and the same grapes, from Jerez, used in making sherry. (This aging method is discussed in an upcoming sidebar.)

Spanish and French distillers use the same varietal white grapes for making their brandies, proving that sometimes great good grows out of disaster. In the late 19th century, *Phylloxera,* a grape-vine destroying aphid, virtually destroyed almost all the carefully tended grapevines in France. The Spanish vintners found some root stock for Ugni Blanc — the most important grape used in making brandy. That root stock hadn't been infected, so the Spanish helped their colleagues in France by sending the stock north.

Italy

Because the Italians are the third largest winemakers in the world, they don't particularly like to mess with brandies. The exception was introducing their Trebbiano grape to the rest of Europe, which, it turns out, is the same grape as the Ugni Blanc.

However, most of their wine brandies are made on column stills, which naturally makes them lighter and less complex. So, they find it hard to compete with the more artisanal types of French and Spanish brandies.

But the Italians do make and sell a lot of grappa on the world market. They make two types: the first is relatively raw, aged only long enough to smooth it out without changing the just-made flavor; the second is an expensive grappa made from a single grape varietal, aged for a longer period of time, and usually comes in a very fancy bottle.

The solera aging method

The distillers of the Iberian Peninsula had a jump on all those in other European countries. Distillation came to Europe and the rest of the world from North Africa when the Moors of that region conquered most of Spain. The Moors taught the peninsula dwellers about their alchemic arts, including how to turn fermented fruit into alcohol.

Initially brandy, much as other alcohol beverage types, was considered a medicine and a casual accompaniment for religious and celebratory occasions. Few vintners cared that their products tasted the same year after year. This meant that the producer of brandy might lose a customer the following year because his beverage didn't taste the same.

The Spaniards and Portuguese found a way to offset this commercial problem by aging their spirits using the solera method. The name *solera* either comes from the word *suelo*, meaning *ground* or *land,* or *solar,* meaning *the tradition that holds families together* ("solidarity" in English).

In this system, a series of oak barrels are placed in tiers sometimes ten barrels high. The bottom tier is called the solera. On top of that, the barrels range in age with the youngest (called *criadaras)* at the top.

The first wine removed from the tier is the bottom row, which is replaced by those on the next tier up. The solera barrels are used to fill the top tier barrels, which had been left half empty. This goes on continually.

Wine isn't allowed to be siphoned from one tier to the next one down, and by law, no more than one-third of a barrel can be removed at a time.

The reason for all this up-and-down? The infusion of older wines can "tame" the younger wines by taking away some of their original harshness. Removing the wine from the bottom barrel into a sealed container also allows it to "breathe" for a while in the open air.

Does it work? That's for your taste to decide.

United States

Before Prohibition, brandy was a big item for California wineries, dating back to 18th-century Spanish missionaries who introduced winemaking to the region. It became such an important item in world trade that for a time Leland Stanford (yes, the University endower) was the leading brandy producer in the world.

The triple bogey of Phylloxera, Prohibition, and the Plague of Worldwide War virtually destroyed the brandy business in the United States. With the help of expert vintners at the University of California–Davis, a California-style brandy was created. It was made on continuous stills, aged from 2 to 12 years in oak, and had a light uncomplicated flavor thanks to the table grape varieties (including Thompson seedless) that were used.

However, as the industry matured, some vintners started making their brandies from the traditional French white varietal grapes. They arrived at a brandy style ideal for drink making because of its clean taste. Like American tastes in wine, the California-style brandies have found wide acceptance in the mass global market. Another brandy gaining popularity is Slivovitz, made in Oregon and California from a black plum (called Mirabelle in France).

Another recent entry into the category is a number of brandies, including grappa, that are made from New York state fruits. Most are bottled in slender, very modern looking bottles at 80 proof (40 percent ABV). These brandies are beginning to get some serious attention, particularly from restaurant owners and those who like to try the latest "new thing."

Probably the oldest spirit made in the U.S. isn't from California, which wasn't even thought of in 1780 when Laird's was founded in New Jersey and issued distillery license #1 (see the nearby sidebar for more information).

Other places, other brandies

Brandy is produced in plenty of places around the world. You may not find the products listed in this section at your local tavern, but they may be worth trying when traveling in the vicinity of the producing country. You may even consider stopping at an airport duty-free shop on the way home.

Australia

Aussies aren't much for drinking brandy, but so much wine is available that it would be foolish not to use the excess for brandy. The spirit of the grape from Oz is generally light and on the lower alcohol side — sort of like California-style brandy. It's good for the money, particularly in cocktail making.

Black Sea region

Georgia and Armenia both make good brandies, including some for export. Drawing on their early teaching by monks, the brandies are intensely flavored using local grapes along with imported grapes, such as French Muscadine and Sercial and Verdelho from Madeira.

U.S. Distillery License #1

When William Laird from Scotland's County Fyfe landed in the New World in 1698, he had no idea that he would establish a family dynasty that would introduce a unique product that's still popular more than 300 years later.

William was a farmer who had a knowledge of distilling. He was looking around for a farm to develop in the new land of New Jersey, and he saw an abundance of apple trees. "Eureka" (or the Scottish equivalent), he said: The apples would be easy to distill into apple brandy, and so he did.

It's estimated that his first sale of Laird's Apple Brandy came in 1770 or thereabouts, but the first record of a sale was found in an operations account book maintained by his son Robert, who ran the Colts Neck Inn, in 1777. It recorded a sale at the price of "four shillings, six pence per gallon of cyder spirits." Later to be called Apple Jack.

Robert joined General Washington in the fight to establish a new nation and also played host to the army. He even found time to make the big boss feel better by sending him a requested recipe for cider along with some to drink.

When the new republic began licensing the production of alcohol beverages, Laird's was granted Distillery License #1, and they remained in their Scobeyville, New Jersey, location from then on. Laird's became the "oldest native distilled beverage in the United States," according to a state legislature proclamation of 1980.

Even during Prohibition, Laird's was given a special recognition and was permitted to continue distilling and selling apple brandy for medicinal purposes only. They also made nonalcohol sweet cider and applesauce.

The company is still prospering today under the guidance of William's descendants. Proving once again, quality and persistence pay off.

Eastern Europe

The best-known plum brandy is Slivovitz, which is made throughout the region of the Balkans and Eastern Europe and now in the United States. Several brands are available in many countries. Among them is *Manastirka* ("from the monastery"), a double distilled brandy made in Serbia from a black plum called *Madjarka*. It's aged for a minimum of ten years.

Germany

Using the German word *weinbrand*, German distillers have been making brandy since the 14th century (they formed their distillers' guild in 1588), primarily using imported wines.

Today, most German brandies are made on pot stills and aged for a minimum of six months. Those aged longer are identified as *uralt,* which means *older.* The best of them resemble Cognac, only lighter and with a sweeter finish.

Greece

The Greeks make a lot of brandies, the most globally famous of which is Metaxa. It's a wine with the herbal flavoring of a liqueur that's distilled two times, qualifying it as a brandy. The number of stars on the label indicate the age (*** = 3 years old).

Another popular Greek spirit is Ouzo, which is similar to Absinthe. It's a brandy-based wine flavored with anise that turns milky white when water is added.

Israel

Winemaking in Israel is as old as The Bible, but brandy only began in the 1880s when Baron Edmond de Rothschild established the modern Israeli wine industry. The brandies are made in the French style, similar to Cognac.

Latin America

Because the Spanish were the first Europeans to open trade with Latin America, brandy was introduced to the area in the 16th century. It wasn't generally taken to by the populations, except for those in Mexico. There, nearly all the wine made from Mexican-grown seedless Thompson, Ugni Blanc, and Palomino grapes is used for the production of brandy. And brandy is the most popular spirit in the country, beating out Tequila and rum.

Other than that, almost all other brandies in Latin America are made strictly for domestic consumption. The exception is the Andean region's Pisco, made primarily in Chile and Peru from Muscat grapes. Pisco has a light, slightly sweet flavor that makes it ideal for cocktail mixing, especially in the popular Pisco Sour.

South Africa

Brandy production started in South Africa in the 17th century with the arrival of the Dutch, but the spirit was so rough that it was called *witbits* (white lightning). Modern brandies, first produced in the 20th century, are made from the standard grape varieties plus Palomino grapes. Aging for a minimum of three years makes them far tamer than the original entries.

Brandy by Type

Regardless of where they're made, all brandies fall — more or less comfortably — into one of these three broad general classifications:

- ✔ Wine brandy
- ✔ Fruit brandy
- ✔ Pomace brandy

And just to complicate things a bit, some are known as *fine brandies,* while others, made with a different distilling method are called *mass produced.* Both methods are explained later, in the section "Distilling Brandies."

Wine brandies

Wine brandies, distilled from fruit wines, are the brandies that are most commonly available. They're the ones the average consumer is most likely to have tasted. More often than not, the wine from which the brandy is distilled was made from grapes, but, in fact, virtually every fruit wine — including oddities such as kiwi or pomegranate — has been used somewhere, by someone, to make brandy.

Fruit brandies

Fruit brandies aren't distilled from fruit wines; they're made by macerating (soaking) actual fruit, such as apples, in small amounts of high alcohol distillates to extract the flavor of the fruit. The newly-flavored alcohol is then used to produce the brandy.

Because fruit brandies are most commonly made from locally grown fruits that ferment easily, they aren't very expensive. As a result, they're very popular. Two well-known (and popular) fruit brandies (both made from apples) are Calvados and Apple Jack. As you can tell from the names, the first was born in France, the second in the United States.

Pomace brandies

When winemakers press the juice of fruit to make wine, what's left is *pomace:* skins, stems, seeds, and leaves. Not being folks who like to waste anything, winemakers put this aside to use for distilling (what else?) *pomace brandies,* high-proof spirits bottled with minimal (if any) aging.

The best-known and most popular of the pomace brandies is *grappa,* named for the Italian town Bassano del Grappa in the Veneto where it was first produced. Another Italian name for pomace brandy is *bagaceira.*

Other countries have still different names for their pomace brandies:

- ✓ Aguardiente or ourip (Spain)
- ✓ Alcool blance, eau-de-vie, or marc (France)
- ✓ Dop (the Netherlands)
- ✓ Testerschnapps (Germany)

Whatever they call it, though, it's definitely a brandy.

Distilling Brandies

The distillation of brandy is similar to the distillation of all other spirits. For the complete process, check Chapter 2. For the particulars on brandy, read on.

Choosing a base

The base for distilling brandy is a fermentable liquid, most commonly wine made from the traditional white varietal grapes. However, virtually any plant or vegetable product containing sugars may be used. From soft fruits, such as berries, to sugar cane, honey, rice, milk, grains, and tubers (yes, potatoes too).

During World War II, Londoners who really must have wanted their brandy, made wine out of cabbage leaves and carrot peels. They then distilled what must have been strangely flavored wines, and made equally strangely flavored brandies. And to be clear: There is no record of Winston Churchill, patriot that he may have been, ever dunking his cigar into a glass of cabbage brandy.

Bringing out the spirit

The initial step in brandy production is to allow the base to ferment in a large vat for about five days as the sugars are converted to alcohol. As a rule, white grape wines usually ferment to about 10 percent alcohol content.

Berry good, thank you

Every kind of fruit (except grapes) falls into the fruit brandy category. Not "fruit-fla-vored," which is another thing entirely. How come? Simple. Fruit-flavored brandies are actually cordials to which sugar must be added to differentiate them from true brandies. True brandies are sugary enough naturally. And grapes contain the most sugar of any fruit used for distillation.

To make a fruit brandy, the fruit is first crushed, and then macerated (soaked) in a high-proof spirit. The blended extract is then removed and distilled once at a low proof. In this way, the flavor is preserved as fresh and natural.

As in other distillations, the fermented liquid is pumped through a series of filters into either a pot still or a continuous (column) still. It's then heated to boiling so that the alcohol (which boils at a lower temperature than water) rises to be captured and condensed into a liquid that's about 52 to 64 proof (26 to 32 percent ABV).

A second distillation, which the French call *la bonne chauffe,* produces a liquid that's about 72 proof (36 percent ABV).

 When distilling other spirit types, such as whiskey, distillers strive to produce a distillate free of most flavors and aromas. Not so with brandy. Here, distillers prefer to hold as much flavor in the distillate as possible in order to qualify it as brandy.

Aging

Having reached a recommended level of alcohol, the brandy is then pumped from the still into wooden casks/barrels (generally oak). There, it rests for anywhere from 2 to more than 50 years, absorbing flavor from the casks themselves and losing about 1 percent of its alcohol a year through evaporation (called "the angel's share").

Even though they're made from fruit wine, brandies don't get mellower with age after they're bottled. The time in the barrel is what counts here. When you take into account that percentage of alcohol that's lost while the brandy is in those barrels, you can understand why connoisseurs relish a well-aged brandy. It has less alcohol but a more pronounced fruit flavor.

Material that was filtered out of the wine before distillation is compacted to concentrate the remaining juice. The entire mass is distilled again to make pomace brandy, which retains the taste of the original wine used. While the other brandy types are then aged, pomace brandies are filtered again and bottled to preserve that original wine flavor, which can be lowered or even lost entirely when aged in wood.

Blending

A fine brandy such as Cognac is actually a blend of various Cognacs from various sections of the appellation district and aged a varying length of time.

Before removal from the barrel and before bottling, distilled water may be added to the oldest of the brandies. This addition keeps the alcohol at around 80 proof (40 percent ABV). Sugar and caramel may also be added to make the color of the brandy consistent from year to year.

How did that great big pear get into the little bottle?

One of the more unusual brandies is *poire,* made mostly in Austria and Switzerland. It's set apart from other fruit brandies because, instead of merely the fruit essence, it actually has a fully ripe pear in every bottle. The pear is macerating in the pear brandy.

Many people buy a bottle of poire not for the taste — which is terrific if you like pears, and who doesn't? — but to keep on the mantle for guests to marvel at and ask, as practically everyone does, "How do they get the pear into the bottle?"

Easy: First the brandy-making fruit farmer culls through his pear trees — Anjou pears for Poire William, the best-selling brand — to find one or more with pears that have ripened just to the size of a grape. He gently manipulates the branch, with the pear still growing on it, into a brandy bottle.

Then he waits until the pear is mature, cuts away the branch, washes the pear (inside the bottle), and fills the bottle with pear brandy.

Voila, as the French might say — a big pear in a little bottle.

Tasting Brandy

Tasting is tasting.

The instructions on how to structure a tasting in Chapter 3 are as valid for brandy as for any other spirit.

Of course, I do have some special adaptations. Right here. Read on. But first, create your tasting sheet by copying this sample in Table 13-1 or drawing up your own.

Then read on.

Table 13-1	Brandy Tasting		
Brand	*Appearance*	*Aroma*	*Flavors*
#1			
#2			
#3			
#4			
#5			

Tasting by type

If you're tasting by type, just follow these steps:

1. Decide which type of brandy you wish to taste.

2. Consult your favorite liquor store.

3. Choose two or three brands.

4. Taste.

Most experts recommend beginning with the French Big Two, Cognac and Armagnac. Just pick some bottles with the appropriate type on the label. If they're all from France, French law makes sure that you're getting the proper spirit.

Comparing Calvados with an American apple brandy such as Laird's is a more interesting experiment in the effects of geography and culture on brandy.

Pomace brandies are an acquired taste, but if you sample two or three, you may soon be able to distinguish different flavor notes in brandies from different countries.

Tasting by country

Another way to taste brandies is to pick out an entry from several countries and taste them all at one sitting (around the world on brandy).

Use Spanish brandy as your baseline, and then move on to those non-solera method aged brandies from California, noting the differences in flavor and aroma. Table 13-2 is full of selected examples for this kind of tasting.

Table 13-2	Selected Examples of Brandies from Different Countries
Country	*Brand-name Brandies*
Armenia	One of the earliest brandy producing regions. Their best-known brand-name is Ararat, which is currently being made and distributed by Israel's Carmel Wines because of the problematic political situation in Armenia.
Australia	Virtually any reputable wine producer, such as Penfold's, makes a brandy or two as well as their usually well made wines. The problem is getting them. Because the wineries make so little brandy, most of it is consumed domestically.
Germany	One of the best-known modern German brandies is the well known Asbach Uralt. It has a robust but very smooth taste because of its cask aging (uralt means *old*) and French-style blending.

(continued)

Table 13-2 (continued)	
Country	**Brand-name Brandies**
Israel	Winemaking in Israel is as old as, or older than, The Bible. But French interests subsidized the making of kosher brandy in the mid-19th century. Initially on the sweet side, today the brandies, such as Yarden and Carmel, are based on the French model and have found a non-kosher audience as well.
Mexico	Mexicans vote with their money when it comes to selecting a brandy. Among the many brands offered in the country is their number-one favorite, Presidente, which is also the best-selling brandy in the world. It's made in the Spanish style, and a solera-aged version is available too.
Peru	Peru and Chile have been actively battling in the courts for decades about where Pisco originated. Until the argument is settled, let's just say it's an Andean region style of brandy that's very popular. Now generally available anywhere in the world is Capel Pisco.

Tasting by price

Price comparisons are probably the worst way to select brandies for tasting. Unlike some other beverage types, brandy isn't terribly susceptible to wildly changing prices.

Rule of thumb? The older a brandy, the higher the price. Why? Because the distiller has to recoup the investment he made while the brandy sat quietly mellowing in his cellar.

Obviously then, a 50-year Cognac is exponentially more costly than a virtual baby of only four years. But some people prefer the lighter (younger) brandies — even if they aren't the ones legends are built around.

You won't know until you try.

What you taste (and smell) when you sniff and sip

Table 13-3 tells you all about the flavors and aromas of the various types of brandy. Incidentally, when you're talking about how spirit affects your nose, use the word *aroma* rather than *smell* — particularly with an upscale product like brandy. And when you're discussing how it affects your palate, it's always more sophisticated to say *flavor*, referring to the sensual experience, rather than *taste*, which makes it sound like a Twinkie ("My, that tastes good.").

Table 13-3	Brandy Flavors and Aromas
Brandy Type	**Flavors and Aromas**
Cognac	Caramel, chocolate, cigars (and the wooden box), cloves, honey, molasses, nuts, oak (from aging barrels), prunes, smoke, vanilla
Armagnac	Various floral scents, various dried fruit flavors
Calvados/Apple Jack	Apples, oak, vanilla (plus many of the flavor components in Cognac and Armagnac)
Fruit Brandies	Fruit from which the brandy was made (plus many of the flavor components in Cognac and Armagnac)

Serving Brandy: Neat or Mixed? Warm or Cool?

What's so great about drinking brandy? Here's what Samuel Johnson (1709–1784), the eminent British writer and philosopher, had to say:

> "Claret is the liquor for boys, port for men, but he who aspires to be a hero must drink brandy."

Brandy works as an aperitif, as a cooler mixed with club soda, or, in the traditional fashion: sipped in the drawing room as a substitute for a really rich dessert.

Brandy should never be frozen. The flavor is too delicate to take much ice, which is not to say that it has to be heated. Room temperature is usually the right serving temperature. If someone wants it chilled, drop in an ice cube or two. Let the aroma out before drinking by letting the bottle stand open for a few minutes before you start.

The final decision about the tasting is how to serve the brandy. Some brandies are light enough and designed to be mixed with a lot of other things, including colas. Other brandies turn up their noses (and yours) against diluting their wonderful aged taste with some upstart soft drink or even fresh fruit juice.

The top brandies are the product of centuries of experience and years of skilled work. The Cognac producers are highly honored in France for their endeavors. The recommendation of all those who appreciate the top of the spirits line is not to mix Cognac with anything, but to save it for after the meal. Drinking good aged brandy, seated in front of a roaring fire on a chilly winter's eve following a hearty meal while smoking a great cigar is a cliché, but it's also something that everyone should try at least once.

Modern brandy drinkers, however, accept the idea that a lighter, California-style brandy makes the perfect base for fruit or fruit-flavored cocktails. Examples of brandy in cocktails are the Brandy Alexander or brandy as a substitute for Bourbon in a Mint Julep. (See the classic drink recipes in Chapter 15).

For more brandy cocktails, check out the master source: *Bartending For Dummies,* 3rd Edition, by Ray Foley (Wiley).

Pairing Brandy and Food

Brandy's richness goes well with lush, high-fat, fully flavored foods such as

- Pate de fois gras
- Roast meats and poultry (duck, goose, beef, lamb, venison)
- Whole milk cheeses
- Whole milk desserts (ice cream, crème caramel)
- Rich egg desserts (zabaglione)
- Dense, moist cakes (fruit cake, pound cake)

Brandy is also a welcome ingredient in an elegant sauce with peppercorns for duck à l'orange or steak. Or you can simply add a little to your French onion soup, pour it over vanilla ice cream, or stir it into your coffee. Sometimes, as architect Frank Lloyd Wright said, "Less is more."

Flambé — with care

Who enjoys the theatrical moment of a dessert or a cocktail that bursts into brilliant flame right before his very eyes? Everyone.

Who totally hates to see the napkins go up in flames along with the dessert or drink? Everyone.

Flambé is an art not to be practiced by the unschooled. Professionals prevent conflagrations simply by remembering that every 80 proof (40 percent ABV) brandy burns easily at room temperature.

So first they chill the bottle, and then they pour the brandy into a heated spoon or ladle over the serving bowl or glass, dropping a sugar cube in the brandy to serve as a "wick" for the flame.

Then they light the thing . . . very carefully, at a safe distance from the drinker or diner.

If you're moved to try this, don't. Not without a really good lesson from a really good teacher. That's my fire prevention lesson for the week.

Winston and brandy: A classic twosome

One of the truly great men of the 20th century, Winston Leonard Spenser Churchill (1874–1965) served as Prime Minister of England during World War II. Even in times of deepest crisis, he never missed his brandy and cigars.

Every evening Churchill took the time for a good cigar and a good glass of Cognac (he preferred Hine). So seriously did he enjoy these nowadays guilty pleasures that legend credits him with the notion of dipping a cigar into the brandy to give the cigar a special richer flavor.

Not that Sir Winston invented the ritual of cigars-and-brandy for the guys after dinner. Credit for that generally goes to the Prince of Wales who became King Edward VII, and who drove his mother Queen Victoria to distraction because she hated smoking.

The ritual has changed a lot since then. Today, where smoking is permitted (Sir Winston would surely wince at that!), the ladies are likely to light up alongside the gents as all lift their brandy glasses to toast one of those moments that makes life just a little better.

Chapter 14

Collecting Cordials, Lining Up Liqueurs

In This Chapter

▶ The sweet side of alcohol

▶ How an alcohol beverage started as a medicine and ended up a dessert

▶ The difference between generic and proprietary

▶ Choosing what to taste among hundreds of types

*I*n the 12th century came the discovery by alchemists of how to bring out the essence of agricultural products to create *al-kohl,* the medieval cure-all.

Next came teaching others the many ways to make and use this remarkable "water of life." It took about 800 years from the discovery of distillation in the 9th century until monks in France learned how valuable the sweet-tasting, health-giving benefits could be in saving lives if they added flavors to alcohol.

So were born *liqueurs* in the form of two that taste so good they remain popular to this very day: Chartreuse and Benedictine. Both were named in honor of the monastic orders where they were first created.

The further development of the most complex, colorful, tasteful, and varied of all distilled spirit types has blossomed (like many of the plants and flowers used in their production) since the 1600s. These new products used combinations of so-called *neutral spirits* (clear with little or no flavor) made from grain or wine or other agricultural products with (or over) fruits, flowers, plants, their juices, or other flavoring materials. And the monks used various means to bring out the best of their flavors in a controlled and standardized manner.

They turned these early pharmaceuticals into a tremendous variety of colorful, different-flavored, spirit products. And that led to the huge industry known and enjoyed all over the world today as cordials or liqueurs. The popularity of cordials has never dimmed; popularity that lasts for 400 years must mean something. In the case of these beauties, it means variety, reasonably low cost, generally lower alcohol, and great use in drinks and in cooking.

The Birth of the Liqueur

Many historians attribute the first compounding of sweetened herbs and alcohol to Italy's Salerno University of Medicine and Science. The art of turning medicine-taking from "ugh" to "wow!" was ultimately obtained by Catherine de Medici, who was a member of one of Italy's ruling classes (and also one of the world's great poisoners). In 1536, she introduced her new husband, King Henry II of France, and his French court to what is today called a *cocktail*. The Rossoli was a varied mixture of everything from jasmine leaves to chamomile and sugar steeped in alcohol by Italian peasants to ward off "the Death" (the superstitious peasantry's term for the Bubonic Plague).

In very short time, this "medicine" became a favorite of the French aristocracy. They most likely appreciated the mood altering capabilities more than they did the effectiveness in warding off the plague and other death-dealing ailments.

During the Renaissance, the practice of adding alcohol to well-known medications became far more prevalent among the elite. Many upper-class households had a dedicated "still room" for making distilled spirits to be used in cosmetics as well as for drinking. Women of the house used the same distillation methods to make rosewater to improve complexions, and water of ground up cloves to relieve stomachache, obesity, and worms.

Further proof of the Italian origin of these remarkable variations on an ancient theme arrived in London in 1749 in the person of Giacomo Justerini. He brought with him a number of complex recipes for making liqueurs. Signore Justerini's name and his "apothecary" shop have lived on. So has his partnership with Alfred Brooks, which made J&B Scotch whisky a household name among the British Royal family and today's more moderate drinkers as well.

While people in many countries were creating more types of medicinal liqueurs, innovative distillation was growing on a parallel track. It didn't take too long for the two to join hands.

The monks were the first to realize the potential benefits of adding aqua vitae to a distillate of herbs, leaves, or even plant roots. They quickly started using the new method to get patients to take their medicine. In the 16th and 17th centuries, hundreds of concoctions were born (naturally including "love" potions). In 1510, Benedictine monk Dom Vincelli created the still-used recipe for Benedictine Liqueur. Only in more recent times has scientific progress discovered the chemical agents that made those homely plants and flowers a preventive for heart attacks. Now they can be put into a simple pill or capsule, eliminating the original bad taste as well as the alcohol. Only in the last generation have the facts been learned about how the healthful effects of these botanicals continue to operate even in an alcohol base.

Today virtually hundreds of cordials/liqueurs use fruits and other ingredients to add flavors undreamed of by the Moor Jabir, the world's first distiller. Modern liqueurs are the biggest category of all spirits if you look at the number of brands, and it's the third best-selling category worldwide. Not surprising considering that cordials come at a far lower cost than other, more heavily taxed types of spirit.

The first "medicines"

Prior to World War I, the only "medicines" available were first concocted as far back as prehistoric times by using plants and herbs found in local regions. If you're watching all the ads on TV today, that's hard to believe. But back then, botanicals were ground up and water was added, and then, often over much protestation, they were administered — foul tasting or not. The "medicine man" could always blame the water — and he would generally be correct. These initial attempts to provide sick people with some relief through the wonders of chemistry may have worked, sort of, but they were rarely taken as prescribed and they certainly weren't enjoyed.

As tastes grew more sophisticated to the point where meat was cooked before eating, the flavor of these locally produced medicines didn't sit so well with the masses. They blamed the "doctors" for not making the medicines more effective.

Then came the discovery of honey, and later, sugar cane (see Chapter 12). Medicine men quickly realized that, as Mary Poppins sang many centuries later, "a spoonful of sugar helps the medicine go down." In a desire to make their medicines more effective, the pharmacists of the day added a little sweetness by adding honey, dates, figs, or the ground up sugar cane to make their medical selections more palatable.

When they mixed the powders with alcohol instead of water — wow! — the difference in their patients' moods and attitudes were markedly less hostile.

Cordial? Liqueur? A tale of two words

Before I go any further, you should know that the words *cordial* and *liqueur* refer to the same alcohol beverage type. The only difference is that *cordial* is more common in the United States, while the Frenchification of the word *liquor* into *liqueur* belongs to the Europeans.

Interestingly, both words have Latin roots. Cordial is from the Latin word *cor,* which means *heart* in English. Liqueur is taken from the English word *liquefaction,* which in turn is from the same word in Latin that means *the process of liquification,* and that's particularly apt when applied to creating a liqueur made from ground up ginseng roots, for example.

The United States Standards of Identity originally gave the category the designation of *cordial.* But liqueur has a more upscale tone to it, so it became more common throughout the world.

According to every standard of identification worldwide, cordials and liqueurs are made by "mixing or redistilling distilled spirits with, or over, fruits, flowers, plants or [their] pure juices, or other natural flavoring materials or with extracts derived from infusions, percolation, or maceration." They must contain sugar, dextrose, or levulose not less than 2.5 percent by weight of the finished product.

A host of other controls factor into production, and are shown on the label. Examples include the use of imitation flavors, the type of spirit used as a base, and so on.

Cordially Yours: The Making

Cordials have a wide spectrum of flavors available from the potential basic flavoring ingredients. So, the tastes offered depend to a large extent on the experience and skill of the distiller, the ways in which the flavors are obtained, and the exact formulation of ingredients. Making cordials is a skill and an art. It requires a wide knowledge of the earth's plants, flowers, fruits, herbs, vegetables, and almost every other botanical product found even in the most remote parts of the world.

As an example or two, consider the recent introduction of a pome-granate cordial — a fruit mentioned lovingly in the Bible — or the awareness of the fruit of an African tree, the marula. It was reborn as a cordial called Amarula, which has a delightful taste when per-colated into an unflavored spirit.

When someone goes to make a cordial, he or she takes this very complex knowledge and puts it to use in basically the same way that other distillers use their knowledge to create other spirit types. Liqueurs are made by using many types of spirits for a base, ranging from grain neutral spirits through brandy and rum and surprisingly even to already-juniper-berry-flavored gin. To the base spirit, the distiller adds the flavoring agents compiled from his secret recipe and then mixes with care and attention.

Choosing the base spirit

Distillers select the base spirit of a cordial on the basis of flavor, availability, and blending potential with the prime flavoring agent. Each different spirit has a distinctive taste. Will the earthy notes of Tequila go well with a scented flower? Alternatively, can the juniper-laden gin blend in with a pomegranate flavor? Or, can a sweet sugary rum match up with a sweet herb?

Economic choices are also involved. If brandy is the base, it doesn't make economic sense to use a vintage Cognac. Or does it? Should a vodka made from low cost wheat or corn be used, or should the more exotic vodkas from grapes make the flavor base?

Finally, a decision must be made on how high the final price of the liqueur should be — value priced, premium, super-premium? That too has a definite effect on how much the distiller pays for all the ingredients.

Marking the differences

Years ago, the trade agreed that in order to keep order in the mar-ketplace, various price ranges designating the quality level of the liqueur inside should be set and given names. In a bow to the French, they were *Ordinair* for the lowest quality, up the ladder through *Demi-fine* to *Fine,* and ultimately to the top, *Surfine.* In these days of global marketing, you rarely see these designations, but they're in the pricing if not on the label.

To further assist the consumer, however, all liqueurs are still classi-fied as *Crème* when they're thick and extra sweet; *Balm,* which has a thick consistency; or *Water, Extract,* or *Elixir,* which are all lighter.

Today, liqueurs are also classified by the flavor type. Most confusing of these are *Crème* and *Cream*. The first is a category generally indicating a single flavoring agent, such as crème de cacao, which is a sweeter, more heavily sugared liqueur with a cocoa flavor. Cream, as in Bailey's Irish Cream, is a category that came into being in the 1980s. These liqueurs are made by using a technology invented in Holland to stabilize dairy cream and give it a shelf life of about two months without refrigeration. Cream liqueurs are blends, usually of a whiskey and fresh stabilized dairy cream. You can also find rum creams and even an Amarula cream. The most common flavorings come from chocolate, mint, and coffee. The best part of these dessert liqueurs is that they last for a long time and still taste fresh. But shelf life isn't much of a worry in your refrigerator — the drinks are so delicious that they don't generally last two months.

Generic liqueurs are usually classified as non-descriptive *Liqueurs*. This class includes Sloe Gin, which is made from sloe berries on a neutral spirit base.

Another category of liqueurs are *Fruit Brandies,* which are a colorless neutral brandy base to which a blending of similar fruit flavors have been added. The use of flavored brandy most likely arose years ago in the Cognac region of France where flavored Cognac was often a preferred way to drink their native classic. Alizè is a flavored Cognac and therefore classified as a liqueur.

Finally, you have *Schnapps,* which is similar to a flavored *eaux-de-vie* (the French version of vodka) but with no added sugar. In the United States, even schnapps must adhere to the requirement that all cordials have a given percentage of sugar added.

Adding the flavor

Having determined the spirit to use as a base, the next step in making a liqueur is determining how to get the flavor into the finished product.

The most common methods for extracting flavor from a botanical include the following:

- ✔ **Maceration:** The flavoring agents for the recipes are soaked in the spirit and agitated. When the maximum flavor has been leached from the botanicals, they're removed, and the remaining solids are filtered out. Maceration is generally used for delicate fruits, such as berries and bananas, where the flavor can't stand up to harsher methods.

✔ **Infusion:** This method is similar to maceration, and it's the most inexpensive way to capture the essences of dried leaves and plants. If you know how to "steep" tea, you know how to infuse. The botanical material is moistened until it's soft. Then it's covered with the base spirit and allowed to steep in that. This results in much of the flavor being transferred to the base.

✔ **Percolation:** Have you ever brewed coffee? This is the same thing. The heated spirit is pumped through the flavoring ingredients over and over again. It's generally used with tough-covered flavorings, such as beans or pods.

✔ **Distillation:** This method is very similar to the way gin is made except that juniper berries are rarely, if ever, used. Botanicals are dried and put into a pot still. The base spirit goes directly into the pot still with the botanicals, or into a special type of tray placed at the "head" of the still. Then the material is put through the still, which condenses the vapors from the alcohol and the botanicals together. Generally, a second distillation is used to make certain that objectionable flavors are totally removed. This is the costliest way of getting the base spirit and flavor together. Distillation is generally reserved for rinds, flowers, and other more highly flavored botanicals.

The final touches

After going through one or more of the processes I describe in the previous section, the resulting flavored liqueur that comes off the still can be as high as 100 proof. Pure water is used to reduce the proof. Most of the modern liqueurs are in the low-alcohol range, between 25 proof (40 percent alcohol by volume, or ABV) and 70 proof (35 percent ABV). The mandated alcohol level for fruit brandies is 70 proof. Some liqueurs, such as Chartreuse and Curaçaos, are permitted to be bottled at a higher 110 proof (55 percent ABV).

Next, the mixture is sweetened with simple sugar, honey, dextrose, or another type of natural sugar. Then the liqueur is aged for a short time to help all the flavors "marry." Blends in which distillers want to avoid any additional accidental flavoring are aged in stainless steel tanks. On the other hand, if the distiller wants more flavor, the liqueur can be aged in wood casks to bring the wood's extra flavor agents into the blend. Some macerated liqueurs aren't aged at all.

After this, the distiller adds color — usually natural — if desired. A few liqueurs are chilled before filtering to remove certain unwanted oils that could cause clouding. If the liqueur contains colloidal materials, they can be "fined" by being filtered through albumen or milk that sinks to the bottom of the vat where it attracts particles that are undesirable and makes it easier to remove them.

With the constant demand for new and improved flavor thrills in liqueurs, many distillers have turned to food technology. Using mixtures of natural and manmade flavors, for example, can produce flavors that taste cold when you take the first sip of a liqueur and then turn hot in your mouth. Nothing is wrong with using this technology, provided the ingredients have been approved for food and drink consumption.

This kind of innovation, however, is frowned on by many high-end producers. Marie Brizard, for example, has been making all natural liqueurs since 1755 when, legend has it, nurse Marie brought a sailor back to health. In appreciation, he gave her a recipe for an "elixir" that could cure all ills. She and her nephew, Jean-Baptiste Roger, set up a company to produce this remarkable product and called it Anisette. The company is still making it the same way.

The two types of cordials

Not all cordials are equal.

Some are "generic," made using a single commonly known and commonly found flavoring agent. These cordials are used primarily in cocktail making. About 40 are generally available, including such standard items as banana, cassis (black currants), cherry, coffee, kümmel, peppermint, sloe gin (sloe berry), spearmint, triple sec (orange), and a back bar full of others.

The other types are called "proprietary" because they're made from exclusive recipes created and maintained by the brand producer. Many of these cordials may use one of the generics as part of their mixture, but they all add their own special secret ingredients. Some of the most famous proprietary cordials are listed in Table 14-1.

Table 14-1	Famous Proprietary Cordials	
Cordial	*Primary Flavor/ Made From*	*Country of Origin*
Absinthe (now legal)	Wormwood	France
Amarula	Tree fruit	South Africa

Cordial	Primary Flavor/ Made From	Country of Origin
Chambord	Raspberry	France
Cherry Heering	Cherry	Denmark
Cointreau	Orange	France
Dr. McGillicuddy's	Cinnamon	Canada
Elisir du Dr. Roux	Herbal	France
Frangelico	Nut flavor	Italy
Hpnotiq	Tropical fruits	France
Irish Mist	Whiskey	Ireland
Jägermeister	Licorice	Germany
Kahlua	Coffee	Mexico
Southern Comfort	Bourbon	USA
Villa Massa	Lemon	Italy
Vermeer	Chocolate	Holland

Cordials by the Ingredients

Because of the already vast number of products called liqueurs, some way to put them in order had to be established. The following sections tell you about the general categorization used by cordial producers. Please keep in mind that with the current rush to flavor, questions arise as to whether (or even why) a gin should be flavored with raspberry. And, if it is, is it a cordial or just another in a line of gins from one distiller? That conundrum gets even worse when dealing with vodka because vodka has no flavor of its own — that's one of its major selling points. So, is it vodka when it tastes like mangos?

All these questions are just a way of leading into the excuse that if you get confused by the categories and the products that are in them, think how you would feel if you had to deal with those questions every day of the week.

Fruit flavors

One of the most popular flavor families used in liqueurs are fruit flavors. The offerings are expanding rapidly as tropical fruits, such as mango, kiwi, marula, and maybe even some fruits yet to be known are added to the arsenal.

Sometimes the distiller can use the entire fruit, including the pit (as in apricots), and sometimes he can use only the flavorful part, such as the peels of citrus fruits.

Eaux-de-vie (see Chapter 13) that's on the shelves in the U.S. isn't a true brandy. Rather, these products are fruit-flavored brandies that are generally at lower alcohol levels than the true eaux-de-vie. And even fruit-flavored brandies may be flavored with something unusual.

Table 14-2 lists a generic type of cordial, and then, where there are any, gives a brand name or two of liqueurs made with that flavor in **bold face.**

Table 14-2	Fruit-Flavored Cordials
Flavor Source	*Generic Description (Brand(s) in Bold)*
Apple	This is the alcohol version of apple cider, the all-American drink. Low alcohol level. Not to be confused with Apple Jack, which is a true brandy.
Apricot	Another fruit that can be either a liqueur or a flavored brandy. Made from the kernel. **Marie Brizard Apry.**
Banana	Sweet and heavy with a sometimes-overpowering banana flavor. Inexpensive versions sometimes smell like furniture polish. **Pisang Ambon** (Holland).
Blackberry	Made as a liqueur and a flavored brandy. The brandy is a traditional liqueur with purported medicinal properties.
Cassis (Currant)	Crème de cassis made in the U.S. has a very berry taste. When mixed with a good white wine, it makes a very tasty Kir. The best drink and the best cassis come from around Dijon in Burgundy, France, where both originated.

Flavor Source	*Generic Description (Brand(s) in Bold)*
Cherry	Made as a liqueur and a flavored brandy. Bright red with a so-so cherry flavor. European cherry liqueurs have a much brighter flavor. **Maraschino** is distinctive liqueur made only from Marasca cherries from Italy and the Dalmatian coast by distilling the pits and the pomace left from cherry wine. **Stock** (Italy). Most famous cherry liqueur: **Cherry Heering** from Denmark.
Cranberry	Bright red with an astringent taste. Made in the U.S.
Lemon	Growing in popularity throughout the world is **Limóncello,** the low alcohol modern Italian liqueur often found in European bars where no other liqueur is served. Pungent lemon-lime flavor is very cooling. Made by many producers from local citrus. **Villa Massa** is particularly good quality.
Lime	Light green; made with lime peel. Fairly sweet and 40 proof (80 percent ABV). **Freezolime.**
Melon	Light green with a pleasant honeydew flavor. **Midori.**
Orange	Two generic types. **Curaçao,** first made on the Dutch Caribbean island of the same name uses peels of the local bitter orange. Also available in blue. **Triple Sec** is made from both bitter and sweet peels in the U.S. **Grand Marnier** is a triple sec made on a base of Cognac. **Cointreau** is double distilled to get a "dry" flavor said to be three times drier than regular orange liqueurs, which gave birth to the "triple sec" designation.
Peach	Made as a liqueur and as a brandy. Not very "peachy" until Hiram Walker made **Peachtree Schnapps,** which turned the whole peach business upside down. **Southern Comfort** is made on a Bourbon base. It starts as a 100 proof (50 percent ABV) whiskey that's mixed with peaches and peach liqueur to bring the alcohol level down. Is it a liqueur or a whiskey? This purely American drink can usually be found on the liqueur shelves. It was originated by Louis Herron, a St. Louis bartender who later moved to New Orleans and named it.
Pear	Wonderful pear aroma, but taste is hard to duplicate. **Marie Brizard** and most other French labels are better.

(continued)

Table 14-2 (continued)

Flavor Source	Generic Description (Brand(s) in Bold)
Raspberry	Not many made in the U.S., and those from France are rated as far superior. **Chambord Royal** black raspberry is ranked among the best for color and aroma.
Sloe berry	Called sloe gin, but the sloe berry is actually a plum. The liqueur is made with cherries and other flavorings that give it a bright red color. Despite its name, it isn't made from a gin base.
Strawberry	Very tough to make liqueurs that taste like strawberries. Best versions of strawberry flavor are from France and made with wild berries.
Tangerine	**Mandarine Napoleón** is made on a Cognac base using North African tangerines. Other versions are made with South African tangerines, also on a brandy base.

Seeds and nuts

Fruits aren't the only flavor bases for liqueurs. Other botanicals, like seeds and nuts, also make for great beverages. Check out Table 14-3.

Table 14-3   Seed and Nut Cordials

Flavor Source	Generic Description (Brand(s) in Bold)
Absinthe	The famed French *Fèe Verte* ("Green Fairy") was said to cause madness and was ultimately banned from all European countries and the U.S. It was made from anise and wormwood, which was deemed to be poisonous. Traditionally, the 72 proof (36 percent ABV) liqueur was diluted with water, and poured over a sugar cube while it turned pearly white. In the last few years, chemists determined that what made Absinthe so dangerous was a poisonous substance called *thujone*. Removing that made Absinthe once again legal, and it's now available in the U.S.
Anise	One of the most widely used flavors — licorice — is from this seed. **Anisette** includes some other flavorings to add depth to the licorice-like taste. It's usually clear but occasionally tinted red. European versions are more complex than those made in the U.S.

Flavor Source	*Generic Description (Brand(s) in Bold)*
Anise Aperitifs	A broad range of liqueurs with a licorice-like taste were made in imitation of the then-banned Absinthe. Usually with an alcohol volume of 90 proof (45.5 percent ABV). Clear, but when water is added, they turn pearly white. Best examples of these: **Pastis,** a French generic (except for one produced by **Ricard**), **Ouzo** (from Greece), **Raki** (from Turkey), **Herbsaint** (from the U.S.). Generic types are also made in Spain and Italy.
Caraway	Used in making Kümmel, which was originally made in Holland in the 16th century. This liqueur also includes cumin seed and has an aftertaste of anise. The **Allash Kümmel** made in Germany is regarded as being top quality.
Chocolate	Crème de cacao is the primary liqueur that uses chocolate. It can be either brown or clear, and it's primarily for use in making cocktails. A lot of generic types have chocolate blended with coffee, mint, or fruits. Among the proprietaries are: **Droste Bittersweet,** which tastes like a Nestle chocolate bar; the Swiss **Marmot,** which has actual pieces of chocolate floating in it; **Sabra** from Israel, which is a chocolate-orange liqueur; from Holland, **Vandermint,** which, as indicated, is a blend of chocolate and mint; and **CocoRibe,** made with Virgin Islands rum. The most recent famous chocolate names added to the liqueur lists are **Godiva Chocolate, White Chocolate,** and a ready-to-drink cocktail with vodka.
Coffee	Crème de café, crème de mocha, and coffee liqueur are all names given to some generic types of coffee liqueur. Coffee-flavored brandy has a higher proof and uses brandy as a base. Finally, branded proprietaries include the first coffee based liqueur, **Kahlua,** which possibly adds molasses for smoothness. **Tia Marie,** a product of Jamaica, has a lighter body.
Elder Bush	The fruit of this bush has a unique flavor and is used in making higher alcohol (80 proof or 40 percent ABV) and a sweet slightly licorice flavor. **Sambucca Romano** is probably the best-known.

(continued)

Table 14-3 *(continued)*

Flavor Source	*Generic Description (Brand(s) in Bold)*
Herbal	**Goldschlager** is one of the more unusual liqueurs because it has real flakes of gold — a mythical aphrodisiac — in its mixture of herbal flavors. **Galliano,** the liqueur that started the rush to highly flavored products with the Harvey Wallbanger after World War II, is made in Italy and is named for an Italian war hero. The herbal vanilla flavor is less complex than similar liqueurs made in France and gets very little aging. **Jägermeister** is a huge recent success story in the U.S., although it's been made in Germany since 1878, where it's designated as bitters. It's best enjoyed chilled and downed quickly. **Licor 43** ("Cuarente Tres") is named for the 43 ingredients that go into its making; it's based on an ancient farmer-made drink. **Tuaca Liquore** has a lighter than typical herbal-vanilla flavor and a light amber glow.
Pits and kernels	Fruit pit kernels, such as those found in peaches and cherries, give a bitter almond flavor to a number of nut-flavored liqueurs and fruit-flavored types. **Amaretto Disaronno** is the first and best example of a bitter almond version. **Frangelico** is another favorite made from nuts, but this one is made from hazelnuts. The generic crème de noyaux and crème de almond are made from almond and fruit pit kernels.
Mint	Crème de menthe is one of the most classic generic liqueurs. It's colorless but is sometimes tinted green, red, or occasionally gold. Peppermint Schnapps is a colorless, drier version.
Spices	Spices are generally used as accent flavors, but you can find Cinnamon Schnapps and Ginger Schnapps as well as a ginger-flavored brandy.
Tea	**Suntory Green Tea** is the best-known brand, but with the increased interest in tea as a dinnertime beverage, new types are coming onto the market nearly every month. Like tea? You'll love tea liqueur.

Branded, spirit-based

Some liqueurs are derived from a flavored whiskey base. These liqueurs weren't hugely successful until recently; their growth in popularity could be due to the more accepted use of spirits in general, specifically whiskey.

✔ **Bourbon:** The exact ingredients in Southern Comfort are still a mystery, but it is known to be based on Bourbon, which is logical given the name. Used as a mixer for many years, it's still a favorite among young adult drinkers.

✔ **Canadian whisky:** Yukon Jack has a citrus flavor blended with herbs and a long Canadian whisky finish. It's 72 proof (36 percent ABV).

✔ **Irish whiskey:** Irish Mist was born in the mists of time when warring clans ruled the land and the recipe for making "Heather Wine" was closely guarded. The formula disappeared when Ireland was invaded. In the 19th century, distillers tried to fathom the recipe but failed. The story is that in 1948, an Austrian refugee turned up at a distillery with his family's recipe for a heather liqueur known to be of Irish descent. It was tried and the Heather Wine was discovered again — or maybe that's just a typical Irish yarn.

✔ **Scotch whisky:** Drambuie has a touch of honey to sweeten the herb-spice blend, and it has a touch of Scottish peat. Drambuie Cream adds stabilized fresh dairy cream to smooth things out. This secret recipe was held by the McKinnon family from 1745 until 1906 when the liqueur finally went public. It started as a gift, after the Scottish Rebellion of 1745, from Bonnie Prince Charlie to Charles McKinnon, who had given him sanctuary. The prince gave McKinnon the recipe, calling it *an dram buidheach* (the drink that satisfies). Everyone knows the name, but the recipe remains a secret.

Cream liqueurs

A number of attempts to produce liqueurs with a fresh cream taste had failed to meet the shelf life test; they turned sour quickly while waiting for a customer. The most public examples were the low-priced, ready-to-drink cocktails called Heublein Cows — they tasted wonderful but turned sour in a couple of weeks. This notable failure turned most producers sour, too. Almost a decade later, Dutch technicians finally found a way to stabilize fresh dairy cream.

The increased shelf life of at least two months opened the way to an entirely new kind of cordial. A recipe was developed for Bailey's Irish Cream made on an Irish whiskey base with light chocolate, coffee, and coconut flavors.

Bailey's success encouraged others, and soon the market had a number of cream cordials — enough to warrant a new category. Today you can find a number of whiskey-based cream cordials as well as Myers's Rum Cream; Droste Cream, flavored with bittersweet chocolate from Holland; Kahlua Cream with coffee and cream; and even Venetian Cream, based on Italian brandy with almond, butterscotch, and coconut. One of the latest cream liqueurs is Tequila Rose, which, despite its name, is a strawberry-flavored liqueur with a Tequila base.

Oh yes, Bailey's now offers caramel and mint variations.

Bitters

Bitters aren't really liqueurs in the popular sense, but they're classified as such because they use the same kinds of ingredients. Bitters, however, are more closely related to the era when concoctions of known curative botanicals were added to alcohol. They were intended, then and now, as a medicine to relieve stomachaches and hangovers, and to aid digestion. And they really taste like that's what they're meant to do.

All bitters are just what they're called, and some of the most popular are:

- ✔ **Amer Picon** is made in France using cinchona bark and, thank goodness, bitter orange to disguise the flavor. Cinchona bark is also used to make quinine, which helps alleviate malaria. French fans drink Amer Picon over ice and never mix it with anything else.

- ✔ **Angostura Bitters,** now made in Trinidad, were originally concocted in Angostura, Venezuela (now Ciudad Bolivar, Venezuela) by a Dr. Sigert. The good doctor was intent on developing a medicine to help ward off tropical diseases. With 45 percent ABV, it was actually a pleasure to drink. Today, most important is its contribution as a flavor enhancer for food and in cocktails.

- ✔ **Cynar** (pronounced *chee' nar*) is a perfect trivia question because it's the only spirit made from artichoke leaves. In Italy, it's garnished with a slice of orange and served as an aperitif. Cynar is also frequently used in cocktails where its distinct herbal flavor is an addition.

- ✔ **Campari** is the world's favorite bitter today. It was developed in 1860 to celebrate Italy's unification, and the same formula is still in use. That consists of herbs and fruits "from four continents," which are aged in oak. Campari is also the main ingredient in two classic cocktails — the Americano and the Negroni.

- ✔ **Fernet Branca** has been available since 1845. In the U.S., it could be sold in food stores until about 1960 when the IRS insisted that it be sold only in licensed liquor stores. It's hard to believe that the combination of 40 herbs and spices could be an effective digestif, but millions swear it is.

✔ **Peychaud's Bitters** is a purely American product. It was first made in New Orleans in 1793 by Antoine Peychaud, a refugee Haitian apothecary. It's no longer used for curing every tropical disease, but it lends its unique flavor — a few drops at a time — to Creole cuisine or cocktails with Southern flair.

✔ **Punt e Mes** is a bitter vermouth with a recipe dating back to the 1700s. The name means "point and a half," and legend has it that the name was given to the product by an Italian stockbroker.

Two classic liqueurs

Chartreuse is called "the world's most mysterious liqueur." Its recipe was recorded in the 16th century by an alchemist who gave it to local Carthusian monks as a "health liqueur." The monks perfected it and protected it from hundreds of nefarious folk who wanted it for themselves. Even in the face of torture during the French Revolution, the monks never disclosed the recipe. In 1817, when France was a little more hospitable, they resumed production of the liqueur.

The recipe for Benedictine was first recorded in 1510 by its creator Dom Bernardo Vincelli, a monk at the Benedictine abbey in Fècamp, France. The abbey was destroyed during the French Revolution. Seventy years after the Revolution was over, one M. LeGrand reintroduced the liqueur commercially. An arrangement with the Benedictine order permits use of the name and the initials D.O.M. The initials stand for *Deo Optimo Maximus* (to God, most good, most great). Brandy was added in 1920 along with the two-headed bottle and bottleneck that permitted mixing from a single source.

A Cordial Tasting

You can go to your favorite liquor store and enlist the clerk's assistance in selecting the kind of tasting you want to do. Here are the two most common types:

✔ **Horizontal:** Try this kind of tasting if you want to sample the entire output of a single producer.

✔ **Vertical:** For this kind of tasting, you select the type of liqueur that most interests you and compare the flavor, color, and general appeal of a liqueur from one distiller with the same product from another distiller.

Want to make your own liqueurs? Here's how

Once upon a time, farmers and others made spirits as a hobby. Many of the liqueurs shown in these pages originated that way. A peach farmer took some of his tastiest peaches, squeezed out the juice, and mixed it in with the local whiskey. Then he aged it a little and put it in a bottle — *voila,* as they say in France — peach liqueur.

There's a gentleman by the name of James A. Duke, PhD, who has four books published on the subject of turning regular garden herbs into tasty liqueurs and healthful teas. Dr. Duke was a specialist in medicinal plants for the U.S. Department of Agriculture Research Center for many years until his retirement.

His books mention that using homegrown materials to make liqueurs may or may not help your health, but they can help your mood. The books, several of which are available through Amazon.com, include *Living Liqueurs, The Green Pharmacy, Herbs of the Bible, Dr. Duke's Essential Herbs,* and *The Handbook of Medicinal Herbs.*

The living ingredients in *Living Liqueurs* are identified by handsome pen and ink illustrations. The book gives a complete history of every one of more than 175 ingredients suitable for use in making your own liqueurs.

After you decide which liqueurs you want to taste, the next step is to open the bottles to let them air for a short time. Then pour some of the liquid into suitable cordial glasses, and use a tasting sheet like the one in Chapter 3 to start recording your observations.

Liqueurs are probably the most versatile type of spirits that you can possibly use. They're occasionally enjoyed neat, or with carbonated nonalcohol beverages, or as an ingredient in either a cocktail of your own imagination or a replica of a classic.

In tasting, keep in mind that the products under scrutiny should always be the center of attention. Some liqueurs should be chilled, but none should be frozen. The objective is to taste the balance and complexity of the blend. That's hard to do when the bottle has been kept in the fridge for a day or two.

Just follow these steps for a successful tasting:

1. If the room is warm, chill the liqueur bottles slightly before opening to hold down the alcohol bite, to tone down the more strident flavors, and to let the fruit flavors shine.

2. Open the bottle and pour into one of the many lovely cordial glasses that are available today.

Using cordial glasses is important because they have a wide mouth to let the aroma out. A cordial's aroma sets the stage for what's to follow, the color provides the setting, and the taste is the star.

3. Try the same liqueur three different ways. First, neat and warm; next slightly chilled; and finally through a layer of crushed ice in a taller glass.

Step three may seem to be a lot of trouble to go through for a taste or two of one liqueur, but keep in mind the difficulties some of the early distillers — such as the Benedictines — had. You may be scorned, but you'll never be beheaded for not doing it the "right" way.

That's became there is no right way to serve liqueurs except to enjoy them in their crazy variety and to remember the history of the type, which adds to the romance of drinking them.

Here's a toast to offer during the tasting:

May the roof above us never fall in, and may we friends gathered below never fall out.

And if you really want to show off, check out the Pousse Café sidebar for the most difficult cocktail ever conceived.

Pairing Foods with Cordials and Liqueurs

Clearly, liqueurs are meant to be enjoyed before, during, or after a meal. Many liqueurs are specifically designed to be enjoyed before dinner to whet the appetite for what's to follow. Our suggestion is to serve lightly flavored liqueurs as aperitifs, particularly if the meal is to feature a robust entrée.

During the meal, choose a liqueur as a cooking accompaniment. The flavor of the liqueur should go well with the foods being served. For instance, ⅓ cup of Kahlua with ½ teaspoon of mustard stirred in can be a basting syrup for ham that may have your guests asking for the recipe. Pretend you're a master chef who just invented a new sauce and must keep it secret.

Fish soup for dinner? Why not add ¼ cup of Irish Mist to the fish soup? The heathery taste will add a grace note to the rest of your seasoning.

Of course, it's dessert time when liqueurs really shine. Dine out at a top restaurant and watch for the cordial tray to come out with an array of delectable flavors to try.

For a fancy dessert at home, try thin dessert pancakes. Add 2 ounces of Grand Marnier to the pancakes and keep them thin, because you're going to pretend they're crepes. When browned on both sides, fold the pancakes, pour another 2 ounces of Grand Marnier over the top, light a long fireplace match, and keep your hand away from the pancakes: whoosh — flambé.

Always be careful where you set fire to your pancakes. If the flames go too high, you could scorch a ceiling or your best table. Keep a large plate on hand to smother any possible escaping flames. If all goes well, just make yourself a certificate from the Cordon Black and Blue — you earned it.

Liqueurs are fun no matter how you use them. So, have some fun with them. They'll cooperate.

The Pousse Café

In French, the name Pousse Café literally means "push the coffee down." In this case, you're pushing five types of liqueur and one base spirit. The name grew out of the fact that this drink is served most often with dessert as an after-dinner digestif, along with good, strong coffee. It's pronounced "poose ka-FAY."

Start making the drink in the most logical place, the bottom. That's important because if you do it correctly, you'll wind up with several layers of different colors (and densities, which is what keeps them separate).

First get a clean tall glass with straight sides, and start pouring with a very steady hand. Grenadine goes on the bottom. Then take a small spoon and, with the bowl side down, slowly drip one part Yellow Chartreuse over the spoon bowl so that it drips on top of the Grenadine. Next, get a clean spoon and repeat the layering with one part White Crème de Menthe. This ingredient should be followed by a layer of one part Sloe Gin (tinted red), followed by one part Green Chartreuse. Finish it off with one part Brandy.

This monster originated in New Orleans in the mid 19th century and became the rage of cities around the U.S. in the early 1900s.

(Recipe from Bartending For Dummies *with the compliments of author Ray Foley who says he can make one of these with his eyes closed — that's because he's dreaming.)*

Part V
The Part of Tens

"Oh, come on, you're just drinking it! You're not even tasting it..."

In this part . . .

This section, also known as "the fun part" of any *For Dummies* book, serves up classic spirits cocktails. You get the history as well as the recipes. I also give you recipes for ten delicious dishes made with spirits, and ten reasons why moderate drinking can be healthful. And if you're wondering just how nutritious your evening glass of spirits is, I give you nutritional information for ten popular spirits and cocktails.

Chapter 15

Ten (or so) Classic Spirits Cocktails

. . . .

In This Chapter

▶ Explaining the origin of the cocktail

▶ Turning Martinez into a Martini

▶ Identifying Bloody Mary

▶ Naming the sailors who fathered the gimlet

. . . .

*W*hen you're dining out and everyone is reading the menu, how often have you heard "I think I'll have a cocktail before eating"?

Now for the quiz: What is a cocktail anyway? Whether you're dining out or at home, the modern cocktail is defined as any alcohol-based drink with more than one ingredient — no umbrellas or pink cherries required. Read on to learn where it all comes from.

This chapter, being one of the Part of Tens, serves up ten classic spirits cocktails. Then, like any good barkeep, we add one more for the road.

The majority of the recipes in this chapter come from *Bartending For Dummies,* 3rd Edition, by Ray Foley (Wiley). Some recipes come from the *Mr. Boston Platinum Edition* (Wiley).

Oops! Tomato Juice on My Blouse: The Bloody Mary

Vodka first saw the light of day in Russia, or maybe, as Chapter 10 explains, Poland. After World War I, the spicy morning-after pick-me-up combination of vodka and tomato juice was whipped up by

American-born Fernand Petiot (ca 1900–1975) at the famed hangout of American expatriates, Harry's New York Bar in Paris. In the mid-1920s, the drink made the clear spirit a favorite with his clientele.

Petiot may or may not have named his drink after a barmaid at Chicago's Bucket of Blood tavern, where he had served as a bartender. And he may or may not have named it for a customer who, having spilled some over her white blouse, noted that it made her look like "Bloody Mary," the beheaded Scottish Queen, sister of Queen Elizabeth I.

For sure, when Petiot came to America in 1934 to become head bartender at New York City's St. Regis Hotel, the management at that ritzy establishment considered "Bloody Mary" vulgar and changed it to "Red Snapper." But customers who had met the drink in Paris insisted on the original name, and, just like that, a new bar star was born.

Petiot's own recipe was simplicity itself. Half vodka, half tomato juice. Period. By the time he got back to America, he was tossing a bit of this, a little of that — black pepper, cayenne pepper, Worcestershire sauce, Tabasco sauce, lemon juice — into the original half-and-half. Modern bartenders have taken it upon themselves to codify the quantities into something that looks like the following.

What's a cocktail?

According to the *Online Etymology Dictionary,* the word *cocktail* first surfaced around the turn of the 19th century. No one knows for sure where it came from, although H.L. Mencken, the eminent Baltimore journalist and essayist, lists no fewer than seven possible points of linguistic origin, including a drink stirred with the tail feather of a rooster.

Another legend has it that a barmaid in New York State used a rooster's tail to stir the hot toddies she provided to male visitors because folktales based on the virility of roosters had it that the cock's tail had aphrodisiac qualities.

Perhaps the most likely antecedent is the French word *coquetier* (eggcup). This proposal is bolstered by the fact that New Orleans apothecary Antoine Amédée Peychaud (the man who created the still-famous Peychaud bitters in mid-18th-century New Orleans) is reported to have held social gatherings in his drugstore, where he mixed brandy with bitters and served the drink in, yes, an eggcup. In other words, the *coquetier,* which in English sounded like *cocktay* and slid seamlessly into *cocktail.*

You pays your money and you takes your choice.

Bloody Mary (from *Bartending For Dummies*)

> 1¼ ounce vodka
>
> 2½ ounces tomato juice
>
> Dash Worcestershire sauce
>
> Dash Tabasco sauce
>
> Dash salt and pepper

Pour vodka over ice in a glass. Fill with tomato juice. Add a dash or two of Worcestershire sauce and Tabasco sauce. To make it spicier, add a little horseradish. Stir, garnish with a celery stalk, and serve.

Alexander! Another Brandy!

Brandy fans generally warm their spirit, holding the round glass in their hands to "excite" the aroma molecules in the liquid so that they dance above the surface of the brandy, their grapey scent available to anyone who sticks his or her nose into the sniff.

However, in 1922, when the bartender at London's Ciro Hotel was asked to create an unusual and elegant after-dinner drink to serve at the wedding of Princess Mary of England to Lord Alexander Lascelles, he went another way. His innovation? The chilled Brandy Alexander, a creamy delight that was soon a favorite with elegant ladies in southern American cities, particularly New Orleans.

Their men may still warm their brandy and drink it the classic way, while smoking a fragrant cigar. If, that is, they can find a place where smoking is still legal!

Brandy Alexander (from *Bartending For Dummies*)

> 1½ ounces brandy or Cognac
>
> ½ ounce Dark Crème de Cacao
>
> 1 ounce sweet cream or ice cream

Shake with ice. Strain into glass.

War Is Hell, so Pass the Rum — in a Daiquiri, if You Please

Remember the *Maine?* The newest and finest American battleship of its day mysteriously exploded and burned on February 15, 1898 while docked in Havana harbor, and 300 crew members were lost. However, the country gained a really good excuse to move into aiding Cubans rebelling against the Spanish Empire.

The Spanish-American War began on April 25. Soon after, the members of the U.S. army — not to mention the war correspondents and Theodore Roosevelt — found themselves beating off not only the Spanish but also malaria transmitted by billions of omnipresent mosquitoes.

The victims had no effective medicine available, so they tended to rely on a mixture of locally made rum and various flavorings for relief. Eventually Jennings Cox, a member of the ever-resourceful Corps of Engineers, christened the cocktail the Daiquiri after the city on the east coast of Cuba where he and his troops were stationed.

Daiquiri (from *Bartending For Dummies*)

> 1¼ ounce light rum
>
> ½ ounce sweetened lemon juice

Shake or blend with ice.

The local rum was Bacardi, which created the drink in 1896 and then spent until 1936 protecting it as a Bacardi Daiquiri. The New York State Supreme Court ruled that the cocktail should be called the Bacardi Daiquiri and that was the rum to be used. Here's the original recipe.

Bacardi Daiquiri (the original recipe)

> 2 ounces Bacardi Silver Rum
>
> Juice of half a fresh lime
>
> ½ teaspoon of sugar or sugar syrup to taste
>
> Club Soda

Mix all ingredients with cracked ice in a shaker or blender; shake or blend until smooth. Strain into a chilled cocktail glass.

A Shipboard Romance: The Gimlet

In the late 18th century, Britannia ruled the waves — except when the waves bit back and sailors developed scurvy. This potentially fatal vitamin C deficiency disease laid them low on long voyages and often killed them.

In 1747, while serving on the HMS Salisbury, a Scottish surgeon named James Lind set up an experiment. He wanted to see whether changing the sailors' diet could protect them from scurvy's weakness and hemorrhages. Lind chose 12 Salisbury sailors suffering from scurvy and divided them into six pairs. Each pair received a different dietary supplement: cider; seawater; a garlic/mustard/horseradish mush; vinegar; or one of two citrus fruits (oranges or lemons).

You know which ones recovered: the sailors who ate the citrus fruits. Lind's discovery wasn't exactly new — lime juice was already recognized as an anti-scorbutic (a remedy for scurvy) — but it was conclusive. Now the problem was getting the sailors to drink the juice of bitter limes, the citrus fruit most likely to survive long voyages intact.

The official *Eureka!* moment came when a British Naval Surgeon named Gimlette recommended mixing the lime juice into the sailors' daily *tot* (a ration generally of London dry gin). The unofficial, and more likely, explanation is that the sailors took it upon themselves to open the kegs filled with lime juice and add the juice to take away the taste of the gin. The device used to open the keg was a corkscrew-like shipboard tool called — you guessed it — a gimlet.

Naval etiquette has changed a lot since then, but the simple recipe for a Gimlet has never been improved, except for those who don't particularly like gin. Today you can always substitute vodka.

Gimlet (from *Mr. Boston Platinum Edition*)

> 1 ounce fresh squeezed lime
>
> 1 teaspoon superfine sugar or simple syrup
>
> 1½ ounces gin

Shake with ice and strain into a chilled cocktail glass.

And here's the vodka substitution recipe:

Vodka Gimlet (from *Bartending For Dummies*)

> 1¼ ounce vodka
>
> ½ ounce fresh lime juice

Mix vodka with lime juice in a glass with ice. Strain and serve in a cocktail glass. Garnish with a lime twist.

Uptown, Downtown: The Manhattan

New York City prides itself on being the very center of the known universe, and the center of New York City is the island called Manhattan. There, in mid-Island, at the end of the 19th century, a very special cocktail was born. The natives say that it was created to please Jennie Jerome, the American beauty who later crossed the Big Pond to marry Lord Randolph Churchill; she later became the mother of Winston Churchill.

Jennie is said to have asked the bartender at the exclusive Manhattan Club to create a drink to honor the election of Governor Samuel J. Tilden — yes, the same man who lost the presidential election of 1876 in the Electoral College despite winning the popular vote. That's a recorded fact.

But, unfortunately, you can find dozens of different reports of exactly what the bartender put into the glass. However, if you order a Manhattan in a restaurant near the Empire State Building, which stands on the spot that once housed the Manhattan Club, this is probably what you'll get:

The Manhattan (from *Bartending For Dummies*)

> 2 ounces American or Canadian (blended) whiskey
>
> Splash sweet or dry vermouth
>
> Dash Angostura bitters

Stir with ice; strain into cocktail glass. Garnish with a cherry.

If You Knew Margie Like I Know Margie: The Margarita

During Prohibition, the Hollywood elite found an oasis in nearby Mexico. The liquor was plentiful, cheap, and legal. Especially the Tequila, served in a cocktail glass rimmed with salt and decorated with a wedge of lime. The drink was a favorite with the young Californians. They took it back to the States, where it became standard fare at cocktail hour — and at other times, as well.

As they say in Hollywood, flash forward now to several years later. The story shows Margarita Soames, a Texas socialite, looking for a new way to serve an old favorite at the annual holiday celebration in her Acapulco villa. She carefully adds an extra ingredient to the locally famous cocktail — the strong, clear, orange liqueur triple sec. Margarita's guests immediately vote her recipe *Numero Uno* and name the drink in her honor. As they say in documentaries, *olé*. The Margarita today is America's most popular cocktail after the Martini.

Margarita (from *Bartending For Dummies*)

> 1 ounce tequila
>
> 1 ounce Cointreau or triple sec
>
> 1 ounce sweet and sour mix or fresh lime juice

Blend with crushed ice. Serve in a salt-rimmed glass. Garnish with a lime wheel.

Margarita (from *Mr. Boston Platinum Edition*)

> 1½ ounces tequila
>
> ½ ounce triple sec
>
> 1 ounce lemon juice
>
> Coarse (Kosher) salt

Mix liquid ingredients with ice in a shaker or blender. Rub rim of chilled cocktail glass with a slice of cut lime. Rub the glass lip in a plate of coarse salt. Strain and pour liquids into the glass. Garnish with a lime slice.

The World's Most Famous Cocktail: The Martini

No one knows for sure who first decided to soften Dutch gin with dry vermouth. But most people are pretty sure that the event occurred on the U.S. West Coast, where the drink was created either by a San Francisco bartender named Martinez or by a traveler on his way to Martinez, California.

Others take a more jaundiced view, claiming the Italian winemakers Martini developed the cocktail to promote sales of the company's vermouth. In fact, as early as 1890, Martini sold bottles of a pre-mixed "American Drink" called the Martini, which rather suggests that they, too, gave credit to the Yanks.

Finally, you have the New York claim to Martini fame: The tale says that a Knickerbocker Hotel bartender named Martini mixed a drink that was half gin, half dry vermouth, shook it with ice and strained it into a chilled glass. He served the world's first crystal clear, dry Martini to (who else?) John D. Rockefeller.

If it was made with Old Tom, a popular Dutch gin, the original Martinez was slightly pink. Today, it may be multicolored — blue with added Curaçao, red with grenadine, yellow with citrus juice, green with apple flavored mixes, or brownish with coffee. True aficionados consider these an abomination, preferring them clear, the Knickerbocker way.

Martinez (from multiple sources)

> 1 ounce sweet vermouth
>
> 1 ounce gin
>
> Dash bitters
>
> 2 dashes Maraschino
>
> ¼ teaspoon triple sec

Stir with "two small lumps of ice" and strain into chilled glass.

Martini (from *Bartending For Dummies*)

> 2 ounces gin
>
> Dash extra dry vermouth

Shake or stir gin and vermouth over ice. Strain and serve in a cocktail glass straight up or over ice. Garnish with a lemon twist or an olive (even two).

A Cuban Cup of Cheer: The Mojito

Like the Bloody Mary, the Mojito (mo-HEE -to) is a drink whose origins are cloaked in legend. Its creation is variously attributed to pirates, slaves, and the scion of a very famous family distiller.

The pirate was Richard Drake, who mixed aguardiente (an unrefined rum), sugar, lime, and mint into a concoction he called *El Draque* (the dragon), the nickname of Sir Francis Drake (no relation). Drake was the 16th century Cuban-based British explorer who made his bones terrorizing ships in the Caribbean and ports along the coast of South America where El Draque (the cocktail, not the pirate) was enthusiastically welcomed.

A second story attributes the Mojito to African slaves working in the Cuban sugar fields, although many drinks historians think this tale confuses the Mojito with the Daiquiri, another Cuban-born delight.

Modern distillers give credit for the Mojito to a 19th century Cuban distiller named Don Segundo Bacardi. He is said to have mixed a few naturally available ingredients — sugar, limes, and mint — into his evening rum. This creation was a refreshing drink that was necessary after a day in the field or after dinner in the warm Cuban evening. When the Bacardis moved their distillery to Puerto Rico, Don Segundo's cooler became a favorite there, as well. Today, it ranks among the four most popular cocktails in the United States, along with the Martini in all its forms, the Margarita, and the Cosmopolitan.

In other words, if you mix it, they will come. To drink. In droves.

The Mojito (from *Bartending For Dummies*)

   2 ounces Bacardi light rum

   Eight mint leaves

   Juice of ½ lime

   2 teaspoons sugar

   4 ounces club soda

In a Collins glass, place mint leaves and lime juice, crush with a muddler or the back of a spoon, and add sugar. Fill glass with ice, add rum, and top with club soda. Stir well and garnish with a sprig of mint.

The Highland Fling: Rob Roy

The Scots aren't given to diluting their fine whisky with anything other than clear mountain water, if that. The Rob Roy is as close as they come to a national mixed drink. The drink was named for Robert MacGregor (1871–1734), a Lowlands sort of Scottish Robin Hood, who was celebrated in novel and poem by Sir Walter Scott and William Wordsworth.

Some New York food writers and theater historians say the drink was actually created in 1894 by a bartender at the original Waldorf Astoria. The hotel was located near Herald Square, around the corner, so to speak, from where a new operetta called "Rob Roy" had taken the city by storm. What better way to pay tribute to the show than to name a drink in honor of its hero?

Who's right? As usual, who knows? But once again, the pleasure of the drink is certain.

Rob Roy (from *Bartending For Dummies*)

> 2 ounces blended Scotch whisky
>
> Dash sweet or dry vermouth

Stir over ice and strain into a cocktail glass.

Simple Perfection: The Whiskey Sour

The very first recipe for a whisky sour appeared appropriately in the very first book of drink recipes, compiled and published in 1862 by British-born bartender Jerry Thomas (1825–1885). Thomas (also known as The Professor or The Father of the Cocktail) was as much a showman as a barkeep. He traveled the U.S., putting on stage demonstrations of his bartending skills. Ultimately, he wound up for a while at San Francisco's Hotel Occidental, where he's also credited with creating the Blue Blazer. He's known as the first man to create an organized system of drink families and categories.

The book is a 236-recipe soft cover called *The Bartender's Guide* or *How To Mix Drinks*. It's still useful for its information on recipes for homemade cocktails and cordials. Facsimile copies from New Day Publishing aren't available on Amazon.com at the moment, but you can see an image of the cover. Other versions were revised by Herbert Asbury, a New York newspaperman, in 1865 an d 1872. Vintage Books, a French publisher, has a copies available (in English) at www.vintagebook.net. You can also find it online at www.theartofdrink.com/book.

Classic Whisk(e)y Sour (from *Bartending For Dummies*)

> 1½ ounce rye whisky
>
> ¾ ounce sweetened lemon juice
>
> 1 teaspoon superfine sugar

Shake with ice. Serve straight up or over ice.

Horses, Grass, and Mint: The Mint Julep

You can get a good, brisk discussion going among Bourbon versus rum aficionados by asking which came first: the Mojito or the Mint Julep. Each side is likely to consider the other's candidate second in line.

In fact, the Mojito probably wins the race. According to *Famous New Orleans Drinks and How to Mix 'Em,* published by New Orleans bartender Stanley Clisby Arthur in 1937 and in print ever since, the Mint Julep arrived in Louisiana around the turn of the 19th century. It came to town along with aristocrats expelled from San Domingo, where the Mojito was already a favorite. Not surprisingly, Arthur's recipe for the original Julep is made with rum.

Eventually, of course, the Julep spread across the American South and north to Kentucky, where the Lords of the Land of Bourbon recast it as an American drink, made with American Bourbon. After the Julep was named the official drink of the Kentucky Derby, its place in spirits history was assured. And well deserved.

Mint Julep (from *Bartending For Dummies*)

> 2 ounces Bourbon
>
> ¼ ounce sugar syrup
>
> Five mint leaves

In a silver cup, mash four mint leaves with sugar syrup. Fill the cup with crushed ice. Add Bourbon and garnish with a mint leaf.

Shaker, shaker, who's got the shaker?

Serving spirits is generally a breeze: Open bottle. Pour spirits into glass. Drink.

Serving cocktails is another thing entirely: Mash. Muddle. Crush. Shake. Strain. Pour. Just getting to "drink" can be exhausting.

To make the job easier, the smart cocktail maker keeps several basic tools close at hand.

✔ **Blender:** Use it to smooth some drinks. In a pinch, a blender with a "crush ice" setting can be used to crush ice. No setting, no crushing. Unless you're the do-it-yourself type. If so, wrap the ice in a dishtowel, put the towel on a cutting board, and whack away with a meat mallet.

✔ **Cocktail shaker:** A two-piece container that looks like two large stainless steel or glass drinking glasses. Pour the ingredients into the larger half, clap on the top, and shake away.

✔ **Cocktail strainer:** A strainer that fits over the larger half of the cocktail shaker so that you can pour your cocktail into a glass minus pieces of ice and other floating stuff.

✔ **Long spoon:** Similar to an ice teaspoon, this tool is long enough to reach into the shaker and give everything a good stir.

✔ **Measuring cup:** A 1½-ounce jigger is good; an 8-ounce measuring cup is more versatile.

✔ **Muddler:** Cooks call this a pestle; the wooden or marble bat used to crush herbs and spices in the bowl is known as a mortar.

Chapter 16

Ten Spirited Dishes

In This Chapter

▶ Cooking with spirits

▶ Perusing Web sites with spirited recipes

Distilled spirits aren't just for drinking. In fact, from soup to nuts (actually, nut cookies), whiskey and other distilled spirits are valuable flavor additions to food recipes.

In other words, the ten recipes I share here — for starters, main dishes, side dishes, and desserts — are barely the tip of the ice cube, sorry, iceberg. But what a delicious beginning!

If you're interested in more examples of cooking with spirits, check out the Web sites in Table 16-1. The recipes in this chapter come from these sites but represent just a small sampling of what the distillers have to offer.

Table 16-1	Sources for Spirited Recipes	
Spirit	**Source**	**Web Address**
Applejack	Laird & Company	www.lairdand company.com
Bourbon	Wild Turkey	www.wildturkey bourbon.com
Gin and vodka	Gin and Vodka Association	www.ginvodka.orgz
Irish whiskey	Irish Distillers (Pernod Ricard)	www.jameson whiskey.com
Rum	Bacardi Distillers	www.bacardi.com

(continued)

Table 16-1 (continued)

Spirit	Source	Web Address
Scotch whisky	Scotch Whisky Association	www.scotch-whisky.org.uk
Tennessee whiskey	Jack Daniel Distillery	www.jackdaniels.com
Tequila	Jose Cuervo	www.cuervo.com

Chilled Melon Pepper Soup with Glazed Shrimp

This is a dish made for dining on a cool veranda on a warm evening in the Caribbean. The sun is setting over your shoulder as your waiter puts this chilled spicy dish before you and you dip in your spoon . . . wait! You can do that just as well sitting in your very own dining room as the air conditioner whirls, the same sun sets, and this cool soup with a hint of hot spice begins your elegant lunch or dinner. Lovely.

Yield: 6 servings

Ingredients

2 tablespoons Bacardi 8 Rum

2 red bell peppers, seeded and chopped

½ cantaloupe, seeded and cut into chunks

4 scallions (green onions), white parts only, chopped

1 small hot red pepper, seeded

1 cup orange juice

2 tablespoons lime juice

¼ teaspoon salt

1 cup plain yogurt

Ingredients (shrimp)

2 tablespoons Bacardi 8 Rum

2 tablespoons honey

Pinch salt

18 medium-to-large shrimp

Preparation (soup)

1. In a blender, puree Bacardi 8 Rum, red peppers, cantaloupe, scallions, hot red pepper, orange juice, lime juice, and salt.

2. Strain the liquid through a sieve into a large bowl.

3. Stir in yogurt.

4. Cover and refrigerate until cold, at least 2 hours or as long as 24 hours.

Preparation (shrimp)

1. Combine Bacardi 8 Rum, honey, and salt in small bowl and set aside.

2. Light a charcoal fire in a grill or preheat a stovetop grill pan.

3. Thread the shrimp onto skewers and grill 30 seconds per side.

4. Brush the shrimp generously with the rum glaze and grill 1 minute longer.

5. Ladle cold soup into six chilled soup bowls. Garnish each bowl with three hot glazed shrimp, and serve.

Game Pâté Terrine

So the local supermarket is out of the goose livers you need to make an authentic pâté de foie gras. Not to worry. Plain chicken livers with a dash of this and that — particularly your favorite gin — will do nicely. Serve the terrine with toast points, flash a mysterious Mona Lisa smile when complimented on the dish, and who will guess those livers aren't duck? No one, that's who.

Note: A *terrine* is a loaf made of pieces of meat or vegetables, cooked or chilled in a dish or pan with straight sides. The dish or pan itself is also called a terrine.

Yield: 8 to 10 servings

Ingredients

2 garlic cloves, peeled and crushed

1 teaspoon salt

7 ounces (200 mg) chicken livers, finely minced

5 ounces (150 mg) fresh pork belly, finely minced

5 fluid ounces (150 ml) gin

1 tablespoon grated orange peel

1 teaspoon ground allspice

1 teaspoon dried marjoram

Salt & freshly ground black pepper to taste

5 fluid ounces (150 ml) whipping cream

1 egg

1 tablespoon unsalted butter or margarine

Orange segments and watercress for garnish

Preparation

1. Mix the garlic with the salt to make a paste.

2. Stir together the garlic paste with the chicken livers, pork belly, gin, grated orange peel, allspice, and marjoram, and chill the mixture overnight in the refrigerator.

3. Thoroughly butter a terrine dish and set aside.

4. Beat the egg and cream together, mix into the chilled ingredients, and pack the mixture into the buttered terrine dish.

5. Scatter bits of butter on top of the mixture and bake for 45 minutes to 1 hour at 400 degrees F (200 degrees C).

6. Cool the baked terrine in the refrigerator. To serve, turn the chilled terrine out on a platter and garnish with orange segments and watercress.

Marinated Salmon

This recipe melds Scotch whisky with another famous Scottish export: salmon. The dish itself does double duty as the perfect illustration of proverbial Scottish practicality. Translation: You can serve it either as a cool appetizer in winter followed by a warm entrée, or as a cool main event at a summer lunch or dinner.

Yield: 2 to 3 servings

Ingredients

2 tablespoons Scotch whisky

2 tablespoons lemon juice

8 ounce boned, tail fillet of salmon

Salt and pepper to taste

½ teaspoon sugar

1 teaspoon chopped chives

1 tablespoon chopped dill

Preparation

1. Mix the whisky and lemon juice together and set aside.

2. Place the salmon on a platter, cover, and chill in freezer for 1 hour.

3. Use a very sharp knife to slice the chilled fish as finely as possible across the grain.

4. Lay the fish slices in a single layer on a plate.

5. Drizzle the whisky and lemon juice over the salmon; season with salt and pepper; sprinkle on sugar and herbs.

6. Allow the salmon to marinate (covered) in the refrigerator for least 1 hour or overnight, basting with the juices two or three times before serving.

Penne à la Vodka

When you think of pasta, the alcohol beverages that spring most quickly to mind are usually wines, red or white. This classic recipe, however, eschews wine for a distilled spirit, a surprising but delicious combination that goes well with white wine to match the color of the white pasta and sauce, red wine for contrast, or a vodka and tonic for consistency. Your choice.

Yield: 4 servings

Ingredients

1 pound penne, or other tubular pasta such as rigatoni

¼ cup unsalted butter

3 tablespoons tomato paste, diluted with ¼ cup hot water

1 hot pepper

⅔ cup fresh cream

¼ to ⅓ cup vodka

1 teaspoon brandy

1 cup freshly grated Parmesan cheese

Preparation

1. Cook the pasta according to the package instructions.
2. For the sauce, melt the butter in a large pot and stir in the diluted tomato paste and the hot pepper.
3. Let the mixture simmer over a low flame for a couple of minutes.
4. Stir in the cream.
5. When the sauce comes back to a boil, add the vodka and brandy.
6. Fish out and discard the pepper, stir in the grated cheese, and continue stirring gently until the sauce is well mixed and creamy.
7. Drain the cooked pasta and transfer it into the sauce.
8. Cook the pasta and sauce over a brisk flame, stirring for about 1 minute to help the pasta absorb the sauce.
9. Serve in warmed bowls.

Chicken Fajitas

In the mood for something spicy yet totally nutritious? Try this classic high-protein, fiber-rich, low-fat combination of chicken, beans, and grains (the tortillas).

Yield: 6 servings

Ingredients

1 tablespoon vegetable oil

4 boneless chicken breast halves cut into ½-inch strips

1 cup black beans, cooked

1 tablespoon grenadine (syrup made from pomegranates)

¼ cup orange juice

⅛ teaspoon chili powder

3 tablespoons Jose Cuervo Especial

¼ teaspoon garlic powder

1 cup chicken stock

2 tablespoons cornstarch

½ cup cold water

1 tomato, diced

6 flour tortillas, warmed

Preparation

1. Heat oil in nonstick skillet on medium-high heat.
2. Add chicken to skillet and cook 6 to 8 minutes.
3. Stir in the black beans, grenadine, orange juice, chili powder, tequila, garlic powder, and chicken stock.
4. Lower the heat to medium, and cook for 5 minutes.
5. In separate bowl, combine cornstarch and water until dissolved, and add it to the skillet mixture. Stir until thickened.
6. Add tomato, and heat through.
7. Divide the mixture evenly among the tortillas, fold the tortillas, and serve immediately.

Filet Mignon with Whiskey Sauce

The filet is generally considered the most tender cut of beef. But while the filet has tenderness and silky smoothness in spades, it lacks a little in the flavor department compared to other cuts of beef such as sirloin or rib eye. That's why it's a great idea to sauce up your filet, and that's where this recipe comes in.

Yield: 4 servings

Ingredients

4 small filet mignons (4 ounce each)

2 tablespoons butter

1 clove garlic, diced

1 teaspoon finely diced shallots

1½ cups mushrooms, chopped

1 teaspoon honey

½ teaspoon wholegrain mustard

1 ounce Jameson Irish Whiskey

¾ cup beef stock

¾ cup heavy (double) cream

Freshly ground black pepper to taste

Preparation

1. Melt the butter in a skillet over medium-high heat.
2. Add the filets and sauté until they're done to your preference. Transfer the filets from the pan to a heated platter, and cover them with foil to keep warm.
3. To the skillet, add the garlic, shallots, and mushrooms, and sauté over medium heat until soft.
4. Add honey and wholegrain mustard to the pan and stir.
5. Add the whiskey, and turn up the heat so that the sauce boils for 1 minute as the alcohol evaporates.

6. Turn down the heat and stir in the beef stock. Boil gently until the amount of sauce in the pan is reduced by half.

7. Stir in the cream, and continuing stirring until the sauce thickens.

8. Give the sauce a quick taste, and add salt and pepper as needed.

9. To serve, slice the filets, put them on plate, and pour the sauce over the top.

Green Beans with Toasted Pine Nuts

Never thought of adding spirits to veggies? Think again. The Bourbon whiskey in this side dish adds a surprising but delicious sweetness to the beans. Try this once, and you'll never go back to plain boiled string beans.

Yield: 4 servings

Ingredients

2 cups green beans

1 to 2 tablespoons vegetable oil

¼ cup pine nuts

2 tablespoons Wild Turkey Bourbon

Melted butter to taste

Salt and pepper to taste

Preparation

1. Immerse green beans in boiling water for 1 to 2 minutes. Drain, and set aside.

2. Heat vegetable oil in a medium sauté pan, add pine nuts, and toast until golden, about 1 to 2 minutes.

3. Remove the nuts from the pan (but don't wash the pan). Drain the pine nuts on a paper towel and set aside.

4. Put the green beans in the sauté pan, add the Wild Turkey Bourbon, and boil over high heat for 1 minute to cook off the alcohol.

5. Turn the heat down to medium-low and add the nuts. Stir the mixture over the heat for 1 to 2 minutes.

6. Serve hot with melted butter and salt and pepper.

Note: You can vary the recipe by substituting snow peas for the green beans and slivered almonds or shelled pumpkin seeds for the pine nuts.

Tennessee Whiskey Candied Apples

For a tart firm treat, use green or Granny Smith apples; Rome apples hold their shape as well as green apples, but deliver a slightly sweeter flavor. As you might guess, this dish goes particularly well as a side with roasted meats and poultry, but you could also top it with a dollop of unsweetened whipped cream and serve it as a warm or chilled dessert.

Yield: 6 servings

Ingredients
6 cups peeled and sliced apples

¼ cup butter

2 to 3 cups white sugar

Jack Daniel's Tennessee Whiskey to taste

Preparation
1. Combine apples, butter, and sugar in a large skillet.

2. Cook slowly over low-to-medium heat until the apple slices are tender but still hold their shape

3. Add the whiskey, and stir over high heat for 5 minutes to cook off the alcohol. Serve while warm.

AppleJack Pound Cake

AppleJack, an apple brandy, adds a warm, rich flavor to this traditional pound cake. To make an even richer dessert, toast slices of cake on a flat, nonstick pan, and top them with unsweetened whipped cream or vanilla ice cream.

Yield: 8 to 10 servings

Ingredients

1 pound butter or margarine

3 cups sugar, divided

8 eggs, separated

3 cups sifted all-purpose flour

2 teaspoons vanilla

⅓ cup Laird's AppleJack

½ cup chopped pecans

Preparation

1. Cream butter and 2 cups of sugar until light and fluffy.
2. Add the egg yolks one at a time, beating thoroughly after each addition.
3. Add flour alternately with vanilla and AppleJack (beginning and ending with flour), one third at a time, beating the mixture smooth after each addition.
4. In a separate bowl, beat the egg whites until stiff but not dry.
5. Stir the remaining sugar into the egg whites gradually and gently.
6. Fold the butter mixture gently into the egg whites.
7. Sprinkle pecans in the bottom of a well-buttered 10-inch tube pan.
8. Carefully pour the cake batter into the pan. Bake in a 350-degree oven for 1½ hours.
9. Turn the cake out onto cake rack to cool completely, and then slide it onto a cake plate for slicing and serving.

Nut Ball Cookies

Making cookies from cookies sounds over-the top, but trust me on this one. This combination of wafer crumbs, walnuts, and rum is a sure winner. And keep in mind that these cookies make a delectable gift for a really special friend.

Yield: 2½ dozen cookies

Ingredients

2 cups ground walnuts (from 2½ cups chopped walnuts)

1½ cups vanilla wafer crumbs

¼ cup Bacardi Superior Rum

¼ cup honey

Confectioners' sugar

Preparation

1. In a medium bowl, combine walnuts and wafer crumbs.

2. Stir in Bacardi's Superior Rum and honey.

3. Shape the dough into 1-inch balls.

4. Roll each ball in confectioners' sugar.

5. Store the cookies in a tightly covered container.

Chapter 17

Ten Nutrition Profiles of Alcohol Beverages

In This Chapter

▶ Listing the nutrients in your drink of choice

▶ Introducing the USDA's incredible online database

▶ Going beyond the basics to find out which beverages have more nutrients

*A*re distilled spirits food? Yes. Do they provide any nutrients other than calories? Sometimes. This chapter gives you basic nutritional facts for ten distilled beverages. It's enough info to satisfy the moderately curious.

If you really want to know just about all there is to know about the nutritional content of your favorite spirit, check out the USDA National Nutrient Database for Standard Reference, a long name for an incredibly handy database. It's available online at www.nal. usda.gov/fnic/foodcomp/search.

The entries listed here show you the basic nutrients — calories, protein, fat, and carbs. But some alcohol beverages have other goodies. For example, click onto the USDA site and call up coffee liqueur with cream. Yes, it has caffeine. No surprise there. But it also has a little calcium. Very little, to be sure, but there it is. Who knew? Pull up some other alcohol beverage products on the database to see what else is in your glass.

A note for cocktail fans: The cocktails listed in this chapter are the ones sold in cans. True, they don't provide the same delicate balance of flavors you get with a freshly made drink at your favorite watering hole. However, the USDA chose these versions for its database because they pour the same serving size and nutrients every single time. Consider them simply a nutritional guide.

Rum

The nutritional information for one jigger, or 1.5 fluid ounces, of 80 proof (40 percent ABV) rum is as follows:

- ✔ Calories: 97
- ✔ Protein: 0 g
- ✔ Fat: 0 g
- ✔ Carbohydrates: 0 g
- ✔ Ethyl alcohol: 14 g

Gin

For one jigger, or 1.5 fluid ounces, of 90 proof (45 percent ABV) gin, you get the following nutrients:

- ✔ Calories: 110
- ✔ Protein: 0 g
- ✔ Fat: 0 g
- ✔ Carbohydrates: 0 g
- ✔ Ethyl alcohol: 15.9 g

Vodka

One jigger, or 1.5 fluid ounces, of vodka at 80 proof (40 percent ABV) has these nutrients:

- ✔ Calories: 97
- ✔ Protein: 0 g
- ✔ Fat: 0 g
- ✔ Carbohydrates: 0.04 g
- ✔ Ethyl alcohol: 14 g

Whiskey

For one jigger, or 1.5 fluid ounces, of whiskey at 86 proof (43 percent ABV), you get:

- ✔ Calories: 105
- ✔ Protein: 0 g
- ✔ Fat: 0 g
- ✔ Carbohydrates: 0 g
- ✔ Ethyl alcohol: 15.2 g

Coffee Liqueur

Coffee Liqueur, 53 proof (27 percent ABV), has the following nutrients in one jigger, or 1.5 fluid ounces:

- ✔ Calories: 175
- ✔ Protein: 0.05 g
- ✔ Fat: 0.16 g
- ✔ Carbohydrates: 24.3 g
- ✔ Ethyl alcohol: 11.3 g

Coffee with Cream Liqueur

For one jigger, or 1.5 fluid ounces, of coffee with cream liqueur, you get a 34-proof (17 percent ABV) beverage and the following:

- ✔ Calories: 154
- ✔ Protein: 1.3 g
- ✔ Fat: 7.3 g
- ✔ Carbohydrates: 9.8 g
- ✔ Ethyl alcohol: 6.5 g

Whiskey Sour (Cocktail, Made from a Powdered Mix)

One serving with 2 ounces of mix and 1.5 fluid ounces of whiskey (106 g total) contains the following:

- ✔ Calories: 162
- ✔ Protein: 0.06 g

- ✔ Fat: 0.06 g
- ✔ Carbohydrates: 13.6 g
- ✔ Ethyl alcohol: 15.4 g

Tequila Sunrise (Cocktail, Canned)

The following nutrients are in one 6.8-ounce serving:

- ✔ Calories: 232
- ✔ Protein: 0.63 g
- ✔ Fat: 0.21 g
- ✔ Carbohydrates: 23.8 g
- ✔ Ethyl alcohol: 19.8 g

Piña Colada (Cocktail, Canned)

One 6.8-ounce serving has the following nutritional value:

- ✔ Calories: 526
- ✔ Protein: 1.3 g
- ✔ Fat: 16.9 g
- ✔ Carbohydrates: 61.3 g
- ✔ Ethyl alcohol: 20 g

Daiquiri (Cocktail, Canned)

One 6.8-ounce serving has the following nutritional value:

- ✔ Calories: 259
- ✔ Protein: 0.0 g
- ✔ Fat: 0.0 g
- ✔ Carbohydrates: 32.5 g
- ✔ Ethyl alcohol: 19.9 g

Chapter 18

Ten (or so) Health Benefits of Moderate Drinking

In This Chapter

▶ Defining moderate drinking

▶ Evaluating alcohol's effects on heart health

▶ Explaining the link between moderate drinking and longevity

▶ Listing some real risks of alcohol abuse

*A*ccording to the experts at the U.S. Departments of Agriculture (USDA) and Health and Human Services (HHS) — the authors of the Dietary Guidelines for Americans 2005 — people who drink in moderation have the lowest *all-cause mortality* (science speak for d-e-a-t-h from all causes).

The guidelines define moderation as one drink a day for a woman and two drinks a day for a man. One drink is equal to 1.5 ounces of 80 proof spirits, or 5 ounces of wine, or 12 ounces of regular (as opposed to low-cal) beer.

Government stats, in the U.S. and around the world, show that people who stick to these guidelines not only live longer, but they also live healthier than people who either drink too much or avoid alcohol altogether. Those in the Moderate Middle have fewer heart attacks and strokes. They're less likely to suffer from high blood pressure, Alzheimer's disease, diabetes, rheumatoid arthritis, broken or weakened bones, Parkinson's disease, hepatitis A, pancreatic cancer, macular degeneration (a major cause of blindness), duodenal ulcer, erectile dysfunction, hearing loss, gallstones, liver disease, and — believe it or not — the common cold.

In addition, just feeling good may not be up there with avoiding a heart attack or broken bones, but it's nothing to sneeze at either. One drink before or with a meal may improve digestion or offer a soothing respite at the end of a stressful day, and the occasional drink with friends can be a social pleasure. In other words, the physical and psychological effects of moderate drinking are components of a comfortable life.

Best of all, unlike some of life's other pleasures, the health benefits of moderate drinking actually seem to get more beneficial as a person gets older. The British Medical Journal reports that among men younger than 35 and women younger than 55, nondrinkers have a lower risk of death than do moderate drinkers. But hit the magic 65, and things change. Among senior citizens, moderate drinking may save as many as 5,000 older lives a year, perhaps because older drinkers have learned to avoid the risky behavior that trips younger drinkers into potentially fatal accidents.

This chapter is an annotated list of ten (or so) good things associated with moderate drinking, from the well-known (improved heart health) to the new and surprising (that increased resistance to the common cold).

And remember: When one drinker toasts another with the words, "To your health," he or she is right on the mark.

Heartening News

The evidence that moderate drinking benefits the heart comes from reliable studies funded and/or run by reliable organizations like the American Cancer Society (ACS) and the American Heart Association (AHA).

Riding the curve

When scientists talk about the relationship between alcohol and heart health, the term "J-curve" often pops up. What's a J-curve? A statistical graph in the shape of a J.

In terms of alcohol and your risk of heart attack, the lower peak on the left of the J shows the risk among teetotalers, the high spike on the right shows the risk among those who drink too much, and the curve in the center shows the risk in the moderate middle. In other words, the J-curve says that people who drink moderately have a lower risk of heart attack than do either people who drink too much or not at all. Several studies say that the J-curve may also apply to a moderate drinker's risk of stroke.

The best known study may be the ACS Cancer Prevention Study 1, a research project that followed more than one million Americans in 25 states for 12 years. Analyzing the lifestyles of 276,802 middle-aged men and the circumstances of those who died during the study period, the researchers concluded that moderate alcohol intake had an "apparent protective effect on coronary heart disease." Translation: Men who drink moderately lower their risk of heart attack. The risk is 21 percent lower for men who have one drink a day than for men who never drink.

A similar analysis of the data for nearly 600,000 women in the same study showed that, like men, women who drink occasionally or have one drink a day are less likely to die of heart attack than women who don't drink at all.

The two most likely explanations for these facts are alcohol's ability to make blood less sticky, reducing the risk of an artery-clogging blood clot, and its tendency to raise the level of HDL, the "good" fat and protein particles that ferry cholesterol out of the body.

Lowering Bad Cholesterol, Raising Good Cholesterol

Moderate amounts of any type of beverage alcohol lower blood levels of low density lipoproteins (LDL), the "bad" fat and protein particles that carry cholesterol into arteries, while raising the blood levels of high-density lipoproteins (HDL), the "good" fat and protein particles that ferry cholesterol out of the body.

To counter the idea that wine is the only alcohol beverage that accomplishes this phenomenon, researchers at Hebrew University Hadassah Medical School in Jerusalem divided 48 men with coronary artery disease in two groups. The first got 12 ounces of Pale Lager a day for a month; the second got mineral water. Both groups ate a fruit-and-veggie-rich diet.

The results, released in 2003, showed that 21 of the 24 beer drinkers had lowered their bad cholesterol, raised their good cholesterol, and reduced the activity of fibrinogen, a natural clot-maker in blood. None of these changes occurred among those drinking mineral water, but, on the other hand, nobody in either group had a heart attack during the study.

Busting Blood Clots

Cut yourself and you'll bleed, but soon tiny particles in blood, called *platelets,* glom onto a sticky net made of a naturally occurring substance, called *fibrinogen,* to form a scab. This series of events, most visible when skin is cut, also occurs when the inside surface of a blood vessel is injured, perhaps by a passing piece of cholesterol.

Forming a scab over a cut on the skin is good. Building a scab over an injury inside a blood vessel isn't. Inside an artery, the "scab" can catch more particles that stick on, eventually creating a pile of gunk that may be large enough to block the artery and cause a heart attack.

Alcohol beverages reduce the risk of forming that pile of gunk by temporarily lessening the stickiness of fibrinogen and other naturally occurring clotting factors that normally make platelets stick together.

As a result, blood clots are less likely to form in an artery, another reason why moderate drinking appears to protect the heart.

Lowering the Pressure

When the alcohol from a (moderate) drink flows through the bloodstream into the heart, the heart muscles relax, reducing the force of their contractions (or *beats*). As a result, your heart pumps out slightly less blood for a few minutes, blood vessels all over your body relax, and your blood pressure goes down.

The contractions of your heart muscle soon return to normal, but your blood vessels may remain relaxed and your blood pressure may stay lower for as long as half an hour. How important is this lowered blood pressure?

In 2002, researchers at the Nurses' Health Study issued a new report on 70,891 women who had been 25 to 42 years old when the study began in 1989. According to this report, women in the study who took one quarter to one half of a drink a day — in real life, two or three drinks a week — were 15 percent less likely to develop high blood pressure than were women who never drink. The results applied to all kinds of alcohol — that is, beer, wine, and spirits.

The inevitable bad news — sorry about this — is that women who take more than 10 drinks a week are 30 percent more likely to have high blood pressure. Once again, moderation is the key.

Reviewing resveratrol

Resveratrol, found in grapes and peanuts, is a *flavonoid,* one of a group of plant chemicals credited with lowering cholesterol and thus reducing your risk of heart attack. It's also linked to a lower risk of some forms of cancer, but that's another book.

In 2001, two reports — one in the American Heart Association's *Circulation,* the other in *Atherosclerosis* — confirmed earlier speculation that resveratrol powers up antioxidants, such as vitamin E and vitamin C. These compounds prevent molecule fragments from linking up to form rogue molecules that damage body cells.

Juice from purple grapes has more resveratrol than the juice from red grapes, which has more resveratrol than the juice from white grapes (get the red wine connection?). To be even more specific, in 1998, a team of food scientists from the USDA Agricultural Research Service and Mississippi identified a native American grape, the muscadine, as an unusually potent source of resveratrol.

About half of all muscadines grown in the United States are used to make grape juice. With that in mind, you can see that teetotalers can get their resveratrol from grapes and grape juice. Don't you love it when science serves up something for everybody?

But suppose you also absolutely, positively hate grape juice. What to do? Easy: Just pick a pack of peanuts.

A 1998 analysis from the USDA Agricultural Research Service in Raleigh, North Carolina, shows that peanuts have 1.7 to 3.7 mcg (micrograms) of resveratrol per gram versus the 0.6 to 8.0 mcg of resveratrol per gram in red wine. This fact may explain data from the long-running Harvard University/Brigham and Women's Hospital Nurses Health Study, which shows that women who eat an ounce of nuts a day have a lower risk of heart disease. To review: Wine, grape juice, peanuts — all tools to lengthen life.

Wait. There's more. Resveratrol pills may be looming on the health horizon.

The whole world knows by now that cutting calories is one way to lose weight, and that cutting lots and lots of calories may lengthen life, at least in laboratory mice for which seriously low-calorie diets appear to increase lifespan to the human equivalent of 162 years. No jokes about the quality of that life, please.

In 2006, researchers at Harvard Medical School announced that feeding resveratrol to the mice does the same thing, by "turning on long life genes shared by almost all living organisms," in the words of study coauthor and molecular biologist David Sinclair.

Unfortunately, to get the amount of resveratrol needed to produce this effect in mice, human beings would have to down gazillions of glasses of red wine a day. But one can practically hear the hoof beats of drug companies in the distance rushing into to find out how to pack the necessary resveratrol into a human size pill.

To which one can only say, "Get a move on, guy. The world is waiting."

Staving Off Stroke

In 2006, scientists at Johns Hopkins University in Maryland fed laboratory mice a moderate dose of resveratrol, a naturally occurring compound in red grape skins and seeds. Then they induced stroke in the mice and found that animals given the resveratrol experienced about 40 percent less brain damage than mice that weren't treated with resveratrol before a stroke.

The suspicion is that resveratrol increases levels of *heme oxygenase,* an enzyme in the brain that protects nerve cells. Naturally, more studies are required before anyone can say that drinking red wine prevents stroke damage, but, hey, it's a start.

Beer and distilled spirits have no resveratrol, so right now this particular good news may (or may not) apply only to red wine. But an any-type-of-alcohol-plus-caffeine cocktail may prevent additional brain damage after a stroke strikes.

In 2004, neurologist James C. Grotta and a team of researchers at the University of Texas-Houston Medical School whipped up an experimental drug they named *caffeinol.* They designed one dose to deliver as much caffeine as two cups of strong coffee plus the alcohol in one drink of any type of alcohol.

The Texans induced stroke in laboratory rats and gave caffeinol to half the injured rats within two hours of the stroke. The treated animals had up to 80 percent less brain damage than the untreated ones. Human tests say caffeinol is safe; future studies will tell whether it's effective. If so, look for Irish coffee on the menu in every ER.

Just kidding.

Deterring Diabetes

In 2002, the Journal of the American Medical Association reported the results of a study at the U.S. Department of Agriculture's Agricultural Research Service (ARS) Lab in Beltsville, Maryland, designed to evaluate the effects of moderate drinking alcohol on insulin resistance, a risk factor for both diabetes and heart disease.

The scientists randomly assigned 53 healthy, post-menopausal, women volunteers to one of three once-a-day drink plans: Plain orange juice or orange juice with half an ounce of alcohol (the equivalent of one standard drink), or orange juice with one ounce of alcohol (the equivalent of two standard drinks).

Yes, the Dietary Guidelines for Americans say that one standard drink is 1.5 ounces of distilled spirits, 5 ounces of wine, or 12 ounces of beer. But the actual amount of pure alcohol in that amount of beer, wine, or spirits is 0.5 ounces of alcohol. Remember: When spirits are distilled, and when wine and beer are fermented and bottled, the alcohol is diluted with water.

The 51 women who completed the study took blood tests to measure their *fasting insulin levels* (the level of insulin in the blood after 12 hours without food or drink).

Among women who drank orange juice with one ounce of alcohol each day, fasting insulin levels went down 19 percent versus no change for those drinking less alcohol or none at all. Levels of *triglycerides,* a form of fat found in blood that's a risk factor for both heart disease and diabetes, also fell among the women who drank either one half or one ounce of alcohol a day.

Protecting Intelligence

MRI (magnetic resonance imaging) studies of the brain have clearly shown that even moderate drinking knocks off some brain cells. The surprise is that this loss may not correlate with a loss of intellect.

Typically, a human being's score on tests for memory, reasoning, and decision-making declines about one point per decade before age 60 and two to three points every ten years after that.

But data from a 12-year, 1,488-person survey at Johns Hopkins University in Maryland strongly suggests that moderate drinkers score better than teetotalers over time on the Mini-Mental State Examination (MMSE), a standard test of intelligence and cognition. (In addition, a recent study among French senior citizens pinpointed a 75 percent lower risk for Alzheimer's disease and an 80 percent lower risk for senile dementia among moderate drinkers versus teetotalers. Vive la France.)

What makes this news fascinating is that MRI studies showing alcohol-related brain shrinkage and the new alcohol-and-intelligence survey were both done at Johns Hopkins.

Talk about your left hand (or brain) not knowing what your right hand (or brain) is doing.

Preserving the Brain

Can it be? Yes, it can. According to Monique M.B. Breteler and her colleagues at the Erasmus Medical Centre in Rotterdam, the Netherlands, people who drink moderately as they grow older are less likely than abstainers or heavy drinkers to develop Alzheimer's and other forms of dementia, including dementia triggered by repeated small blood-clot-related strokes.

To reach that conclusion, from 1990 to 1999, the Dutch team collected data for 5,395 healthy people age 55 and older with no signs of dementia. After adjusting the data to account for gender, age, weight, blood pressure, smoking, and all the other nasty factors that affect the risk of dementia, the researchers discovered that the people in the survey who took one to three drinks a day of any kind of beverage alcohol were only half as likely as those who drank more (or less) to develop dementia.

Anyone here know how to say "to your health" in Dutch?

Boosting Bones

Alcohol abuse is linked to an increased risk of fractures, not simply to an intoxicated person's higher risk of falling, but also to a documented alcohol-related loss of bone density (the concentration of minerals such as calcium in bones), particularly in postmenopausal women, a group at high risk of weakened bones.

But moderate drinkers don't have the same problem. When researchers at the Bone Metabolism Unit and the Cardiac Center of Creighton University School of Medicine in Omaha, Nebraska, measured bone density among 445 women ages 65 to 77, they found that the women who drank moderately (about an ounce a day) had higher total bone density, higher spinal bone density, and higher forearm bone density than the women who drank more or less or none at all.

How come? The body destroys old bone and builds new bone every day. With age, the body continues to break down old bone at the same rate but builds new bone more slowly. Hence, the characteristic loss of bone called age-related osteoporosis.

The Creighton researchers suggest that alcohol may lower the concentration of anti-bone hormones, thus preserving existing bone. Worth another study, doncha think?

Enhancing Appetite

Appetite is the desire for food, a psychological reaction (looks good! smells good!) that stimulates hunger pangs, the involuntary contractions triggered by the secretion of gastric acids in an empty stomach that say, "Time to eat."

In America, as any casual observer of bulging bodies knows, most people have no trouble shoveling in the food even in the absence of hunger pangs.

But for those whose weight is under control, a moderate drink before dinner can enhance the pleasure of dining. In addition, appetite declines with age so that older people often eat less than they should, raising the possibility of malnutrition. Luckily, several studies in nursing homes and hospitals have suggested that a moderate amount of alcohol at dinnertime may benefit healthy seniors who aren't physically or mentally impaired or taking any medication that can interact with the alcohol.

Controlling Weight

Yes, a balanced diet is important. But so is balanced consumption of beverage alcohol.

The figure comes from researchers at Texas Tech University Health Sciences Center and the Mayo Clinic. Based on a detailed analysis of the drinking habits and body mass index (BMI) for 8,236 non-smokers, they concluded that moderate drinkers (up to five drinks per week) are 46 percent less likely than either abstainers or alcohol abusers to end up obese.

Their final word, in their report in *BMC Public Health,* an online medical journal that publishes original peer-reviewed research articles, is this: "The evidence reported here argues against a strategy of promoting complete abstention at least among those who regularly consume alcohol."

People who don't already drink shouldn't start drinking to control their weight. But you know that.

Countering the Common Cold

Sometimes you have to wonder whether researchers really have enough to do. With all the health problems humans face, did they actually need to study the relationship between beverage alcohol and the common cold?

Heck, why not.

Seeking to test the idea that smoking and/or drinking makes a person more susceptible to viral infections, five scientists at the Department of Psychology at Carnegie Mellon University in Pittsburgh, Pennsylvania, exposed 391 volunteers to one of five different respiratory viruses (a control group of 26 volunteers was exposed to plain saltwater). Then the researchers sat back to see who got a cold.

Soon enough, they discovered that smokers had a higher risk of getting a cold than did nonsmokers. But nonsmokers who drank were less likely than smokers to end up sneezing. In the words of the researchers, "moderate drinkers have been found to be more resistant than abstainers to five strains of the common cold virus." Compared to abstainers, the resistance was lowered

- 85 percent for people who consumed two to three drinks a day
- 65 percent for people who consumed one to two drinks a day
- 30 percent for people who consumed less than one drink a day

The other side of the glass

The term *alcohol abuse* usually means drinking so much so frequently that it interferes with the ability to live a normal, productive life. Alcohol abuse is also hazardous to your health because it's a serious risk factor for liver damage, high blood pressure, and cancer of the esophagus and stomach, not to mention injury, violence, and death from accidents. In addition, for some people, even moderate amounts of alcohol may be too much. The obvious examples are young people; pregnant women; people taking medicines, such as sedatives, that interact with alcohol; and those who plan to participate in sports or an activity — such as filling out tax forms — that requires really clear thinking. As for drinking and driving, fuggedaboudit. Period.

Index

• A •

Aalborg Akavit, 182
absinthe, 266
Absolut vodka, 175, 178, 180, 182
abstinence, 133
ABV (alcohol by volume), 25, 39
The Adams Liquor Handbook, 186
ADH (alcohol dehydrogenase), 58
agave
  harvesting, 200
  mezcal and, 203
  pressing, 199
  Tequila and, 192–193
  types of, 198
aging
  after bottling, 19
  of Bourbon and Tennessee whiskey,
    106–107
  of brandy, 246–247
  in oak barrel, 36–37
  overview of, 35–36
  requirements for, 37
  of rum, 215
  of Scotch whisky, 86, 93
  of Tequila, 201–202
aguardiente, 211, 245
akavit
  choosing, 182
  origins of, 13, 170
  in Scandinavia, 173
al-ambiq, 11–12
alchemist, 12
alcohol
  discovery of, 12
  as diuretic, 58
  as medicine, 133, 149–150
  names for, 13
alcohol abuse, 316

Alcohol Administration Act, 16
alcohol by volume (ABV), 25, 39
alcohol dehydrogenase (ADH), 58
alcoholic beverage
  nutrition profile of, 303–306
  trade and, 14
  as term, 21
aldehydes, 31
alembic still, 12, 29
Alizè Cognac, 180
Allash Kümmel, 267
Allison, Young E. (poet), 223
Amaretto Disaronno, 268
Amarula, 259
Amer Picon, 270
American blended whiskey
  building, 119
  choosing for blending, 120–121
  choosing for tasting, 121–123
  combining food with, 124
  description of, 118
  history of, 18, 116–119
  taste of, 119
  tasting, 121
American Distilling Institute, 31
American gin, 159–160, 167
American Medicinal Spirits Company,
    102–103
American whiskey. *See* American
    blended whiskey; Bourbon;
    Tennessee whiskey
American Whiskey Trail, 124–125
Amsterdam, Morey (entertainer), 222
Añejo Tequila, 202, 206, 208
angelica root, 165
Angostura Bitters, 270
Angostura rum, 222
anise, 166
Anisette, 262, 266

Antigua, rum from, 218–219
antioxidants, 311
aperitif, 76, 273
appellation of origin, 196–197
appetite, 315
apple cordial, 264
AppleJack, 242, 244
AppleJack Pound Cake, 301
Appleton Estate rum, 220
aqua vitae, 13, 62, 170
aquamiel, 200
aquavit, 173, 182
arak, 210
Armagnac, 235, 237–238
Armenia, brandy from, 249
Arnald of Villanova (professor), 13
aroma
  of American blended whiskey, 123
  of Bourbon or Tennessee whiskey,
    110–111
  of brandy, 250–251
  evaluating, 49
  of gin, 155, 165
  of Irish whiskey, 74
  of Scotch whisky, 93–94
  of Tequila, 207
aromatic esters, 31
Arthur, Stanley Clisby, *Famous New
    Orleans Drinks and How to Mix
    'Em,* 288
artichoke, 50
Asia, rum from, 224
Association of Canadian Distillers,
    140
Australia
  brandy from, 241, 249
  rum from, 224
Aztec pulque, 191, 193

• *B* •

Bacardi
  Daiquiri, 280
  Límon, 180
  rum, 216–217, 221

Bacardi, Segundo (distiller), 285
Bailey's Irish Cream, 68, 269
Barbados, rum from, 211, 219
barley
  Irish whiskey and, 66–67
  malting, 83
  Scotch whisky and, 82
barrel, charred wood, 36, 68, 106
The Bartender's Guide (Thomas), 287
Bartending For Dummies (Foley), 274,
    277
Barton gin, 160
base spirit of cordial, 259
batch, 25
batch distilling, 30
bathtub gin, 20, 153
bay rum, 212
Beam & Hart Distillery, 102
Beam, James Beauregard (distiller),
    102
Beefeater London distilled dry gin,
    157
beer, discovery of, 10
Beerhouse Act, 152
Benchley, Robert (author), 133, 154
Benedictine, 150, 257, 271
benefits, health
  to appetite, 315
  to blood clots, 310
  to blood pressure, 310
  to bones, 314
  to brain, 313–314
  to cholesterol, 309
  common cold and, 316
  diabetes and, 312–313
  drinking in moderation and, 307–308
  to heart, 308–309
  stroke and, 312
  to weight, 315
Bermuda, rum from, 224
bitters, 270–271
Black Bush whiskey, 71
Black Sea region, brandy from, 241

Black Velvet
  Reserve 8 Year Old, 142
  3 Year Old minimum, 142
blackberry liqueur or brandy, 264
blackstrap molasses, 214
Blanco Tequila, 202, 206, 208
blended grain whisky, 86, 90
blended Irish whiskey, 76
blended Scotch whisky, 86, 89–91
blended spirits, 38–40
blended whiskey. *See also* American
      blended whiskey
  after Prohibition, 65
  description of, 18
  Irish, 76
  making, 39–40
  Scotch, 86, 89–91
blender, 289
blending
  brandy, 247
  liqueurs, 261–262
  overview of, 37–38
  rum, 215–216
blood clot, 310
blood pressure, 310
Bloody Mary, 277–279
Blue Weber agave, 198
body, 49
Bombay distilled London dry gin,
      156–157
bone density, 314
bootlegger, 134
booze, 19
Burrough, James (distiller), 155, 157
botanicals
  in gin, 149, 154–155, 165
  in medicine, 256–257
Bottled-in-Bond, 108
bottling
  choosing model bottle, 40
  size of bottle, 42
  for vodka, 178
bottling line, 40–42

Bourbon
  branch water and, 112
  choosing for tasting, 108–110
  combining food with, 111
  description of, 18
  history of, 98–102
  making, 104–107
  mash bill of, 26
  tasting, 108–111
  touring distilleries, 112–113
  types of, 107–108
Bourbon balls, 111
Bourbon County, Kentucky, 101, 105
Bradstreet, Bradley (sea captain), 159
brain, benefits to, 313–314
branch water, 112
brandy
  aging, 246–247
  blending, 247
  combining with food, 252–253
  description of, 18
  flavors and aromas of, 250–251
  from France, 235–238
  from Italy, 239
  making, 245–246
  origins of, 234
  from other countries, 241–243
  overview of, 233–234
  serving, 251–252
  from Spain, 239
  tasting by country, 249–250
  tasting by price, 250
  tasting by type, 248–249
  types of, 244–245
  from United States, 240–241
Brandy Alexander, 279
brandy snifter, 57
Brazil, rum from, 210–211, 225
brentwine, 150
Breteler, Monique M.B. (scientist),
      314
British gins, 156–158
British Royal Navy and rum, 226
Brizard, Marie (distiller), 262

Bronfman, Allan (distiller), 135
Bronfman, Samuel (distiller), 38,
    117–118, 135–136, 174
Brooks, Alfred (distiller), 256
Brown-Forman Beverages, 110
Brown-Forman Woodford Reserve
    Kentucky Bourbon, 31
Brugal rum, 220
Burnett's London dry gin, 160
Burns, Robert (poet), 95
Bushmills distillery
  contact information, 77
  history of, 63
  location of, 71
  Original whiskey, 71
  Single Malts, 44, 71
buying on Internet, 54

• C •

cachaça, 225
Calvados, 235, 237, 244
Campari, 270
Campbeltown region of Scotland, 89
Canada. *See also* Canadian whisky
  history of, 145
  quiz about, 146
  rum from, 225
  traveling to, 136
Canadian Club
  Reserve 6 Year Old, 141
  6 Year Old, 142
Canadian Ice Wines, 143
Canadian Mist 3 Year Old minimum,
    142
Canadian whisky
  after Prohibition, 117
  choosing samples for tasting,
    140–143
  combining with food, 144–145
  description of, 18, 136
  flavor of, 143–144
  history of, 131–136
  making, 137–139

popular priced brands of, 142
  premium priced brands of, 141
  value priced brands of, 142–143
cane juice, 213–214
cane syrup, 214
Captain Morgan Spiced Rum, 216, 221
carbohydrates
  distilling and, 26
  yeasts and, 28
carbon dioxide, 28
cardamon, 166
Caribbean rum
  from Antigua, 218–219
  from Barbados, 219
  from Cuba, 219
  from Dominican Republic, 219–220
  from Haiti, 220
  from Jamaica, 220–221
  from Martinique, 221
  overview of, 217–218
  from Puerto Rico, 221–222
  from Trinidad and Tobago, 222–223
  from Virgin Islands, 223
Casa Herradura, 199
Casa Noble Tequila, 199
Catherine de Medici (queen), 256
Catherine the Great (ruler), 172
Chambord Royal, 266
charcoal filtering, 106–107
charred wood barrel, 36, 68, 106
Chartreuse, 271
Cherry Heering, 265
Chicken Fajitas, 297
Chilled Melon Pepper Soup with
    Glazed Shrimp, 292–293
Chivas Regal Royal Salute, 45
cholesterol, 309
Churchill Downs, 114
Churchill, Winston (prime minister),
    253, 282
cigar and brandy ritual, 253
Cinco de Mayo, 195
cinnamon, 166
Cinnamon Schnapps, 268

classification of liqueur, 259–260

clear spirits, 17–18

Cock 'n' Bull, 174

cocktail glass, 57

cocktails, classic

  Bloody Mary, 277–279

  Brandy Alexander, 279

  Daiquiri, 280

  description of, 277

  equipment for making, 289

  Gimlet, 281–282

  history of, 256

  Manhattan, 282

  Margarita, 283

  Martini, 284–285

  Mint Julep, 288

  Mojito, 285–286

  nutritional profile of, 305–306

  Rob Roy, 286

  use of term, 213, 278

  Whiskey Sour, 287

CocoRibe, 267

coffee liqueur, 267, 305

coffee with cream liqueur, nutritional profile of, 305

Coffey, Aneas (still inventor), 35

Cognac, 235–236, 238, 247, 252

Cointreau, 265

color

  of American blended whiskey, 123

  of Bourbon and Tennessee whiskey, 106–107

  evaluating, 48–49

  of gin, 164

  of Irish whiskey, 73–74

  of Scotch whisky, 93

  of Tequila, 207

Columbus, Christopher (explorer), 210

column still

  description of, 33

  number of columns, 34–35

  rum and, 214

  Scotch whisky and, 84–85

  workings of, 33–34

combining food and spirits. *See also* recipes

  American blended whiskey, 124

  Bourbon or Tennessee whiskey, 111

  brandy, 252–253

  Canadian whisky, 144–145

  cordials and liqueurs, 273–274

  Irish whiskey, 76

  Scotch whisky, 95

  taste buds and, 50

  Tequila, 207–208

  vodka, 188

common cold, 316

compounding gin, 155

congeners

  column still and, 35

  description of, 25

  pot still and, 31–32

Connemara Irish whiskey, 72

continuous still, 34. *See also* column still

Cooley distillery, 44, 71–72, 77

Cor, John (friar), 80

cordial glass, 57

cordials

  Benedictine, 150

  birth of, 255–256

  bitters, 270–271

  blending, 261–262

  branded, spirit-based, 268–269

  classic, 271

  classification of, 259–260

  combining with food, 273–274

  cream, 269–270, 301

  description of, 258

  flavoring, 260–261

  fruit-flavored, 264–266

  Hayman's 1820 gin liqueur, 158

  history of, 256–258

  from Irish whiskey, 68

  making, 258–259

cordials *(continued)*
  making own, 272
  nutritional profile of, 305
  seed- and nut-based, 266–268
  tasting, 271–273
  types of, 262–263
  Yukon Jack, 143
coriander, 166
corn whiskey, 117, 120, 123
corsair, 211
Cortez, Hernando (conquistadore), 194
Cox, Jennings (military man), 280
crackers, for tasting, 46
craft distillers in Canada, 140
craic, 64
Craig, Elijah (minister), 100–101
cream liqueurs, 269–270, 305
crème de almond, 268
crème de cacao, 267
crème de café, 267
crème de cassis, 264
crème de menthe, 268
crème de mocha, 267
crème de noyaux, 268
cross fiber pattern theory of gustatory coding, 50
Crow, James C. (distiller), 103
Crown Royal, 141
Crown Royal Special Reserve, 141
Cruzan rum, 217, 223
Cuba, rum from, 219
Cuervo, José Guadalupe (distiller), 195
cultivated yeast, 28
Curaçao, 265
cure for overindulgence, 58
curragh, 63
Cynar, 270
cynarin, 50

• D •

Daiquiri, 280, 306
Daktulosphaira vitifoliae, 64
Damrak Genever gin, 161
Daniel, Jasper Newton (distiller), 102–103, 129
dark rum, 215
dark spirits
  aging and, 35
  description of, 18
  temperature, for serving, 56
de la Boie, Franciscus (distiller), 150
Demerara rum, 225–226
demon rum, 216
denatured alcohol, 11
dessert pancakes, 274
diabetes, 312–313
Diastase, 67
Dickel, George A. (distiller), 102
Dickens, Charles (author), 152
distillate, 32
distillation
  Arabs and, 12
  basic material for, 26
  of Bourbon and Tennessee whiskey, 106
  column still and, 33–35
  discovery of, 1, 11–12
  in distillery, 28–29
  experiencing, 29
  first book on, 13
  foods used in, 14–15, 26
  of liqueurs, 261
  monks and, 13
  pot still and, 29–32
  process of, 23–24
  of rum, 214
  of Scotch whisky, 84–85
  spread of, 14–15
  of Tequila, 201
  of vodka, 178

Distilled Spirits Council of the United States, 125
distilled spirits, history of, 9–10
distilled water, 112
distilleries. *See also specific distilleries*
  in Ireland, 77
  in Mexico, 199
  in Scotland, 96
  in United States, 112–113, 124–125
distiller's beer, 28, 105
Dominican Republic, rum from, 219–220
Don Q rum, 221
Doornkaat gin, 162
double-casked whisky, 141
Drake, Francis (explorer), 285
Drake, Richard (pirate), 285
Drambuie, 95, 269
drinking in moderation, 58, 307–308
Droste Bittersweet, 267
Droste Cream, 269–270
Duke, James A. (distiller), 272

• E •

Eastern Europe, brandy from, 242
Eaton, Alfred (distiller), 107
eau de vie, 13, 211
eaux-de-vie, 236–237, 260
Edward VII (king), 253
18th Amendment, 15–16
English Harbor 5 Year Old rum, 219
entertaining spirits quiz, 20
equipment for making cocktails, 289
ethanol, 11, 25
Europe, rum from, 225
excise tax
  in United Kingdom, 80, 81
  in United States, 98–99
Extra Añejo tequila, 202, 206, 208

• F •

Famous New Orleans Drinks and How to Mix 'Em (Arthur), 288
feints, 32
fermentation
  discovery of, 9–10
  process of, 23–24
  rum and, 214
  standardization of process of, 10–12
  starting process of, 27–28
fermentation tank, 28
Fernandes "19" rum, 222–223
Fernet Branca, 270–271
Filet Mignon with Whiskey Sauce, 298–299
filtering of Bourbon and Tennessee whiskey, 107
finish, 52
Finlandia vodka, 175, 180, 182
flambé, 252–253, 274
flavonoid, 311
flavor
  of American blended whiskey, 123
  of brandy, 250–251
  of Canadian whisky, 143–144
  of gin, 155, 165–166
  of Irish whiskey, 75
  of Scotch whisky, 94–95
  of Tequila, 207
  of vodka, 179–180, 185
flavoring
  liqueurs, 260–261
  rum, 216–217
  Tequila, 202
  vodka, 180–181
Foley, Ray, *Bartending For Dummies,* 274, 277
foods used in distillation, 14–15, 26
foreshots, 32
Foster, Stephen (songwriter), 114
France
  brandy from, 235–238
  gin from, 161

Frangelico, 268
Freezolime, 265
fruit brandy, 244, 246–247, 260
fusel oils, 31

• G •

Galliano, 268
Game Pâté Terrine, 293–294
gastric alcohol dehydrogenase
    (GADH), 58
Gaudaloupe, rum from, 221
gaugers, 80
Geber (alchemist), 11–12
Gehry, Frank (architect), 178
generic cordial, 262
George Dickel whiskey, 110
Germany
    brandy from, 242–243, 249
    gin from, 154, 162, 167
Getz, Oscar (distiller), 125
Giant's Causeway, 71
Gilbey's London dry gin, 159–160
Gimlet, 281–282
gin
    American, 159–160
    artificially flavored, 166
    botanicals and, 149
    Britain and, 151–152, 156–158
    description of, 17
    flavor of, 155
    French, 161
    German, 162
    Holland and, 150–151, 154, 161
    London dry, 153–154, 156–158, 167
    making, 154
    nutritional profile of, 304
    origins of, 149–150
    Plymouth, 158
    premium brands of, 163–164
    Prohibition and, 153
    reputation of, 153–154
    serving, 167

Spanish, 162–163
super-premium brands of, 164
tasting, 163–166
value brands of, 163
Gin Act, 152
"Gin Lane" (Hogarth), 152
Ginger Schnapps, 268
glass
    in bottles, 41
    serving in proper, 56–57
    for tasting, 46
Glengoyne, 88
The Glenlivet, 81, 91–92
Glenlivet distillery, 90
Godiva Chocolate, 267
Goldschlager, 268
Gordon, Alexander (distiller), 153
Gordon's London dry gin, 159–160
Gosling's Black and Gold Labels,
    224–225
grains
    barley, 66–67, 82, 83
    for Bourbon and Tennessee
        whiskey, 104
    dark spirits and, 18
    vodka and, 177, 185
Grand Marnier, 265
grape juice, 311
grappa, 234, 239, 245
Greece, brandy from, 243
Green Beans with Toasted Pine Nuts,
    299–300
Grey Goose vodka, 175
grog, 226
Guyana, rum from, 225–226

• H •

haggis, 95
Haig & Haig distillery, 35
Haiti, rum from, 220
Hamilton, Alexander (Secretary of
    Treasury), 98

hand-crafted spirits, 30–31
hard liquor, 21
hard water, 67
Hart, Albert (distiller), 102
harvesting
  agave, 200
  peat, 84
Harvey Wallbanger, 268
Havana Club rum, 219
Hayden, R. B. (distiller), 102
Hayman's 1820 gin liqueur, 158
heads, 32
health and sense of taste, 51
health benefits
  to appetite, 315
  to blood clots, 310
  to blood pressure, 310
  to bones, 314
  to brain, 313–314
  to cholesterol, 309
  common cold and, 316
  diabetes and, 312–313
  drinking in moderation and, 307–308
  to heart, 308–309
  stroke and, 312
  to weight, 315
Heaven Hill distiller, 160
heme oxygenase, 312
Hendricks gin, 158
Herbsaint, 267
Heublein, Inc., 174–175
highball glass, 57
higher proof or higher ABV, 21
Highlands, Scottish, 88–89
Hir, Reault (distiller), 129
history
  of American blended whiskey,
    116–119
  of Bourbon, 98–102
  of Canada, 145
  of Canadian whisky, 131–136
  of distilled spirits, 9–10
  of liqueurs, 256–258

of rum, 209–212
of Tennessee whiskey, 98–102
of Tequila, 192–196
of vodka, 170–175
of whisky, 80–81
Hogarth, William (artist), 152
Hokonui whiskey, 128–129
Holland gin, 161, 167
hooch, 19
Hoover, Herbert (president), 16
horizontal tasting, 44
How To Mix Drinks (Thomas), 287

• *I* •

Ice Wines, 143
Icelandic vodka, 178
India, whisky from, 127–128
infusion, 261
intelligence, 313
Internet, buying on, 54
Ireland. *See also* Irish whiskey
  description of, 61
  famines in, 64
  map of, 69
  Shannon airport, 75
  toasts from, 78
  touring, 76–77
Irish coffee, classic, 75
Irish Distillers Company, 68, 72
Irish Mist, 68, 269
Irish whiskey
  barley and, 66–67
  Bushmills, 71
  combining food and, 76
  Cooley, 71–72
  cordials from, 68
  description of, 18
  famine and, 65
  flavors and aromas in, 75
  heating, 67–68
  leading, 68–69
  Midleton, 69–70

Irish whiskey (continued)
origins of, 62
tasting, 73–75
trade and, 63–64
uniqueness of, 66
in United States, 65
water and, 67
Islay, 89
isopropyl alcohol (isoproanol), 11
Israel, brandy from, 243, 250
Italy
brandy from, 239
liqueurs and, 256
Ivan IV (czar), 171–172

• J •

Jabir ibn Hayyam, Abu Musa
(alchemist), 11–12, 210
Jack Daniel distillery, 102–103, 110
Jägermeister, 268
Jalisco, state of, 197
Jamaica, rum from, 220–221
Jameson Irish whiskey, 70
Japan
sake, 18
shochu, 176
whisky from, 126–127
J&B Scotch whisky, 256
J-curve, 308
jenevre, 150–151, 154, 161. See also
gin
Jerome, Jennie (celebrity), 282
Jim Beam Company, 102, 108
jimadores, 200
Johnnie Walker Black, 91–92
Johnson, Samuel (writer), 251
Joseph E. Seagram & Sons, 135–136
Joven Tequila, 202, 206
juniper berries, 165. See also gin
juniper bush, 150
Justerini, Giacomo (distiller), 256

• K •

kabaks, 172
Kahlua, 267
Kahlua Cream, 270
Kanber, Maurice (distiller), 178
Kentucky Derby, 114
Kentucky straight Bourbon, 109
King, Pee Wee (songwriter), 114
Kir, 264
Kubanskaya flavoring, 180
kumis, 26
Kunett, Rudolph (distiller), 173–174

• L •

La Cofradia, 199
label, reading
on Cognac and Armagnac, 238
on spirits, 54–55
Laird, William (distiller), 242
Laphroaig, 89
Larios dry gin, 162–163
Latin America, brandy from, 243
Lee, Harry (general), 99
legs
evaluating, 49
of Irish whiskey, 74
letting spirits open, 45, 48
Licor 43, 268
light rum, 215
Limonaya flavoring, 179–180
Limóncello, 265
Lincoln County Process, 107
Lind, James (surgeon), 281
Linie aquavit, 182
Linnaeus, Carolus (botanist), 193
liqueurs
Benedictine, 150
birth of, 255–256
bitters, 270–271
blending, 261–262
branded, spirit-based, 268–269

classic, 271
classification of, 259–260
combining with food, 273–274
cream, 269–270, 305
description of, 258
flavoring, 260–261
fruit-flavored, 264–266
Hayman's 1820 gin liqueur, 158
history of, 256–258
from Irish whiskey, 68
making, 258–259
making own, 272
nutritional profile of, 305
seed- and nut-based, 266–268
tasting, 271–273
types of, 262–263
Yukon Jack, 143
liquor store, choosing, 53–54
liver alcohol dehydrogenase, 58
Living Liqueurs (Duke), 272
Locke's Distillery Museum, 77
London dry gin, 153–154, 156–158,
    167
Lord Invader (singer), 222
Louisville, Kentucky, 103
low wine, 31
lowball glass, 57
Lowlands, Scottish, 88

• *M* •

Macallan Fine and Rare Collection, 45
maceration, 260
MacGregor, Robert (Scottish hero),
    286
Macquarie, Lachlan (governor), 224
maguey plants, 192–193
Maker's Mark, 103, 110, 121
Mallya, Vijay (distillery owner),
    127–128
malt barn, 83
malting barley, 83
Manastirka brandy, 242
Mandarine Napoleón, 266

Manhattan, 121, 282
Maraschino liqueur, 265
Margarita, 283
Marie Brizard Apry, 264
Marinated Salmon, 295
Marmot, 267
marrying, 35, 139
Martin, John (executive), 174
Martini, 153, 284–285
Martini glass, 57
Martinique, 221
mash
    for Bourbon and Tennessee
        whiskey, 105
    description of, 25, 27
    for Irish whiskey, 66
    for Tequila, 200
    for vodka, 177
mash bill, 25–26
mash tun, 28
Matusalem Grand Reserve rum, 220
McNaughton 3 Year Old minimum,
    142
McShane, Owen (distiller), 128
measuring cup, 289
medicine
    alcohol as, 133, 149–150
    botanicals in, 256–257
    sugar in, 257
Metaxa brandy, 243
methyl alcohol (methanol), 11
metric measurement, 42
Mexican-American war, 195
Mexico. *See also* Tequila
    brandy from, 250
    touring, 199
mezcal
    Cortez and, 194
    description of, 192
    making, 203
    tasting, 205–207
microorganisms. *See also* yeasts
    action of, 23–24
    adding, 28

microvillus, 50
mid-cut, 32
Midleton distillery, 44, 69–70, 77
Midleton Irish whiskey, 70
Midori, 265
Militia Law, 99
mill, 27
Miller, Oliver (farmer), 99, 125
milling, 25–27
Mint Julep, 288
mixed drinks. *See also* cocktails
    American blended whiskey and, 121
    rum and, 229
    vodka and, 187–188
mixto, 198, 203
moderation, drinking in, 58, 307–308
Mojito, 285–286
molasses, 214
Molson, John (brewer), 131–132
Montaño y Cuervo, José Antonio
        (retailer), 194–195
moonshining, 23
Moore County, Tennessee, 105
Moors, 210
Morgan, Henry (captain), 211
Morgan, Jack (restaurant owner), 174
Moscow Mule, 174
moth caterpillar, 204
Motlow, Lem (distiller), 103
Mount Gay distillery, 217
Mount Vernon Distillery, 124
mouthfeel, 51, 123
movies
    about pirates, 229
    about Russia and vodka, 189
muddler, 289
Mundo Cuervo, 199
Muscovado rum, 219
Museum of Tequila, 199
Museum of the American Cocktail,
        126
"My Old Kentucky Home" (Foster),
        114

Myers rum, 220
Myers's Rum Cream, 269

• **N** •

National Distillers, 103
Nearchus (general), 209–210
Nelson, Horatio (naval hero), 226
neutral spirits
    blending whiskey and, 117
    description of, 24–25, 29
    distillation of, 26
New York, brandy from, 241
New Zealand, distilling business in,
        128–129
Noe, Booker (distiller), 102
Nut Ball Cookies, 302
nutrition profiles of alcohol
        beverages, 303–306

• **O** •

oak barrel, aging in, 36–37, 106
oats, 67
Ohio Territory, 100
"Old Bourbon", 101
Old Grand-Dad distillery, 102–103
Old Jameson Museum, 77
Old Mr. Boston drink recipe book, 175
Old Tom gin, 157, 159, 167
old-fashioned glass, 57
The Online Distillery Network for
        Distilleries & Fuel Ethanol Plants
        Worldwide, 16
O.P. Anderson aquavit, 182
opening bottle before tasting, 45
orange peel, 166
osteoporosis, 314
Ouzo, 267
overindulgence, cure for, 58
overproof rum, 221

• *p* •

pairing food and spirits. *See also* recipes
American blended whiskey, 124
Bourbon or Tennessee whiskey, 111
brandy, 252–253
Canadian whisky, 144–145
cordials and liqueurs, 273–274
Irish whiskey, 76
Scotch whisky, 95
taste buds and, 50
Tequila, 207–208
vodka, 188
Palo Viejo rum, 221
Pastis, 267
Patrick (saint), 62
Peachtree Schnapps, 265
peanuts, 311
peat
Irish whiskey and, 67
Scotch whisky and, 82–84
peat firing, 72
Pendryn plant (Welsh Whisky Company), 129–130
Penne à la Vodka, 296
Pennsylvania, 98–99
Pepper, Elijah (distiller), 103
Pepper, James E. (distiller), 103
Pepper, Oscar (distiller), 103
Peppermint Schnapps, 268
perceived value, 179
percolation, 261
Pernod Ricard, 68
Pertsovka flavoring, 179
Peru, brandy from, 250
PET (polyethylene terephthalte), 41
Peter the Great (czar), 171–172
Petiot, Fernand (bartender), 278
Peychaud, Antoine Amédée (apothecary), 278
Peychaud's Bitters, 271
phylloxera, 64

piña, 199, 200, 203
Piña Colada, 306
pirate movie quiz, 229
Pisang Ambon, 264
Pisco brandy, 243
Plymouth gin, 158, 167
poire, 247
poitin, 64
polyethylene terephthalte (PET), 41
pomace brandy, 244–245
porosity of wood, 37
porteros, 198
Portugal, 210
pot still
alchemist and, 12
description of, 29–30
rum and, 214
Scotch whisky and, 84
uses of, 30–31
workings of, 31–32
world's largest, 69
potable spirits, 32
potatoes, 64, 173, 185
Pousse Café, 274
Powers Irish whiskey, 70
pressing agave, 199
pricing of liqueurs, 259
privateer, 211
process of distillation, 23–24
Prohibition
American blended whiskey and, 65, 117
American Medicinal Spirits Company and, 102–103
Bourbon and Tennessee whiskey and, 102
in Canada, 133–134
Canadian whisky and, 134
gin and, 153
impact of, 15–16, 20
Irish whiskey and, 65
Tequila and, 196
proof, 25, 39

proprietary cordial, 262–263
protecting investment, 55–56
Puerto Rico, rum from, 221–222
Puff von Schrick, Michael (author), 13
pulque, 191–193
Punt e Mes, 271
Pusser's Rum, 226

● **Q** ●

Quintessential Gin, 158
quizzes
  about Canada, 146
  about entertaining spirits, 20
  about pirate movies, 229

● **R** ●

Rain vodka, 185
Raki, 267
reading label
  on Cognac and Armagnac, 238
  on spirits, 54–55
recipes
  AppleJack Pound Cake, 301
  Bloody Mary, 279
  Brandy Alexander, 279
  Chicken Fajitas, 297
  Chilled Melon Pepper Soup with
    Glazed Shrimp, 292–293
  Daiquiri, 280
  dessert pancakes, 274
  Filet Mignon with Whiskey Sauce,
    298–299
  Game Pâté Terrine, 293–294
  Gimlet, 281
  Green Beans with Toasted Pine
    Nuts, 299–300
  Irish coffee, classic, 75
  Manhattan, 282
  Margarita, 283
  Marinated Salmon, 295
  Martini, 284
  Mint Julep, 288

Mojito, 285–286
  Nut Ball Cookies, 302
  Penne à la Vodka, 296
  Pousse Café, 274
  Rob Roy, 286
  sources for, 291–292
  Strawberry Vodka Infusion, 180–181
  Tennessee Whiskey Candied Apples,
    300
  Vodka Gimlet, 281
  Whiskey Sour, 287
rectifier, 224
Red Flame rum, 220
Redbreast Irish whiskey, 70
Remy Martin Louis XIII, 233
Reposado Tequila, 202, 206
resveratrol, 311
rhum agricole, 221
Rhum Barbancourt, 220
rhum industriel, 221
Rich and Rare 3 Year Old minimum,
    142
Rob Roy, 286
rocks glass, 57
Roger, Jean-Baptiste (distiller), 262
Ron Barcelo rum, 220
Ron Bermudez rum, 220
Ron Del Barrilito rum, 221
Ron Llave rum, 221
rot gut, 20
Royal Oak rum, 222–223
rum
  aging of, 215
  blending, 215–216
  British Royal Navy and, 226
  Caribbean, 217–223
  description of, 18
  flavoring, 216–217
  history of, 209–212
  making, 212–214
  nutritional profile of, 304
  from other countries, 224–226
  tasting, 227–229
  terminology of, 216

Rum and Coca-Cola, 222
rum-and-mustard, 213
rummy, 216
Rush, Benjamin (Surgeon General), 98, 133
Russia
  movies about, 189
  vodka and, 171–172
rye whiskey, 101, 117, 120, 122

• S •

Sabra, 267
sake, 18
salesperson, finding, 53–54
Sambucca Romano, 267
Samuels, Bill, Sr. (distiller), 103
Sanchez Tagle, Don Pedro (explorer), 194
Sauza Family Museum, 199
Sauza Hornitos, 200
Scandinavian aquavit, 173
Schlichte Steinhager Dry Gin, 162
Schnapps, 260
Scotch whisky
  aging of, 37, 86, 93
  aroma, 93–94
  blended, 89–91
  Campbeltown, 89
  choosing samples for tasting, 92
  combining food and, 95
  description of, 18, 82–83
  distilling, 84–85
  flavors, 94–95
  Highland, 88–89
  Islay, 89
  Lowland, 88
  malting and, 83
  peat and, 83–84
  regions of Scotland and, 86–89
  Speyside, 89
  styles of, 85–86
  tasting, 91–95
  trade and, 81

Scotch Whisky Association, 85–86, 90
Scotland. *See also* Scotch whisky
  geology and climate of, 82
  hiding of distilleries in, 80–81
  map of, 87
  touring, 96
  whisky-making regions of, 86–89
scurvy, 281
Seagram Company
  Bronfman and, 38, 117–119, 135–136, 174
  distilled dry gin, 160
  5 Crown, 135–136
  7&7, 121
  VO Gold 3 Year Old minimum, 142
  VO Gold 8 Year Old, 142
serving
  brandy, 251–252
  gin, 167
  glassware for, 56–57
  temperature for, 56
  vodka, 186–188
7&7, 121
shaker, 289
Shannon airport, 75
shochu, 176
shot glass, 46, 57
sight and tasting, 48. *See also* color
silver rum, 215
Sinclair, David (molecular biologist), 311
single barrel Bourbon, 108–110
single grain whisky, 85
single malt, 66
single malt whisky, 85, 88
size of bottle, 42
Skyy vodka, 178
slavery, 210, 213
Slivovitz brandy, 241–242
sloe gin, 162, 260
slurping, 50–51, 75
small batch Bourbon, 108–109
smell. *See* aroma
Smirnoff, Vladimir (distiller), 173

Smirnoff vodka, 174–175
Smirnov, Piotr (distiller), 173
Smith, George (distiller), 81
smuggling whisky, 81
snifter, 46, 57
Soames, Margarita (socialite), 283
solera aging method, 239–240
sour mash whiskey, 107
South Africa, brandy from, 243
Southern Comfort, 265, 269
Southern Distilling Company, 128–129
Spain
   brandy from, 239
   gin from, 162–163, 167
special bottling, tasting, 45
spent lees, 32
Speyside region of Scotland, 89
spirits. *See also* dark spirits; neutral
      spirits
   blended, 38–40
   clear, 17–18
   distilled, history of, 9–10
   hand-crafted, 30–31
   letting open, 45, 48
   potable, 32
   straight, 38
   types of, 17–18
   vintage of, 19
spirits still, 31
spit bucket, 46
Springbank, 45
Square One vodka, 185
standardization of process of
      fermentation, 10–12
Standards of Identity, 16
Stein, Robert (still inventor), 35
Stevenson, Robert Louis (author),
      223
Stewart, Redd (songwriter), 114
still, 25, 28. *See also* column still; pot
      still
still master, 25, 32
still room, 256
Stock, 265

Stolichnaya
   Límon, 179
   vodka, 175
storage, 55–56
straight spirits, 38
straight whiskey, 18, 107
strainer, 289
Strawberry Vodka Infusion, 180–181
stroke, 312
sugar
   medicines and, 257
   Tequila and, 198
   vodka and, 177
sugar cane, 209–212
Sumerian tablet, 10
Suntory Green Tea, 268

• *T* •

tahona, 200
tails, 32
Taketsuru, Masataka (distiller), 127
Tangle Ridge 10 Year Old, 141
Tanqueray Special Dry English Gin
      and Tanqueray No. TEN, 157
tariffs in India, 128
taste buds, 50–51
tasting
   American blended whiskey, 121–123
   Bourbon and Tennessee whiskey,
      108–110
   brandy, 248–251
   Canadian whisky, 139–144
   choosing spirits for, 44–45
   color and legs, 48–49
   cordials, 271–273
   describing taste, 51–53
   gin, 163–166
   Irish whiskey, 73–75
   nose, 49
   overview of, 43
   practice and, 94
   rum, 227–229
   Scotch whisky, 91–95

setting table for, 45–46
technique for, 50–51
Tequila and mezcal, 205–207
vodka, 181–187
tasting sheet
  for brandy, 248
  example of, 46–47
  for rum, 227
  for Tequila, 205–206
  for vodka, 181
taxes, excise
  in United Kingdom, 80–81
  in United States, 98–99
temperance, 133
temperature, for serving, 56
Ten Cane rum, 222–223
"Tennessee Waltz" (Stewart and
      King), 114
Tennessee whiskey
  choosing for tasting, 110
  combining food with, 111
  description of, 18
  history of, 98–102
  making, 104–107
  tasting, 108
  touring distilleries, 112–113
Tennessee Whiskey Candied Apples,
      300
Tequila
  aging, 201–202
  appellation of origin, 196–197
  brands of, 203–205
  combining with food, 207–208
  description of, 18, 192, 196–197
  flavoring, 202
  history of, 192–196
  making, 198–203
  Prohibition and, 196
  tasting, 205–207
  worm in, 204
Tequila Regulatory Council, 198
Tequila Rose, 270
Tequila Sunrise, 306

terminology
  derogatory, 19–21
  for distillation, 25
  rum and, 216
  Scottish, 82
  for tasting, 52–53
terrine, 293
30 Years War, 150–151
Thomas, Dalby (governor), 212
Thomas, Jerry (bartender), 287
Tia Marie, 267
Tilden, Samuel J. (candidate), 282
toasting
  in Ireland, 78
  in Mexico, 208
  in Scotland, 92–93
  with vodka, 188
tobala, 203
tot, 226, 281
touring
  American Whiskey Trail, 124–125
  Bourbon and Tennessee whiskey
      distilleries, 112–113
  Canada, 136
  Ireland, 76–77
  Scotland, 96
  Tequila Land, 199
trade
  alcohol beverages and, 14
  by Irish, 63–64
  in rum, 211, 213
  by Scots, 81
  in United States, 100
treacle, 93
Treasure Island (Stevenson), 223
Triangle Trade, 213
triglycerides, 313
Trinidad and Tobago, 222–223
triple distilled, 35
Triple Sec, 265
Tuaca Liquore, 268
21st Amendment, 16

type
  of agave, 198
  of Bourbon, 107–108
  of brandy, 244–245, 248–249
  of cordial or liqueur, 262–263
  of spirits, 17–18, 44
  of tasting, selecting spirits by, 44–45
  of yeast, 28
Tyroconnel Irish whiskey, 72

• *U* •

UB group, 127–128
uisege beatha, 13, 62
United States. *See also* American
    blended whiskey
  brandy from, 240–241
  charred wood barrel in, 106
  excise tax in, 98–99
  gin from, 159–160, 167
  rum from, 226
  trade in, 100
USDA National Nutrient Database for
    Standard Reference, 303
Usher, Andrew (stillmaster), 90

• *V* •

Van Winkle, Julian P. (distiller), 103
Vandermint, 267
vatted, 66
vatted or blended malt whisky, 85,
    89–91
Venetian Cream, 270
Vernon, Edward (admiral), 226
vertical tasting, 44
Villa Massa, 265
Vincelli, Bernardo (monk), 150, 271
vintage
  classification by, 19
  Irish whiskey and, 66
vintage Bourbon, 108
Virgin Islands, 223

viscous, 49
vodka
  best-sellers, 186
  choosing, 179
  choosing by base or flavor, 185
  choosing by country of origin, 184
  choosing by price, 182–183
  combining food with, 188
  description of, 18, 169–170, 176
  flavored, 179–180
  history of, 170–175
  making, 176–178
  meaning of term, 13
  in movies, 189
  nutritional profile of, 304
  popular priced, 183
  premium, 183
  serving, 56, 186–188
  tasting sheet, 181
  toasting with, 188
  ultra-premium, 183
  value brand of, 183
Vodka Gimlet, 281
Volstead Act, 16

• *W* •

Wales, distilling business in, 129–130
wash, 23–24
wash still, 31
Washington, George (president), 99,
    124, 242
water
  American blended whiskey and, 121
  branch water, 112
  Canadian whisky and, 138
  Irish whiskey and, 67
  Scotch whisky and, 82–83
  for tasting, 46
  for tasting whiskey, 109
  vodka and, 177
Wathen, Henry Hudson (distiller), 103
Wathen, Richard (executive), 103

Web sites
American Distilling Institute, 30–31
American Whiskey Trail, 125
Bourbon and Tennessee whiskey
distilleries, 112–113
Canadian whisky brands, 140
Mount Vernon Distillery, 124
Museum of the American Cocktail,
126
The Online Distillery Network for
Distilleries & Fuel Ethanol Plants
Worldwide, 16
rum brands, 228
Scotland National Tourist Board, 96
Scottish food, 95
spirited recipes, 291–292
Standards of Identity, 16
Tequila distilleries, 199
Tequila Regulatory Council, 198
USDA National Nutrient Database
for Standard Reference, 303
Weber, Franz (botanist), 193
weight, controlling, 315
Weller, William LaRue (distiller), 103
Welsh Gold, 130
Welsh Whisky Company, Pendryn
plant, 129–130
Western Pennsylvania, 98–99
wheat whiskey, 117, 120–121, 123
whiskey. *See also* American blended
whiskey; Bourbon; Irish whiskey;
Tennessee whiskey
claims for, 79–80
corn, 117, 120, 123
description of, 18
Indian, 127–128
in New Zealand, 128–129
nutritional profile of, 304–305
rye, 101, 117, 120, 122
straight, 18, 107
wheat, 117, 120–121, 123
whisky and, 62

The Whiskey Rebellion, 99
Whiskey Sour, 287, 305–306
whisky. *See also* Canadian whisky;
Scotch whisky
claims for, 79–80
history of, 80–81
Japanese, 126–127
Welsh, 129–130
whiskey and, 62
White Chocolate liqueur, 267
Whitely and Neill gin, 158
Whyte & Mackay, 127–128
wild yeast, 28
Williams, Evan (distiller), 103, 129
wine, 10, 311
wine brandy, 244
wodka, 170. *See also* vodka
wood barrel, charred, 36, 68, 106
worm (part of still), 29, 62
worm in Tequila, 204
wort, 25, 27–28
Wyborowa vodka, 178

• *Y* •

Yak and Coke, 233
yeasts
action of, 23–24
for Bourbon and Tennessee
whiskey, 105
sampling, 27
types of, 28
Yukon Jack, 143, 269

• *Z* •

Zubrowka vodka, 179
Zuidam Dry Gin, 161

Notes

....

Notes

Notes

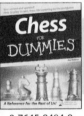

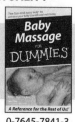
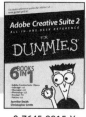

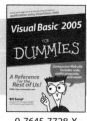

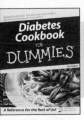
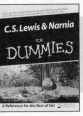